INTERIOR
TOOLS
 INTERIOR
   TACTICS

INTERIOR TOOLS INTERIOR TACTICS

Debates in Interiors Theory and Practice

First published in 2011 by Libri Publishing

Copyright © Libri Publishing Ltd.

Authors retain the rights to individual chapters.

ISBN 978 1 907471 14 8

The right of Edward Hollis, Andy Milligan Frazer Hay, Drew Plunkett and Joyce Fleming to be identified as the editors of this work has been asserted in accordance with the Copyright, Designs and Patents Act, 1988. All rights reserved. No part of this publication may be reproduced, stored in any retrieval system or transmitted in any form or by any means, electronic, mechanical, photocopying, recording or otherwise, without the prior written permission of the copyright holder for which application should be addressed in the first instance to the publishers. No liability shall be attached to the author, the copyright holder or the publishers for loss or damage of any nature suffered as a result of reliance on the reproduction of any of the contents of this publication or any errors or omissions in its contents.

A CIP catalogue record for this book is available from The British Library

Design by Carnegie Publishing

Cover design by Helen Taylor

Printed in the UK by Halstan Printing

Libri Publishing
Brunel House
Volunteer Way
Faringdon
Oxfordshire
SN7 7YR

Tel: +44 (0)845 873 3837

www.libripublishing.co.uk

CONTENTS

FOREWORD — IX
Lois WEINTHAL
University of Texas at Austin

INTERIOR TOOLS INTERIOR TACTICS – AN INTRODUCTION — 1
Edward HOLLIS
Edinburgh College of Art

PLACES AND THEMES OF INTERIORS – CONTEMPORARY RESEARCH WORLDWIDE — 3
Francesca MURIALDO
Politecnico di Milano, Italy

PROFESSIONAL TACTICS — 13

PROFESSIONAL TACTICS – INTRODUCTION — 15
Joyce FLEMING
Glasgow Caledonian University

PROFESSIONAL BODIES IN THE UK, EUROPE AND WIDER — 17
Iris DUNBAR
British Institute of Interior Design

INTERIOR STATUS — 21
Jenny GROVE
The Interior Design School, London

EDUCATIONAL TACTICS: INTRODUCING INTERIORS — 29

INTERIOR TOOLS AND TACTICS – EDUCATION — 31
Joyce FLEMING
Glasgow Caledonian University

LEARNING TO PRACTISE DESIGN — 33
Chris HAY
University of Lincoln

Pam LOCKER
University of Lincoln

RE-THINK THE FIRST-YEAR OFFERING: ADDRESS THE GAP IN STUDENT READINESS   43
Amanda BREYTENBACH
University of Johannesburg

Ian ADAIR JOHNSTON
University of Johannesburg

TACTICS OF DIGITALITY AND MILLENNIAL GENERATIONS   53

TACTICS OF DIGITALITY AND MILLENNIAL GENERATIONS – INTRODUCTION   55
Andy MILLIGAN
DJCAD / University of Dundee

BIM AND I: HOW ADVANCED MODELLING TECHNOLOGY WILL CHANGE STUDIO LEARNING   59
Jana MACALIK
Ryerson University

ENVISAGING THE EXPERIENTIAL   67
Peter WATERS
University for the Creative Arts, Farnham

INTERSPACE: SPATIAL AND TEMPORARY FORMATION OF SENSORY COMMUNITIES WITHIN INTERIOR ENVIRONMENTS   81
Gabriele KNUEPPEL
RMIT University

DIGITAL ORNAMENT: NEW MEANINGS AND SKILLS   93
Annalisa DI ROMA
Polytechnic of Bari

TACTICS IN THE WORKPLACE   101

TACTICS IN THE WORKPLACE – INTRODUCTION   103
Drew PLUNKETT
formerly of Glasgow School of Art

DYNAMIC (SPACE) BUDGETS FOR DYNAMIC (WORKING) ENVIRONMENTS   105
Hugh ANDERSON
haa design limited

SPACES FOR LEARNING   113
Val CLUGSTON
NOMAD Design Associates

TACTICS AT WORK   123
Lynn CHALMERS
University of Manitoba

TACTICS OF THE PERIPATETIC:
ON VENDORS' MAKING AN INTERIOR OF THE STREET   131
Sharn LIM
Studio Daminato, Singapore
RMIT, Melbourne, Australia

TOOLS FOR MODELLING AND MAKING   143

TOOLS FOR MODELLING AND
MAKING – INTRODUCTION   145
Andy MILLIGAN
DJCAD / University of Dundee

MODELLING THE DOMESTIC: REVISITING THE DOLL'S HOUSE   149
Ana ARAUJO
University of the Arts

Ro SPANKIE
University of Westminster

BETWEEN REPRESENTATION AND THE MIRROR –
TACTICS FOR INTERIORISATION   159
Suzie ATTIWILL
RMIT University

WORD, IMAGE, AND THE SPACE BETWEEN: A PRAGMATIC
APPROACH TO LITERARY THEORY AND ARTISTIC PRACTICE   171
Brigid COLLINS
DJCAD / University of Dundee

Valerie ROBILLARD
University of Groenigen

MANUAL MODELLING: A PEDAGOGICAL TOOL   193
Andrea MINA
RMIT University

Peter DOWNTON
RMIT University

THE MODEL AS TEACHING TOOL, EXHIBIT OBJECT AND MUSEUM INSTALLATION – DOMESTIC INTERIORS DESIGNED BY LE CORBUSIER MADE REAL   **205**
Cristina FIORDIMELA
Politecnico di Milano

TACTICS FOR ALTERATION   215

INTRODUCTION – TACTICS FOR ALTERATION   **217**
Edward HOLLIS
Edinburgh College of Art

INTERVIEW WITH FRED SCOTT   **219**
Edward HOLLIS
Edinburgh College of Art

SPOLIA   **223**
Graeme BROOKER and Sally STONE
Manchester Metropolitan University

INTERIOR ROOM URBAN ROOM   **233**
Lorraine FARRELLY and Belinda MITCHELL
University of Portsmouth

MATERIAL TOOLS AND TACTICS   243

MATERIAL TOOLS AND TACTICS   **245**
Andy MILLIGAN
DJCAD / University of Dundee

MATERIAL CHANGE AGENTS AND THEIR DANGEROUS IDEAS   **249**
George VERGHESE
University of Technology Sydney

MATERIALS AND DESIGN EXCHANGE (MADE)   **259**
Andy MILLIGAN
DJCAD / University of Dundee

Written on behalf of

Sumeet BELLARA
formerly of IOM3/MADE

TOOLING A FEMINIST INTERIOR PRACTICE   **263**
Julieanna PRESTON
Massey University, Wellington, New Zealand

ABOUT THE EDITORS   **275**

Lois WEINTHAL
University of Texas at Austin

FOREWORD

To define the profession of interior design raises debates amongst circles ranging from educators to professionals to those that ignore outright all established bodies. Is this because the discipline has ambiguous boundaries, for example the threshold where architecture ends and interior begins, or because of its questionable date of origin in history? Interior design grew from tangential practices – art and architecture – but does not have the same historical foundations or theoretical frameworks, and therefore, is less definitive. Compared to the history of these long established disciplines, it is a relatively new profession in which its own set of tools and tactics have either been re-appropriated from other disciplines or sought anew based upon the latest trends in space, material and form-making.

Constructing interior spaces utilises tools of production such as representation, to tactics that manifest in craftsmanship, identity and function. These tools and tactics are not exclusive to interiors: after all, craftsmanship in the traditional sense applies to furniture making as well as sculpture. It is unavoidable that interior design references these tangential disciplines because they occupy the same space and at times, share the same tools and tactics.

These tangential disciplines can be diagrammed as a nesting of layers, where textiles cover the body but also cover furniture, all of which fill a room that is further defined by properties of light, poché and aesthetics. Traditionally, this diagram includes product, textile and graphic design as influences that appear on the interior, which are themselves undergoing changes with new technologies and trends. Disciplines that may have at one point stood outside the lexicon of everyday interiors are beginning to surface with more visible points of entry, such as the impact engineering can have on the interior, whether in the form of material science or indoor air quality. These influences open the opportunity for interior designers to integrate disciplines located further afield while opening new areas of research and collaboration, at the same time as inviting a new set of tools and tactics to enter the discipline.

What does this mean to the discipline's traditional identity with decoration and ornament?

Historically, personalities such as Elsie de Wolfe have identified interior design as part of a long-standing tradition of decoration, and the interior as a feminine realm. De Wolfe approached design first with a set of tactics followed by tools of production (De Wolfe 1913)[*]. At present, digital fabrication is a tool becoming more commonplace upon which tactics are derived. Unlike de Wolfe's *modus operandi*, where a design strategy was the starting point and tools of the trade followed, technology is currently the tool in-waiting, leaving it up to the designer to decipher the tactic for its use. What would the works of Elsie de Wolfe be like if she were to work with current technologies? Would her preference for soft, feminine interiors, manifested in the knowledge of a fabric's drape, or a correctly set table of dishware, become more like the work of the contemporary designer Elena Manferdini[†] who employs digital tools to fabricate lace-like patterns applied to tea sets, clothing textiles and façade skins (Manferdini 2010)? The comparison between de Wolfe and Manferdini acts as a litmus test for the multitude of tactics that contribute to the making of interiors. Technology and digital fabrication mark a threshold between traditional and experimental methods of working, and reveal a larger set of changes taking place in the discipline.

Interior design is shaped by educators and practitioners and the histories they bring with them. History carries along its paradigms while being confronted with new ones. In specific, technology's influence in drawing and giving shape to three-dimensional forms is one paradigm permeating the discipline, most notably at the level of education. The shift from hand drawing to digital rendering marks a change from the use of tactics that precede tools, to tools that precede tactics. With hand drawing, tactics preceded drawing in order to know how to put the tools to use. A parallel motion and set of triangles offered multiple possibilities and relied upon a designer's knowledge of drawing techniques and physical drawing skills for lines to be generated. With digital rendering, the tools and functions available far out-number those of hand drawing. A simple command offers infinite outcomes that do not necessarily rely upon preconceived tactics. Digital tools allow designers to generate numerous possibilities and then pick the one that best meets the intention. This is unlike hand drawing where a limited number of drawing iterations are produced or continuously worked over on the same sheet. In the case of technology, the tools drive the tactics.

Education is leading the implementation of technology because of the emphasis placed on learning or integrating software programs into courses. Students are

---

[*] De Wolfe, Elsie. *The House in Good Taste*. New York: Arno Press, 1975 [c1913].

[†] Lecture by Elena Manferdini given at The University of Texas at Austin, School of Architecture, March 10, 2010. See also Manferdini's table project *Arktura* at http://www.ateliermanferdini.com/ for a similar process.

exposed to new methods of digital representation and fabrication with laser cutters, CNC routers and 3D printers. When students move into the profession, these tools are less available as they simultaneously bump up against traditional methods of construction. This contrast provides an opportunity for the profession to reassess itself and build upon the knowledge of current trends in education. Similarly, it asks recent graduates to look to the ambiguous boundaries of the interior as a site for cutting-edge technology to merge with traditional methods of construction and learn from long-established practices in the profession.

The overlapping boundary of interiors with related disciplines – from architecture to objects – opens the opportunity for interior designers to shape these endpoints and everything in-between. Methods for giving shape to these elements can take the form of digital fabrication and/or traditional construction practices. In doing so, decisions need to be made about whether tools precede tactics or tactics precede tools. But the ambiguity of which precedes which, together with a hybridisation of fabrication methods, can be used to the discipline's advantage and claim new areas of design in the interior. Where walls are commonplace for the division of space, digital fabrication invites the use of non-structural screen-like modules that rely upon a designer's sensitivity to integrate them into public and private spaces on the interior, something a computer alone cannot determine. Even with digital tools, a designer's sensibility is still needed.

If practitioners, educators and students seize opportunities such as these, the definition of the discipline will become further ambiguous as interior designers take responsibility for elements that typically belong in the disciplines of product design or architecture. This ambiguity should be viewed positively, since it reflects a new genre of work emerging from the discipline, much like the emergence of interior design as a distinct discipline with the rise of Elsie de Wolfe. As this new body of work comes into being, a reflection upon the tools and tactics used to construct it will contribute to a reassessment of the discipline's definition. All together, these multiple readings of the interior will contribute to the ongoing writing of its history and theory.

Edward HOLLIS
Edinburgh College of Art

INTERIOR TOOLS INTERIOR TACTICS – AN INTRODUCTION

When the Interiors Forum Scotland first met in 2005/06, we asked ourselves an apparently simple question: 'What is interior design?' It seemed like a sensible question to ask: we were, after all, the heads of all the interiors degree courses in Scotland.

Our informal discussion soon expanded, and by the next year, we found ourselves running an international symposium, and publishing a book. *Thinking Inside the Box: A Reader in Interiors for the 21st Century* asked the same question; but experience soon taught us that it was a question that had as many answers as there were respondents. Contributions considered the role of education, professional accreditation, gender, materiality, history, and representation, among other fields, and brought together a lively community of researchers from all over the world.

But it was, perhaps, an absurd question to have asked. Interior design is not a thing, but a practice; and our discussions stimulated debate rather than conclusion. Furthermore, these debates were happening without those to whom they were most useful or pertinent: practitioners themselves.

For this reason, this second publication from the Interiors Forum Scotland concerns itself less with what interior design is, and more with how people do it. It is addressed to practitioners as well as to theorists, and it is articulated as a series of debates around key issues in the field.

This book is about the tools of the trade: the role of materials, drawings, models, and computers in the interior design process is discussed, for example. But it is also about the tactics that the designers and the users of interiors employ in using these tools. The computer, for instance, is discussed in terms of the habits of the millennial generation, for instance; and the workplace in terms of its subversion by those who work in it. Materials are considered as provocations to the designer or artist, and education as a challenge to educators as well as to students.

Interior Tools and Tactics is divided into seven debates, to each of which professionals and academics have contributed position papers. These are, namely:

- *Professional Tactics*, which considers how the design of the interior is established, managed, and promoted
- *Educational Tools and Tactics*, in which the diverse roles of the interior educator are discussed
- *Tactics of Digitality and Millennial Generations*; digital tools for the interior designer, and the tactics of their deployment
- *Tactics in the Workplace*, which considers how both designers and users create and subvert places of work and study
- *Tools for Modelling and Making* debates problems in and strategies for representing the interior
- *Tactics for Alteration,* which examines the ways in which interiors alter the buildings that 'host' or contain them
- *Material Tools and Tactics*, which shows how the raw materials of the interior provoke and question innovation in design.

Contributions have come from Australia to Scotland, Canada to Italy, and they originate in a symposium held by the Interiors Forum Scotland at Edinburgh College of Art in 2008. Like this publication, the symposium was staged as a series of debates: participants introduced themselves in a rapid-fire 'pecha kucha' format, and then joined whichever grouping captured their attention most keenly. *Interior Tools Interior Tactics* is intended to convey something of the flavour of this *modus operandi*.

Since the Interiors Forum Scotland was established, the academic debate surrounding interiors has blossomed into a plethora of publications, some dispensing practical advice, some offering philosophical reverie. *Interior Tools Interior Tactics* is intended to complement these, articulating some debates, and, we hope, provoking many more.

Our thanks are due, of course, to our contributors, and to our publishers, Libri Publishing, on whose behalf Celia Cozens and Paul Jervis have shown remarkable patience. We would also like to acknowledge Edinburgh College of Art, which hosted the original Interior Tools Interior Tactics symposium; and Glasgow School of Art, Napier University, Glasgow Caledonian University, and DJCAD Duncan of Jordanstone College of Art and Design / University of Dundee for their support. Thanks go also to Fabian Galama and Ashley Hamilton for their assistance in compiling much of the material of which this book is composed. Our special gratitude is owed to Cathy Brown at DJCAD, without whose sanguine commonsense and tenacity none of this would have happened at all.

Francesca MURIALDO
Politecnico di Milano, Italy

PLACES AND THEMES OF INTERIORS – CONTEMPORARY RESEARCH WORLDWIDE

Introduction

Approaching a PhD course in Interior Architecture and Exhibition Design, one of the most important things is to succeed in explaining to people around you what 'interior' means.

The borders of the interiors discipline often blur with art, design and architecture despite having, particularly in Italy, a strongly based tradition in terms of designers, history and culture. The significance of interiors is quickly growing in terms of projects, courses and debates, but the network is still very weak and unable to update themes and theory on a worldwide discussion basis.

How can we investigate the role and validity of the interiors discipline in the twenty-first century? This is the very simple premise that motivates the PhD course: to enter the discipline without building barriers but rather investigating themes and theories of the contemporary research worldwide. The research that has been developed up till now is an overview of the state of the art, a foundation on which to build a shared knowledge. The ambition of the project is to build up a permanent laboratory in which all the people involved in interiors, on different scales, can access everybody else's point of view. As a starting point the research focused on three main fields on which deep transformation and attention has been focused in the last ten years: domestic, retail and exhibition design.

The thematic area of *domestic* represents both the most traditional field of application of the discipline and the most explored issue at the present time. The interiors definition of the field is traditionally related to the relationship within interior space and people inhabiting that space, particularly related to the home. However, with dwelling becoming a social emergency, the culture of interiors has been contaminated with technological and political issues.

Retail focuses on the spaces characterised by the selling of goods – it is the area favoured by experimental innovation both on the formal and typological side. From one side it is quite a new project field, which has been snubbed in recent decades from the designer's side but, on the other hand, retail is the engine of the globalised world economy, that reflects not only habits and forms of the contemporary society, but also involves thinking about places and methods of the production of goods in the new geography of consumption.

The last field on which the research has concentrated is that of *exhibition design*. Innovation and experimentation have been predominant here for many years: the new technology allows information to be accessible everywhere to anyone and exhibition design is becoming information itself.

The research is an open discussion that started from many questions and concluded with as many questions. Is there a favourite point of view that should characterise the interiors vision or should it use a wider angle? Is it a real necessity that the discipline should be regulated and defined or should it be free and flexible to take from a multitude of contents? The research ran parallel to some questioning focused on the main issues characterising the three thematic areas to "tee off" the international debate.

Which are the new criteria that influence domestic environments and change the significance of "innovation" in our living spaces? How does contemporary research worldwide deal with mobility, sustainability, lack of space and specific societal issues such as disability, aged people and the impact of immigrants in host communities? What are the relationships between traditional domestic environments and new lifestyles? Is it possible to speak widely about domestic spaces despite so many geographical and social differences? What are the qualities of the domestic contemporary environments? How are they influenced by the media technologies, by new materials and lifestyles? Is it still relevant to speak about typologies? And what is the role we attribute today to form and decoration?

How will places for consumption be transformed in the near future? How will the contamination of places and activities evolve? Which are the new production and selling strategies that will affect spaces, materials and finishing? How are selling strategies changing? Will they affect space, materials and finishing? What is the role of shopping in the global community? Are there any social sustainability issues affecting the new consumerism spaces?

What will be the development of exhibition devices between tradition and innovation? Is it still possible to look at exhibition design as an undivided area or are the various fields of application (exhibitions, fairs, museums, events and scenography) opening up to a wider articulation? What will be the role of the visitors/spectators in the near future? How will the exhibition devices change from materiality to immateriality?

Research Methodology

The first goal of the research has been to underline where the interior research centres were located. A second step has been to detect a map of themes, of contents, able to highlight common trends and to preserve cultural differences. These considerations involved also a deep understanding of how the interiors discipline is perceived around the world starting from the university research institutes. The tool chosen for the investigation is the universal open communication instrument, the worldwide web.

As a starting point we took into consideration the world's top 500 universities (taken from *The Times Higher World University Rankings* and the *Institute of Higher Education, Shanghai Jiao Tong University*) checking for each of them if interiors was given some consideration; the research also underlined where, in excellent universities or polytechnics (where faculties of design or architecture are present) there is not any reference to interiors. For each university a form was filled containing a brief description of the research centre, people involved, themes faced. These first grids were reinforced with a deeper analysis of the universities of Europe and of the members of some of the most important associations such as International Federation of Interior Architects/Designers (http://www.ifiworld.org/), European Association for Architectural Education (http://www.eaae.be/), and I.D.E.A. Interior Architecture/Interior Design Educators Association (www.idea-edu.com). Other places of research have been identified mainly in the UK and the USA. The places investigated number more than 800.

It's very important to underline that such a research methodology has many problems determined from technical, cultural, political and linguistic barriers. If it is true that the worldwide web is the most accessible platform for exchange of knowledge, it's also true that many countries have limited access to the free web, many others have no resources to share information and that the language barrier in many cases has been an insurmountable barrier. Work in progress of the research outputs can be viewed at the website: http://www.interiorsforumworld.dpa.polimi.it.

Places

Before going into detail of the main themes identified for each area, the research puts forward evidence of how the interiors discipline is differently perceived around the world: in architecture faculties, in design faculties, as a department in faculties of building environment and in schools of engineering. A very interesting issue is that the last discipline is involving very strongly the fields of humanities with very precise courses of studies in sociology, anthropology, geography and business, especially in Europe (UK) and in the USA. It is no surprise that Europe, North America (USA and Canada) and Australia are the easiest places for networking and, despite some differences, they work on a shared heritage, advantaged by the common use of the English language. It is also true that even in Europe there is a deep gap in between the north and south: the Mediterranean countries, including Italy, Spain, Portugal and Greece are generally very self referenced due to the cultural habits of not publishing in English, with the result that information is getting in but not getting out the country borders. Resources management of the research is another gap to be discussed as tools look to be completely unbalanced against the policy of southern European countries.

The Far East has dramatically different results: Singapore is very active, also hosting important international conferences. China is relatively impenetrable due to lack of communication, Japan treats the Architecture discipline as a department of Engineering and seems to be more focused on technological issues. In Africa, only South Africa seems to face the same dialogue and South America is very difficult to homogenize as characterised from excellence centres and a void around it.

Themes

Domestic

The domestic environment is being studied widely from various perspectives: architecture, design, interior design, art, computer science, sociology, anthropology and geographical studies. Concerning the home, recent architectural research is more concentrated on housing issues oriented toward urban studies, treating urgent issues such as: homelessness; the growth and changing characteristics of housing renovation; remodelling homes for the changing household; new home construction needs and extra small houses for one or two people. There are more than fifteen housing centres in the top architectural universities which rarely take the aspect of the inner space of the house as a main issue of their studies. The home remains the central node of some of the most relevant social and political issues, a privileged place for new technology applications both addressed to sustainability and to new lifestyles.

The widespread adoption of new information technology (IT) today is leading to profound changes in how we communicate with others, shop for goods, receive news, manage finances, deliver and receive medical care and find entertainment. The nature of these activities requires new spatial designs with regard to both *form* and *allocation* of the spaces and with regard to new spatial qualities like lighting, acoustics and degrees of privacy.

Most research is dedicated to the application of new communication with the domestic environment but, except in a few cases [1], mainly concentrates on the application of devices more than to the thinking of the space behind it. Information technology at home supports and encourages social activities from one side, and creates a new relationship between the dwelling and the outside world; traditional boundaries between the home as a private sphere and society as a public sphere have shifted. Work and domestic life are increasingly blurring into each other and e-shopping has brought the retail space into the home [2]. Information technology is also utilised to cope with disability problems through home automation [3].

The concept of the home as an extension of the body, an optimised space which rejects the real landscape and reconstructs another one that can be modulated as required, is another focus of the contemporary research showing a trend of customised houses. The composition of form has made way for the contamination of the container by the content and the interaction between production method and products. One of the most relevant factors that influence lifestyle in the construction of the ideal home is the way in which people create their houses by engaging the media, such as lifestyle magazines, associated building trade literature and the domestic makeover TV shows [4].The discourse of the impact of globalisation and the role of interior designers in contemporary society pose two observations: globalisation leads to standardised design: within the global system, our material lives and experiences are often undervalued [5].

Sustainability attracts a large part of today's studies and research. It comes from the need to change attitudes about the use of the earth's limited resources. The main goal is to save energy. From the universities researched, the sustainability issue takes more than 30 places as an independent study or as part of housing centres. Its application to the home basically applies to solar homes, light wood houses, sustainable life style (energy efficiency), energy analysis (like carbon reduction in building construction), sustainable human behaviour (like recycling or re-use of existing buildings) and remodelling. Their outcomes concentrate on practice, conferences and competitions. As recent research considers the future of our built environment's sustainability, the attempts now are dedicated to build houses from clay, concrete, timber, steel, cardboard, light wood and glass. Its application to the inner space of home is basically seen as a consequence, mainly addressed to furniture issues.

One of the important issues that characterise the contemporary era is that of minimising the dimensions of living spaces – a valuable design issue that involves the concept of multi-functional rooms in minimal spaces. Such minimisation is now widely under study and development as a significant contributory factor of urban and social policies. The *small house*, *xs house* and *minimum house* are contemporary terms in use to refer to a house as a single construction which should have the same properties of medium houses, in terms of comfort and privacy. The idea of the minimum house corresponds to the economic value and the lack of space. Some of those transformations are also coming from social transformation including such issues as the increase in divorce statistics, the rapid progress of the aging society, the scattered family and immigration-related themes [6–12].

Retail

The retail area, in the last few years, has become central to the interiors discipline. After a very long period in which it was snubbed by the designers, now – thanks to big investments from the luxury sector – it has taken centre stage with a great flurry of projects around the world. Places of consumption rethink themselves in order of new places and production methods, new communication, new technologies and radical changes in the society structure. We have been seeing books, exhibitions and conferences proposing themes and innovative ideas able to get off the ground a transformation process that seems to be irreversible and there is an interesting growth in specific university courses in Retail Design that demonstrate that it is a fashionable area [13].

Spatial and typological transformations of commerce and consumer spaces reflect small revolutions that are affecting our lifestyle. The driving force of innovation seems to be linked to macro-economy areas: new places and new production processes are mirrored in goods distribution, both on the macro and the micro scale. Economic policies of the western countries have devolved to commerce issues of land planning and the role of mediation of social conflicts. Shopping is the main activity of our spare time and most of our relationships are mediated by products. At the same time, the products themselves are unloading physical contents to become representative of ideals: in the same way consumption spaces are rapidly changing. The shops of yesterday were characterised by the organisation of the space relating to products; today attention is brought from the product to the consumer-customer in a new environment: perception, experience, emotions seem to be the new keywords and interior design is always more involved. The consumer-customer is the main actor of the new space. The new shops are not more product-oriented but story-tellers and interiors become more complex. Architecture and design join with other disciplines to create a shop that hasn't got any "shopping" characteristics any more. But, if it is true that commercial spaces are gaining a new dignity in the culture of the project, it's also true that research is very much oriented in a few sectors and always design oriented, leaving most of the theoretical themes unexplored and open for future interpretations.

Most of the research identified considers commercial space related to the use of the territory in a urban dimension, often concentrating on policies and specific territorial case studies [14]. Also, the retail theme involves the most important issue of sustainability, being a sensitive part of the consumption process [15]. As we approach relations between the interior space and people acting in that space, it happens that research moves from the architecture-design discipline towards the human studies area. On the retail side of the research, the most interesting matter of fact is that sociology, psychology, anthropology and geography, together with business and marketing, are the main actors of the cultural debate.

Consumer behaviour inspires interesting research focused on the understanding of different consumerism trends [16–17] while business and marketing are trying to trace future trends in store formats and contents [18–20] but also to concentrate on building a conceptual framework of a theory of shopping linking together historical, social and psychological aspects [21].

As the theme is surprisingly new, we detected only a little research into an historical overview of the commercial space related to public space, providing an insight into how architecture and interior design respond to the demands of European urban societies undergoing profound demographic and cultural changes [22–23]. In particular, the new geography seems to play the most innovative part in the investigation of consumers' and consumption's spaces, theorising consumption and the histories of shopping spaces [24–25].

Exhibition Design

Communication, in every possible declination and variable, is a determining and unavoidable characteristic of the society of information. Exhibition design particularly follows this trend and takes advantage from languages and instruments of disciplines such as interior architecture, technology, graphics and communication. We are seeing the contamination of art and scenography, whose techniques and manners of visualisation are exploited by the exhibition design, projecting the beholder into another dimension in which he is the protagonist and the director. Exhibition design becomes entertainment and users become the protagonists able to change the scene itself. The exhibition project also moves the attention from the object-product to the concept-product: the content dematerialises; points of view, perceptions, emotions, exhibits and devices become more and more important. The attempt to deeply analyse these questions drove the research across different layers, going from general considerations towards detailed research into single specific devices. Most of the research is concentrated on Art, Visual Art, Communication and Visual and Cultural Studies courses. The framework is a critical approach to both museums and exhibitions: on the traditional museum side, we did find specific themes also from an historical point of view, while on the temporary exhibitions side, the main research field is concentrated on the contamination with other disciplines such as art, scenography, visual art and cinema. A main issue faced is the relationship between exhibition design and urban spaces: as content is changing, also the container is dealing with different requirements, playing an important role in the definition of public space citizenship. Exhibition design has more often to do with performance. Space, perception and experience of the visitor-actor are central to contemporary research themes [26–27]. Performative devices are not centred on one specific technology and what is characterising performative design is the freedom to experiment with new ways to drag visitors towards new experiences.

The relationship with art and communication is so strong that it's not possible to talk just of contamination. Space design is half way between real and virtual, digital and analogical being always closer to cinema and gaming, relating more to emotions than knowledge [28–29]. Light, sound and colour play a very important role in the exhibition design space and the control of these three variables allows efficient communication of the contents and characteristics of the exhibition.

Devices and technologies directly affect the path chosen by the visitors and the individual experience of the exhibition [29]. Light affects perception and communication and an accurate balance between natural and artificial light becomes central to much research [30]. Colour and sound are also subjects of specific investigations [31]. In general the contributions are not many and do not represent originality in the landscape of the thematic faced in the past years. An interesting element is that exhibition design is considered to be an inexhaustible field of research and this is reinforced by the fact that all the excellent research centres study these themes.

References

[1] The home of the future: Ethnographic Study on New IT in the home, University of California, ARITO center.
[2] A New Physical Space for the Residential Units to come, University of Washington College of Architecture.
[3] Designing the Home to Meet the Needs of Tomorrow, The Robert Gordon University, Faculty of Design.
[4] TV, new media and domestic makeover, Royal College of Art/ Center for the study of Domestic Interior.
[5] Through an exhibition made by the School of Architecture, University of Illinois.
[6] House-n Research Group, Massachusetts Institute of Technology, Department of Architecture.
[7] Home 2020 Studio, Carnegie Mellon University, School of Architecture.
[8] Future Home Institute, University of Art and Design Helsinki.
[9] Centre for the study of Domestic Interior, Royal Institute of Art.
[10] DDTR Digital Home Group: Mapping the digital home, making culture sense of domestic space and place.
[11] Contemporary world interior: survey of the current state of international interior design, Rensselaer Polytechnic Institute, School of Architecture.
[12] The patina of domestic space: from house to home, University of Sheffield, School of Architecture.
[13] MA in Retail design, Piet Zwart Institute, Rotterdam.
[14] Boontharm, D., Contemporary shophouses, C.A.S.A. Center for Advance Studies in Architecture, National University of Singapore, School of Design and Environment.
[15] Fieldson, R., Towards a Framework for Sustainability in Retail Architecture, University of Newcastle upon Tyne, Faculty of Architecture, Planning and Landscape.
[16] Wagner, A. M., Membership identity and Consumer Behaviour: The Case of Consumer Co-operatives, University of Saskatchewan, Department Geography [thesis Degree Master of Arts].
[17] Department of Consumer Studies and Resource Management, Seoul National University, College of Human Ecology.
[18] The Future of Retailing, 26th April 2006, Nyenrode Business Universiteit, Breukelen [conference].
[19] Dawson, J., The future of retailing, 21st February 2002, Edinburgh, The Centre for the Study of Retailing in Scotland (CSRS) [conference].
[20] Woodruffe-Burton, H.R., Eccles, S. and Elliott, R., Towards a theory of shopping: a preliminary conceptual framework, 2002, Lancaster University, Management School, Marketing Department.

[21] Manfred Krafft, M. (University of Muenster, Germany), Mantrala, M., (University of Missouri, Columbia, USA), *Retailing in the 21st century: current and future trends* (Berlin: Springer, 2006).
[22] Pimlott, M., the outside and the inside: studies in the contemporary public interior, Research chair of Architectural Design/ Interior, Delft University of technology, Faculty of Architecture.
[23] Kärrholm, M., Territories of Consumption; design and territorial control in urban commercial spaces, Lund University, Faculty of Architecture and Built Environment.
[24] Crewe, L., New Economic Geographies Research Group, University of Nottingham, Faculty of Human Geography.
[25] Wrigley, N., Lowe, M., Reading retail: a geographical perspective on retailing and consumption space, University of Southampton, Faculty of Geography.
[26] Casson, D., Interactivity in Museum, University College for The Creative Arts, Canterbury.
[27] Brisbin, C., Space in/within Images: Explorations into the Image/space Relation, University of Queensland, Australia / Environmental Design & Technology.
[28] Ullmark, P. (Group Director), Innovative Design_ the boundaries between science, technology, and artistic knowledge, Chalmers University of Technology, Sweden.
[29] Peponis, J. (Georgia Technology University), Wineman, J. (University of Michigan), How Does Space Affect Visitors in Museum Environments.
[30] Behar, D., Capeluto G., Levin M., Light in the art exhibition space, Tecnion, Israel Institute of Technology.

Acknowledgement

The authors gratefully acknowledge the collaboration of the PhD students of the XXII Architettura degli Interni ed Allestimento, Politecnico di Milano, in particular: for the domestic section and references: Mariam Alsaigh and Mariana Siracusa; for exhibition design section and references: Cristina Bergo and Gaetana Russo; and the professors Luca Basso Peressut, Gennaro Postiglione, Francesco Scullica, Imma Forino, for co-ordinating the research.

Francesca MURIALDO
Politecnico di Milano
c/o studiometrico
v. Fontanesi 4
20146 Milano
Italy
francesca.murialdo@studiometrico.com
+39 335 5454685
http://www.interiorsforumworld.dpa.polimi.it/

Professional tactics

Joyce FLEMING

Glasgow Caledonian University and
City of Glasgow College

PROFESSIONAL TACTICS – INTRODUCTION

Interior design is a relatively young profession in the UK; it has historic roots in architectural practice. As far back as 1758, architect Robert Adam, (surely the celebrity decorator of the time) established a business that employed around 2,000 people. This number eclipses even the most commercially-focused design enterprise today. Adam's business produced everything from ornamental plasterwork and carpets to marble chimney pieces and cast-iron down pipes. His holistic approach to architectural design was predominant until the middle of the 20th century, when specialism began to prevail, leaving the way open to the interior design profession that we recognise today.

Formal interior design education still has a strong architectural bias. However, especially in the UK, there are many gifted 'amateurs' who are self taught or have served apprenticeships, usually in the tradition of Adam in a contemporary 'country house' style.

The differences are exposed brutally when interior designers discuss membership of a professional body in any kind of forum. Is this a club we want to join? Who can become a member? What's in it for us? How much pressure can be collectively mustered to influence legislation or the direction of education? The profession ranges from the 'architectural interiorist' who has never specified a wall covering, to the disparaging term 'decorators'. One thing is agreed; the need for wider spread recognition of our professionalism.

Putting together any interior design scheme requires organisational and management skills, and for practice to continue to thrive, a level of business acumen. You may hold a different philosophical stance on the purpose of design from your professional colleagues, or adhere to a different stylistic language but the bottom line is – how can we set quality standards and deliver a professional service?

Hard lessons were learnt in previous economic downturns, when public perception of a designer tag equated to the triumph of expensive style over substance. The profession has moved on and matured. It is more service-focused, the client body is more likely to believe that a professional design service makes good business sense. Interior Design courses produce graduates who have a range of desirable industry-ready skills, but these graduates are being pitched into the job market in the worst economic conditions of a generation.

More than ever, through professional bodies such as BIID, CSD & ECIA, we need to build on the premise that good design makes sound economic sense. The networking opportunities they provide promote insights and links to other businesses and areas of design expertise. They provide an interface to education, to the consumer through advertising, and provide advice on, and influence, legislation that helps facilitate a sustainable and safe future. We need to continue to build trust and the respect that is craved by the profession as a whole. Perhaps we could begin by looking at the work of colleagues who have entered the profession by a different route than our own, and accept that there is room in the profession for us all.

Iris DUNBAR
British Institute of Interior Design

PROFESSIONAL BODIES IN THE UK, EUROPE AND WIDER

One of the subjects included at the 2008 IFS Conference, Tools and Tactics, was professional practice and professional bodies. Representatives from Interior Design bodies were invited to discuss the benefits of membership as part of a panel discussion including representatives of the British Interior Design Association (BIDA), the Chartered Society of Designers (CSD) and European Council of Interior Architects (ECIA). One of the comments from the floor was that there was no body that fully represented Interior Design in the UK. The RCA had dropped Interiors as a discipline and there should be a professional organisation to put the case forward. It was apparent that there was a need for a united voice for Interiors. As Educational Director and the representative from BIDA, I was sympathetic to these comments that came from the Interiors Education sector. Our profession was desperately in need of one body to represent the Interior Design discipline.

To make sense of the current status of professional bodies in the UK and beyond, we need to reflect back on the past. Here is a glimpse into the wealth of expertise, time and effort that has been invested voluntarily by individuals for over 100 years. We say that we are a young profession yet people have been designing, building and constructing interiors for centuries.

In 1899 John Dibble Crace, Decorator located at 38 Wigmore Street, London, met with eight other like-minded decorators from Dublin, Glasgow, Birmingham and Glasgow to start the Incorporated Institute of British Decorators. The first meetings were held in Painters Hall and as the Institute grew so did the districts. The minute book of 1928 highlights: arrears in subscriptions; a lectureship fund appeal for London University; matters of "such national importance" about education in decoration.

There are mentions of Board of Examiners, Regulations and Associate Examinations. In 1953 the word Interior Designer was added to the title in recognition of a new era in expertise. There were close links with colleges who supported the Institute exams - Napier College, Edinburgh; Teesside Polytechnic; Glasgow College of Building; Trent Polytechnic. In 1978, a council meeting was held at the RSA in John Adam Street and a resolution was passed to drop the word decorator and change the name to the British Institute of Interior Design. During the early eighties discussions were held between Michael Giles, President of the BIID and June Fraser, President of the CSD (Chartered Society of Designers) At an Extraordinary general meeting in July 1988 the BIID was amalgamated with CSD.

The Chartered Society of Designers (CSD) is the professional body for designers and the authority on professional design practice. It is the world's largest chartered body of professional designers with members in 33 countries and is unique in representing designers in all disciplines. CSD is governed by Royal Charter and as such its members are required to practice to the highest professional standards. The Society was established in 1930 as the Society of Industrial Artists (SIA), became the Society of Industrial Artists and Designers in 1963, and was granted the Royal Charter in 1986. It is a registered charity working for the benefit of the community and operates accreditation of professional practice to individuals via its own membership programme. The Society is not a trade body or association, and CSD membership is only awarded to designers who prove their professional competences as defined in the CSD Genetic Matrix.

As the CSD represents designers of all disciplines, its remit is to promote design on a general level which is essential for the design industry overall. However, it does not help the Interiors sector. When the BIID merged with the CSD, the identity of a considerable group of Interior specialists was lost within the larger CSD organisation. The Interior Design Discipline sits between Architecture and Design and needs to be recognised in both sectors.

In 1966 another group was established called the Interior Design and Decoration Association who were the UK chapter of the American organisation, the International Interior Design Association. Dual membership encouraged international networking and sharing of views on professional practice. In 2002 the groups merged and became the British Interior Design Association. One of the directives in the BIDA mission statement was actively to seek registration for Interior Designers and over the next few years the executive board of the BIDA redirected the organisation to become an Institute in order to help regulate the profession. In June 2009 the Secretary of State granted Institute status, recognising the British Institute of Interior Design as the pre-eminent body to represent Interior Design in the UK.

It must be stated at this point that it was a sheer coincidence that the chosen combination of name, The British Institute of Interior Design, was the same as that of the organisation that had merged with the CSD. Their corporation no longer existed so Companies House granted the name with no previous recollection of the original BIID.

At the same time that the BIID was going through the rigorous process of becoming an Institute, The British Contract Furnishing Association were in discussions with their designer members who, in 2009, formed the Interior Design Association working principally in the international commercial interiors market with public and private sector clients.

The Society of British Interior Designers was also established in 2009 by a group of past board directors of the British Interior Design Association. Their constitution is driven by the key founders and there is no elected council or published membership.

In Europe, the European Council of Interior Architects (ECIA) was established in 1992 by the North European members of the International Federation of Interior Architects and Designers (IFI), providing a common platform for the exchange of information on best professional practices and established minimum standards of educational and professional profile for the associated member organisations.

On the global stage the IFI was established in 1963 by a small number of European design associations and was very much part of a wider international movement to establish the Interior Design profession as an important tool in business and global trading. By the early 21st century IFI had grown to represent 57 professional associations and institutions in 39 countries in five continents. Currently IFI are undertaking a global initiative to reposition interiors worldwide for an upgraded image, substance, content, respect and clarity in the public's perception. The culmination of this worldwide discussion will be an essential resource for the global interiors profession and industry.

The first decade of this century has been an exploratory stage for professional bodies and as we enter the second decade it is essential that the Interior Design community work together to become a united voice for the profession.

Professional bodies timeline

1899	Incorporated Institute of British Decorators
1930	Society of Industrial Artists
1953	Incorporated Institute of British Decorators and Designers
1963	SIA changes to SIAD
1963	International Federation of Interior Architects and Designers IFI
1965	Interior Design and Decoration Association IIDA
1976	The British Institute of Interior Design BIID
1986	SIAD changes to CSD
1988	BIID merged with CSD
1992	European Council of Interior Architects ECIA

2002   IIDA changed to the British Interior Design Association BIDA

2009   BIDA became The British Institute of Interior Design BIID

2009   IDA – The Interior Design Association – emerged from BCF

2009   SBID –The Society of British Interior Design

2010   IFI Design Futures initiative to establish the Interiors identity

Iris Dunbar studied Interior Design at DJCAD Duncan of Jordanstone College of Art and Design, Dundee and is currently external assessor at Glasgow Caledonian University. She worked with Building Design Partnership before going into practice specialising in office interiors and exhibitions. President 2008-2010 of the British Institute of Interior Design and currently on the Executive board of The International Federation of Interior Design and Architecture, she is also a Fellow of the Chartered Society of Designers and a Fellow of the Royal Society of Arts.

Jenny GROVE
The Interior Design School, London

INTERIOR STATUS

Introduction

Interior design in the UK isn't a profession – it's an industry [1], created by a hard-working, talented, and maverick collection of educated and non-educated designers, striving to manipulate interior spaces at all levels from decoration to architectural design. This unregulated collection of people has created a vibrant and growing industry, but it lacks status. Further, what status we do have has been devalued by populist TV programmes and the use of the title interior designer by those who have received little or no formal training.

At the moment everyone who has anything to do with changing, styling, remodelling or rebuilding an interior space can call him or herself an interior designer. And any project from applying a simple coat of paint to a major museum remodelling can be called interior design.

Within interior design education we try to differentiate ourselves from each other, and remove ourselves from the public perception of interior design as "mdf changing rooms", by calling our courses "Interior Design", "Spatial Design", "Interior Architecture", etc. – anything that removes us from interior decoration.

The number of papers written for *Thinking Inside the Box* [2] that touched on this subject demonstrates that, as practitioners and educators, we are concerned with the status of our industry – for some we are suffering from an inferiority complex that we are not architects, for others we have a superiority complex about being more than decorators.

At the core of this problem is our history. Interior design has developed over a long period of time from decorative embellishment to spatial, architectural and commercial design. Education of interior designers has evolved in a similar way, providing courses at many levels, of differing lengths and content. And our practice of administrating real projects varies from comprehensive and transparent to informal and positively murky. It is this size and scope of what an interior design project can be, the range of courses available, and the variety of methods of practising that have created our diverse and broad industry of Interior Design.

How to define "Interior Design" and who can practise as an "Interior Designer" is a slippery subject. Are these even adequate descriptions of the broad range of skills that we have? Is there an argument for creating a hierarchy that describes us more specifically – ie "interior stylist/styling", "interior design(er)", "spatial design(er)", "interior architect(ure)"? Perhaps a one size fits all approach isn't appropriate, and we shouldn't even try to unify our trade under the singular umbrella of "Interior Design(er)".

How do we raise our status to professional?

Does this mean we need to regulate our irregular industry – to "regulate an irregularity" [3]? Do we want to regulate who is qualified to work within it through education alone, or do we recognise that diverse and unorthodox educational routes, skills and experience can also produce excellent designers?

Will protecting our educational niches, and excluding those without a degree from practising within the industry, be enough to raise our professional profile? Or do we accept the multiple levels of interior design education and explore other ways of professionalising our industry, by introducing a rigorous education in, and implementation of, the practice of interior design?

The practice of interior design

The term professional practice strikes fear and boredom into the hearts of most students, as it is often perceived as the uncreative aspect of design and is unfathomable and remote to their creative hypothetical projects. For us as tutors it is difficult to include it comprehensively into a course, due to the inconsistent and different information and methods from the industry on which we can draw to use as models. Unlike other professions, we have no industry-wide guidelines or codes of practice to use as a reference to manage our projects, ourselves, and our clients. We treat professional practice as a catch-all for anything that is not part of the creative process of design.

An argument for not including more rigorous professional practice into interior design higher education which has been used time and again is that the course is offering an education, not vocational training. As Hilary French, head of the RCA's Architecture and Design School, says "University must be about education first and training second" [4]. However, the RCA also offers business courses and presentation skills, so it recognises that both the industry and students are demanding more than just creative skills. Additional training is becoming more important in order to compete for jobs and projects in the limited interior design market.

But professional practice is not just business knowledge, career development and presentation skills (these can all be taught as vocational courses or CPD training). More essentially it is about gaining an understanding of both the creative and administrative processes in a project, and how they need to run in parallel with each other.

At present we tend to teach project administration separately from conceptual project work, and treat each as separate elements of a design project. But it is impossible to have one without the other. We hope that it is sufficient either introducing a block of professional practice at the end of the course, or presuming it will be picked up by the student once in the workplace. By treating it like this we mystify the design and construction process for students and place a big burden on employers to train them in these essential tools of the stages and progression of a design project.

Project administration should be a core element of the interior design curriculum as it expands, supports and informs the creative processes we already teach so well. If we provide these project administration tools to students we are giving them the ability to realise their projects professionally – they will be able to design and realise their projects to fulfil and even exceed their clients' expectations.

Project administration

However diverse the scope of projects that an interior designer can undertake, from a simple decoration job to a large commercial or institutional refurbishment, the essential outcome for all is to ensure that the expectations for the project are fulfilled for the client, the end user and the designer. This requires the designer to have strong creative skills to be able to develop a conceptual idea; it also requires him or her to be able professionally to practise the objective processes that will actually get the concept successfully built. The constraints of the site, client brief, building regulations, legislations, budgets and timescales add design parameters which force rigorous conceptual thinking and problem solving. They are ultimately what make design projects creatively challenging and move them from indulgent hypothesis to innovative and appropriate interior environments. This project administration tool can enhance the creative toolkit by adding substance and depth. This is why aspects of it should be included in design education and not left for the novice to pick up once in the workplace or solely through CPD training.

What is project administration?

It is fees, it is budgets, it is contracts, it is communications, it is specifications, it is work stages, it is schedules, legislation, CDM and so much more – much of which comes as a shock to the novice designer starting work in the industry. What these things are, when they need to be addressed, who needs to address them, etc., are all things which will smooth a project through to successful completion.

The focus of most interior design education is on the creative process and learning tools and tactics to take a project from initial brief through to detailed design proposals.

No matter what scope and size, all projects go through similar stages of sketch design, presentation, detail design etc. These stages expand and contract in complexity depending on the scope of the project. The administration process is similar in that there is a fundamental process that does not change significantly. It is flexible and adaptable to suit the scope of the project and, most importantly, it runs in parallel to the creative process not separately from it, and on real projects needs to be addressed from the earliest stages.

Professional guidelines

Most professions have guidelines or codes of practice to follow, and for many of them it is not possible to qualify until there has been some practice of their profession in the real world (e.g. architects, lawyers, doctors). If we want to be perceived as a profession, do we need to introduce similar guidelines into our educational systems? As well as including the professional practice of project administration into the curriculum, should we introduce a practice element to include experience in the industry before finally being assessed for qualification?

Incorporating into our educational structure the two elements of a more rigorous approach to teaching professional practice and the application of it to real project experience will start the slow process of raising our status from industry to profession.

The problem with introducing guidelines for interior design practice which we can all adopt is that the industry does not use consistent methods of implementation. The inconsistencies this causes make it very difficult for both clients and novice designers to compare and understand what we do, how we do it, and how we charge for it.

As educators we have the opportunity to change this and begin to professionalise our industry from education upwards. We can begin to unify the methods for administrating projects across the gamut of interior design that then, over time, will infiltrate the industry. Likewise, if we do go down the regulated profession route and have a "body with clout", this aspect of education and practice can be supported and monitored. It is a quantifiable element of interior design education which could form the basis for ultimate qualification into a profession where a certain standard of achievement is expected. This will weed out the amateurs and non-educated who currently call themselves interior designers.

What tools do we have at the moment?

The UK interior design industry has very few tools in terms of reference for project administration. There are many books for architectural projects that are useful, as are parts of the vast tome written for the US market by Christine Piotrowski [5], but there is nothing specific to our UK industry. Like most aspects of what we do, our methods for project administration have evolved in haphazard ways, drawing on methods from heavyweight architectural models to fluffy decorator- and builder- friendly cash and commission models, but this is the reason for a lack of reference material. If we want to raise our professional bar we need to be more consistent in our methods across the board.

The British Institute of Interior Design has produced a document called the Form of Appointment for Interior Design Services (ID/05) [6], which has been written in collaboration with RIBA. It is not the easiest of documents to understand, but it is the only document of its kind for our UK industry which is attempting to rationalise the design process into stages which are clear and practical for projects of most size and scope. It combines the creative processes into a framework that describes what administrative decisions and actions need to be taken and at what point at each stage of a project to take them. It is accompanied by sample client contracts and terms and conditions. This document is only a starting point, but it is at least making an attempt to unify and raise the level of our professional processes. With feedback from educators and practitioners it is a good model from which to form professional, consistent guidelines that will clarify and demystify the processes involved in realising projects – for students, practising designers and clients. The authors of ID/05 have since written the BIID Interior Design Job Book, published by RIBA in September 2010.

As interior designers we are bound by similar constraints to those of architects. Moreover, the boundary between the two disciplines is becoming more obscure as the size of interior projects increases, and the work of architects is including more interior design. The scope of projects may be different to architecture, but the project phases, budget and schedule expectations are similar, as are the requirements for our designs to conform to building and planning legislations. Is the architectural education system a model that we can use? Qualifying as an architect is a long process, Part 1 – 3 year degree, 1 year work experience, Part 2 – 2 years MA, further work experience, Part 3 exam. This length of study is not necessary for interior design, but the model of part study, part work experience and final qualifying assessment is something that we could consider, as there are parallels between architecture and interior design. At the moment we churn out graduates into the industry and they are left to get on with it without any further assessment to establish if they have achieved the skills to practise at a professional level.

Tactics for developing our own models

Clearly we cannot include all aspects of project administration in our existing curriculums. Some elements of it can only be learnt and understood from real experience. But if we take the architectural model and the BIID document as a starting point, the initial stages of project administration that take a project from client briefing to production of installation drawings and documents (Part 1 – The Design Stages) can be included into our current courses (if they are not already). Part 2 – Installation Management, which deals with on-site and contractual supervision, could be taught during or after work experience as a separate course, which is assessed in order to qualify as an interior designer, along with other key professional skills of communication, managing clients, team and multi-project working, budget and scheduling management, identification of further skills and specialisms. If we want to achieve professional status we need to monitor the novice designers' ability to practise on a professional level. This Part 2 course could be based on case studies and/or real projects and be taken on a part-time or distance/online basis.

At present one of the main drawbacks to this model is that there are too many graduates, and not enough placements for them. Employers are reluctant to take on novice designers without experience, as it is difficult to know what to do with them. If we develop a framework for what we expect graduates to learn during their initial work experience, it will make it easier for companies to take on these students as there are clear guidelines for what they need exposure to, and it will develop a culture of mentoring that does not exist at present and hopefully open up more opportunities for placements. It will mean that the graduate is a useful member of the team and as such is a properly paid junior designer.

It also requires the graduate to be proactive in ensuring that he/she is exposed to and gains skills for these areas of knowledge during work experience in order successfully to complete the qualifying assessment. This process will weed out many of the students who are not serious about a career in interior design.

Conclusion

Emma Germain's article in a recent issue of *Design Week* [7] discusses the industry's attitudes to helping students cross over from the isolated world of study into the world of work. She says that:

> "Most designers seem to be in agreement that students should spend time working in studios to comprehend how their creativity can be best applied."

To achieve this we need to work with the industry, be involved in the government's action plan for the creative industries [8] and get support for enabling our students to make the transition from graduate to professional interior designer.

As a more professional educational and industry approach is adopted, encouraged, or even enforced by a professional body with clout, and/or the government [9], interior design courses at all levels will have to raise their professional practice content in order to compete – with each other for high quality students, for government funding, and professional connections.

If we adopt a three-part approach of study, experience, and assessment, it also means that the diverse and unorthodox educational routes, skills and experience, which in the past have produced excellent designers, can continue to offer students several ways into our re-valued profession and find a specialism within it. If we move towards something like what I have proposed then we are raising the awareness of our graduates that there are more jobs within design than the purely creative. If our students are exposed to the full design process it will give them the opportunity to assess where their skills and interests lie, and be able to develop a career path that can make them a specialist within the broader interior design profession.

If we really do want to raise our professional status, we have to change within both education and practice. How we change, what we change and when we change is for debate. The intention of this paper is to explore one area that has been neglected and could provide us with a route to a higher professional profile as perceived by students, the profession and clients.

References

[1] Pearman, H. Are Designers Any Good? *FX Magazine*, 2008, 8(169), 53-54.
[2] Interiors Forum Scotland 2007. *Thinking Inside the Box*, (Middlesex University Press now Libri Publishing, 2007)
[3] Hannay, P. A Regulated Irregularity. *Thinking Inside the Box*, pp107-112 (Middlesex University Press now Libri Publishing, 2007).
[4] Germain, E. Suffering for their craft – Design education doesn't end with graduation – to make it in the real world, placements and apprenticeships are a must. *Design Week*, 2008, 23(17), pp9.
[5] Piotrowski, C. *Interior Design Management: A Handbook for Owners and Managers* (VNR, 1992)
[6] RIBA and BIID. *Form of Appointment for Interior Design Services* (ID/05). (RIBA Publications, 2005).
[7] Germain, E. Suffering for their craft – Design education doesn't end with graduation – to make it in the real world, placements and apprenticeships are a must. *Design Week*, 2008, 23(17), pp9.
[8] For information on government policy go to www.culture.gov.uk/about_us/creativeindustries/
[9] Department for Culture, Media and Sport. Creative Britain: New Talents for the New Economy (Department for Media, Culture and Sport)

Ms Jenny GROVE
The Interior Design School
22 Lonsdale Road
London
NW6 6RD
jennygrove@me.com
+44 7768 394606

Educational tactics: introducing interiors

Joyce FLEMING

Glasgow Caledonian University

INTERIOR TOOLS AND TACTICS – EDUCATION

The papers presented in this part of the symposium posited ideas about how Interior Design educators can address tactically the transition that their students have to make from tuition at school to being critical autonomous learners in Higher Education. Despite rigorous pre-assessment requirements for entry to Interior Design courses there still seems to be a lack of readiness, and a wide range of ability levels, in most cohorts of first-year students.

There is considerable recognition and agreement among educators that this is a problem, and Breyenbach and Johnston's paper 'Rethink the First Year Offering' provides some evidence to verify this. It is difficult to see what further type of objective data could be produced. Their view is widely held by professional educators (and especially our delegates) representing the whole curriculum and in different geographical locations. Therefore this is a problem that must be addressed.

Chris Hay and Pam Locker outline their tactics in "Learning to Practice Design". The intense transition period that has been put in place at Lincoln University's first year collaboration between the Interior Design and the DEM Design for Exhibitions and Museums Programmes rightly focuses on the process of design. By getting students to produce, value, critically reflect and evaluate their work again and again in a continuous loop, their solution is akin to the Breytenbach and Johnston emphasis on a creative tactic that holistically connects heart, hand and mind. Both strategies call for intense tuition, with clear aims and objectives set out and adhered to by the whole teaching team, within a well-defined period of time.

Instilling passion for the praxis and development of the design process is not easy, especially if the students' focus is elsewhere and their learning experiences fragmented or indeed artificial boundaries are erected between creativity, theory and/or design practice. Further, if one methodology is adopted at the beginning of the course it can be interpreted as educational "spoon feeding"; a charge to which delegates and educators in HE are particularly sensitive. However in design education is this not initially what good pedagogy entails? There must be some way in which a tutor can show their students how they would move round a particular problem, to give insight into their design thinking, and share their design ideas. Other methodologies could then be shown, to allow students to adopt and refine their own independent tools and strategies. Coffield et al (2004)[*] describe this as a sheep dip where the learner is covered by as many learning styles as possible. But it is increasingly imperative that new students are given this "leg up", and shown "how to" step by step in one method at the start. For many it will be like a light being switched on in the dark, for most it is the essential foundation of any quality design education.

---

[*] Coffield, F., Ecclestone, K., Hall, E., Mosely, D. (2004) *Learning Styles and Pedagogy in Post 16 – Learning: A Systematic and Critical Review.* http://www.lsnlearning.org.uk/Resourse-32188.aspx Accessed 23.9.10

Chris HAY
University of Lincoln

Pam LOCKER
University of Lincoln

LEARNING TO PRACTISE DESIGN

Introduction

Across all subject areas, higher education has changed. In universities as a whole, student numbers have increased exponentially over the last fifty years and this expansion continues [1]. However there has not been a concomitant increase in resources, and institutions have been under pressure to have "greater efficiency through reduced teaching costs per student" [2]. A recent article suggested that at Manchester University student contact time has halved over the last twenty years [3]. The previous government's ambition that fifty percent of school leavers should continue on to higher education means that students are coming from a wider range of social, cultural and educational backgrounds than ever before. This has generated a range of unfamiliar issues for educators.

Those of us involved in recruitment onto art and design courses in Britain have noticed a dramatic change in the student demographic. The institutional changes into which these students are arriving are themselves also significant. In the main, the institutions are now called universities, rather than art schools or polytechnics, and this in itself has altered the context of art and design education and has important ramifications for our students' learning experiences. Art and design is relatively expensive for institutions to support and across the sector there have been reductions in resources, including staff time and studio space. In this respect our experience at the University of Lincoln can be said to be typical of the higher educational scheme in the United Kingdom today.

This is a situation which is putting considerable pressure on traditional art and design educational practice and which suggests that aspects of that practice need to be challenged and rethought.

It is an awareness of, and a response to, these changing external and internal contexts that our recent work with first year undergraduate students on our joint Design for Exhibitions and Museums(DEM) and Interior Design (ID) honours degree programmes has sought to address.

Problem One: Pre-University

Five years ago both courses moved from Hull to their new home in Lincoln and during this time we were particularly interested in how the change of location might affect recruitment. Over the last two years we have noticed changes that we now realise are not related to our move, but to new and very significant changes in the very nature of the students coming onto our design courses. In order to analyse this change, our starting point was to try and understand why there appeared to be such a marked change and in order to do this we examined students' pre-university experience, their attitudes to study and their expectations of university life.

As institutions, we now function in a consumer-led environment where there is a "systematic conversion of intellectual activity into intellectual capital and hence into intellectual property" [4] which in turn drives a global knowledge economy. We, the producers of educational experiences, have to market ourselves to our potential customers and are well aware that the offer as perceived by the student is a complex mix of location, facilities and social experience where the individual course programme plays but a part. Students talk of being at "Uni" before they say "I am studying design". This is a sometimes sobering thought.

One does not have to go far back in time to find a situation where all art and design courses would have insisted upon all applicants completing a foundation course before entry would even be considered. Without this experience, and the accompanying portfolio of work that evidenced that experience, it was believed that no one was ready to undertake serious study in art and design. Of course there were then far fewer potential students seeking places, and far fewer courses being offered. We have moved from an elite educational model, where the power of admission lay predominantly with the academic and the institution, to one where the student, assuming they have the required points, effectively chooses the institution they wish to attend.

Today, many of our students come straight from sixth forms with no prior foundation experience of any kind and it would appear that Route B entry from foundation courses is almost becoming a luxurious scarcity. Students are accepted onto our programmes from UCAS via Route A on the basis of "A" level points and often we do not meet them until after enrolment. Some students choose to come for interview or are Route B applicants, but the portfolios exhibit different capabilities from students of the past. Although there is evidence of creativity within them, typically these portfolios show that the design projects the students have undertaken are various, but lacking in experimental process or the exploratory investigation offered by the foundation course experience. We see instead clearly defined boundaries and a limiting of possibilities.

Our students are now in the main coming from a pre university experience, which teaches them to see their studies as being made up of discrete self contained elements. They are experienced "box tickers" – providing answers to specific questions. They have been tested again and again and their education has focused on their success in those tests. In comparison with even the recent past, these students appear to have had a very different preparation for art and design in higher education.

Problem Two: Arrival at University

The convergence of the former polytechnics with universities has seen a shift from the Bauhaus traditions of master and student to an expectation of more autonomous learning. No doubt there are institutions which, even today, can still operate the traditional model of one-on-one tutorial-led studio-based teaching, but for the majority – and certainly for us – such a narrow set of criteria would result in the closure of our programmes.

Pedagogically, we expect that on arrival our students will be prepared as independent learners. However, for our new generations of students, this is a questionable and dangerous assumption. They arrive with a different set of skills, which include some strengths but also worrying weaknesses. When a group of thirty-five first year students were asked recently if they understood what "autonomy" meant, not one of them had even heard of the word before. In the main, our new students exhibit extremely limited independent learning skills, they are passive receivers of information and then transmitters of mainly undigested information that they do not appear to understand. They do however exhibit a ready and fluent ability with aspects of digital media, communication between them is often virtual and instant. They are technically sophisticated in terms of networking, but have a limited understanding of graphic and presentation skills.

We have found our students are used to clear unambiguous briefs which ask for straight forward answers. They worry about experimentation or risk taking, and seem to have a very limited understanding of process. Their work is produced for "us" rather than for themselves, and they are reluctant to practise to improve. They do not seem to understand the concept of critical reflection on their own work or that of others. They are very aware of grades and see this as a validation of their progress and ability, constantly asking "What do I do to get a good mark?", and they are very discouraged when they fail to get – as they see it – a straight answer. Students appear however, to be computer-literate and have no problem seeking and finding information on the internet. They are Web 1.0 and Wed 2.0 literate and their social as well as working lives are highly dependent on the computer and its mobility: "I use my laptop. I take it away, it's attached to me, I couldn't survive without it".[5]

This is not an issue of intelligence, it is one of attitude. Students arrive at university with an extremely limited idea of what is expected of them or how to take ownership of their learning. Our point here is that as educators in art and design we can no longer make any assumptions about the skills and expectations that our students will bring with them.

Problem 3: Negotiating Design Process

It is becoming ever clearer that students increasingly do not want to spend time developing alternatives but want to go straight to a "solution". They are very concerned about grades and will focus on the piece of work that in their view achieves the grade. But they want to bring this work into being without any exploration, it needs to arrive immediately – the focus is on the goal not on the journey. If asked to undertake a piece of research the material is usually quickly and efficiently found on the internet, but when a brief asks students to reflect on the meaning of their work, contextualise it in a broader sense or use it to inform their own thinking there is a lack of understanding and resistance. Their interest lies on the surface. They are not interested in, or are as yet unused to, depth.

In effect, students are unable to grasp the importance of practice. Just as the musician needs to repeat actions over time to improve, or the dancer to practice their steps, so the designer needs to develop specific skills relevant to their particular discipline. As Richard Sennett has observed "going over an action, again and again, enables self criticism"[6] He goes on" Modern education, afraid of boring children, deprives them of the experience of studying their own ingrained practice and modulating it from within"[7].

We see in our students this lack of experience in developing work through practice. Within design project work there is a lack of engagement with process and a focus on the end result. Students commonly skip from one idea to another, without exploring any of them in depth or making meaningful connections between them. Their focus has shifted from the learning process itself to its value being expressed as a mark or grade. This phenomenon of undervaluing both process and product, in our experience, takes in two principle forms which are manifestations of the same thing. The first and most serious is the lack of interest in keeping, collating and working with preliminary material of all kinds, both produced by hand and digitally. The second takes the form of discarded expensive printouts left lying in the studio where work is often left unclaimed after a "crit". Their work is discarded, not collated, not valued but thrown out.

There is a paradox at the heart of this as students place value in the images that they can produce, whilst simultaneously discarding the physical manifestation of that image. There is, as Walter Benjamin has pointed out, no original here, no "aura" [8]. In place of their learning is a focus on numbers, "What grade did I get?" is all that matters.

The previous experience of being tested has trained the student to focus on answers not questions. These answers are increasing expressed digitally, and students are (mostly) approaching the computer, the information it generates and the software available to them in an uncritical way. Value is placed on the students' self perception of the "perfect" image, as defined and produced by the software. Once they have succeeded in producing the "first image" they allow themselves to be seduced by it, fixated, and the task is complete.

But this is problematic. They see the value of their work to lie in the perfectibility of the image, which is not surprising given the not-inconsiderable skill required to produce it in the first place. Unlike sketch work where the positive effects of "mistake making" are tangible, computer work enables the constant elimination of errors or mistakes. The image is constantly written and rewritten and the past and its process erased and forgotten.

Mistakes, errors or clumsy work disappear into the ether as to keep any kind of digital or printed record is expensive in terms of money and memory. Ironically, it is potentially within these memories that design learning may lie. Process is seen as mechanical and waste, rather then development and creativity, and is rendered invisible by the action of correction and deletion. The cycle of make (draw/write/model (virtual or physical)) followed by reflection to build cumulative experience is largely absent. The metaphor of placing one brick on top of another to build on one's experience is replaced by make (or download), present and forget. Each new brick that the student makes replaces the last brick. Now there only appears ever to be one brick. Is the process of constructivist learning breaking down?

By treating aspects of their own production as being of no value, as being in effect waste, they are throwing away possibilities and opportunities. John Scanlan has observed that "in the well-ordered society which we like to think we live in, it is easy for the degraded and the worthless to be blocked out. Yet these are the principle categories of "stuff" that the artist dallies with" [9]. He goes on "as with the emergence of knowledge, the performance of artistic creation begins within a conceptual void – with loose associations, with fragmentary ideas and the speculations of curiosity"- the very things in other words that the student discards .

Computer drawing programs, particularly programs like "Sketch-up", have provided an immediacy that has increasingly replaced hand-drawing. The students own estimation of, and confidence in, their own hand work is mostly negative. Through mark making, which is reworked, rubbed out, remembered by the body through the act of drawing, the physical movement of the hand imprints the plan in our memory and it is this experience that cements learning. Sadly, the student's perception is that their own sketching is "bad" as opposed to the accuracy of the computer which they perceive as "good". There is little interest or understanding in the value of accumulating layers of information and thoughts. The "unfinished-ness" of their own sketch work carries ambiguities and suggestions. It is at odds with the pursuit of accuracy that is encouraged in school. It is open and challenging. It is charged with possibilities. It is terrifying.

Paper from the start suggests an origin, which is physical. The mark made by hand is about authorship which carries with it responsibility. The line, materials and colours on the computer are distanced from our (human) experience and their qualities a function of the particular software. Paradoxically, students choose to "trust" that the computer "knows" rather than trust their own self belief that they are the makers and the computer is the recorder. They are thus absolved from thinking, as the software apparently does it for them. We are all familiar with the "badly scaled stone or brick wallpaper" where any sense of mass, weight and texture dissolves into surface and skin. This is not a debate about computer versus pencil. It is a debate about learning to use a new tool whilst struggling to learn how to learn about design. Digital technology is an extremely powerful design tool – once you know how, but in trying to shoehorn this new and constantly evolving "tool" into our teaching pencil cases, terrified of being branded "luddites", we may have misjudged how it should be used in terms of pedagogy.

A clear example of the misuse of the computer as a tool has been noted in relationship to architecture and spatial design and it is to do with scale. Our understanding of space and form and human scale is ingrained. We do not need to think to sit on a chair, navigate round a piece of furniture, or judge the distance required to pick up a cup. We know all this because we understand the relationships between ourselves and the world around us. When student designers begin to produce proposals for new spaces they must translate or transpose this inherent understanding of people and the phenomenological world into a 2- or 3-dimensional representation, whether by means of a drawing or model. In order to do this they have to learn about scale. The computer "impedes the designer in thinking about scale, as opposed to sheer size"[10]. The computer distances the beginner from their own experience. We have observed in our students that the action of drawing by hand a room which they have previously surveyed allows them to register scale and dimension in a way which eludes many on the screen.

Rather then racing blindly ahead, perhaps we need seriously to revisit to exploit the technology more effectively as a teaching and learning tool, particularly in the first year of study. How does theory underpin learning? When should the stabilisers come off?

Seeking Solutions

Understanding Process

During the first eight weeks or so of the 2007/08 academic year we sought to address at least some of the issues identified above. We devised, along with Doug Gittens, senior lecturer in Interior Design, a bridging programme of study which was designed to help students make the transition from their previous experiences to the new challenges of higher education. Doug Gitten's ideas were based on drawing and model making, and emphasised the value of repetition and practice for learning. Projects were kept deliberately short to encourage students to work quickly and to match attention spans and skills levels.

Each group of short concentrated projects focused on the iterative process of drawing, thinking, modelling, thinking, drawing and so on. As well as building on skills, the projects were about understanding process. In particular we stressed the idea of doing things by hand and then doing them again. We sought to register in the students' minds that design was a process of seeing, thinking, doing and reflecting. We were less concerned with the quality of the work, but very concerned that students completed tasks. They were encouraged to work quickly through imaginative engagement to make individual interpretations no matter how tentative. The marks were their marks and they therefore owned their own production.

Adopting Space

The importance of establishing a strong studio culture was key in managing student transition from school or college to university. The studio became the focus for their creative, cultural and social learning landscape. It was a new "home", a place to make friends, mix with other year groups, learn from each other and receive feedback, store work and "play". Through the studio, students could start to develop their identity as "designers" and a sense of security in their space, essential in promoting a comfortable, non-confrontational environment for successful feedback from staff. By encouraging students to use their computers in the studio, rather then elsewhere, this important design tool became interwoven with their design work.

Understanding Autonomy

In parallel to project work, we outlined our expectations of students in terms of adult learning. We started by trying to set aside our assumptions about what they might know and how they might behave. We began from where they were, rather than where we thought they should be. The hope was to help students understand what it means to be autonomous learners and to begin to enjoy and understand the pleasure and responsibility of independence. This was essentially about forming good habits. The students were encouraged to think about self discipline, rigour, attendance, organisation and emotional robustness.

Learning to Reflect

The programme was constructed around the idea of a continuous cycle of production, followed by reflection and evaluation. Core skills were introduced in turn and reiterated through the various project formats which the students were encouraged to practice in the studio and to continue to work on at home. We took the world around us as the context for the work and worked through natural form, mechanical form, human form and letter form. Throughout this period students returned to the same tasks using the same tools but in varying contexts. In this way repetition of skills or practice was slowly built upon, with each layer becoming increasingly difficult. Reflection was built into the process as a continuous cycle of feedback. As students worked through the tasks, they started to become aware and observe their own development, thus criticality entered into the students' thinking and into the process.

Student Producers

We were looking for the production of work. We asked students to fill sketchbooks, to draw expressively in a variety of media and to draw with the precision of the draftsman. Drawing was used to express an idea or concept and to record and delineate the various artefacts, some designed by them, others found for the purpose. Following studio sessions we held regular and public "crits" where all the work was promoted as a celebration of student production. Students were encouraged to bring ALL their work to support their presentations, thus encouraging students to value their work. These occasions were used to pull out students' achievements and were not about measuring or judging the individual. Feedback was about teasing out hidden or partially revealed qualities and sharing that discovery or insight. This served as an opportunity to reinforce learning in a non confrontational context. In this early stage of university life we sought to provide a framework for action, where students knew where they had to be, both physically and in terms of the tasks required. Students could learn to give and receive criticism, within carefully drawn boundaries. We wanted to encourage them to be interactive participants with their learning rather then passive recipients.

Conclusions

What conclusions can we draw from these experiences for our own learning as design educators? For us, it is now clear that the nature and expectations of students coming into DEM and ID has changed. The challenges that face us are great but not insurmountable. There needs to be a renegotiation of our relationship with our students, and a democratisation of their learning to enable a shift from the passive to the interactive as they become independent "student producers". But in order to achieve this, both students and staff need a clear understanding of what we expect from each other as part of a collaborative team. At the end of the year, we as a course team are confident that our approach was highly successful in generating a more settled and engaged year group evidenced by attendance levels and retention.

There was also evidence of clear progression in students' portfolios over the eight week transition period, suggesting that they had built on their learning and made connections between projects and skills. For next year however, the team intend to make the "type" of projects less familiar and more challenging, although the nature of the approach will remain the same. We plan to revisit our pedagogical approach to first year computer learning. This experiment was about process and practice, not product and now we have a better understanding of its potential we can experiment with project work. The biggest challenge will be to engender a more mature culture of reflection encouraging students to look and "see" their own work and that of others more clearly.

In conclusion, we believe this teaching and learning experience to have been positive and encouraging and we have started planning (and practicing) with a sense of satisfaction and optimism.

References

[1] Wolf, A. (2002) Does Education matter? Myths about Education and Economic Growth. London and New York: Penguin Books
[2] Bamber J, Ducklin A and Tett L. (2000) Working with contradictions in the struggle for access. In Thompson J., Stretching the Academy. Leicester: NIACE
[3] Attwood, R (24-30 April 2009) Manchester social science contact time halved since 1988, report shows Times Higher Education
[4] Noble, D. (1998) Digital diploma mills: The automation of Higher Education *First Monday* Vol.3.No.1.
[5] JISC (2007) In their own words: exploring the learner's perspective on e-learning Available at http://www.jiscinfonet.ac.uk/publications/in -their-own-words (accessed April 28, 2008)
[6] Sennett, R. *The Craftsman* Allen Lane, 2008, p. 38
[7] Sennett, R. *The Craftsman* Allen Lane, 2008, p. 38
[8] Benjamin, B. *The Work of Art in the Age of Mechanical Reproduction*, p. 215. Ill*uminations,* Pimlico 1999
[9] Scanlan, J. *On Garbage* Reaktion Books, 2005.
[10] Sennett, R. *The Craftsman* Allen Lane, 2008, p. 41

Acknowledgements

Doug Gittens, Dr Geoff Matthews, Rosie Saunders and to many others in Lincoln School of Architecture for their help and support.

Amanda BREYTENBACH
University of Johannesburg

Ian ADAIR JOHNSTON
University of Johannesburg

RE-THINK THE FIRST-YEAR OFFERING: ADDRESS THE GAP IN STUDENT READINESS

Introduction

Students entering the first year of study in Interior Design represent a diverse group of individuals who vary greatly in the abilities and skills required to execute Interior Design projects. Successful candidates who enter the programme have all met the minimum requirements, which include attaining a predetermined minimum Matric Score (M-Score), and have successfully passed the departmental entrance assessment. The minimum entrance requirements assist the department merely in identifying students from a large group of applicants who could be appropriate to attend the departmental entrance assessment.

However it is apparent to the first-year lecturers that there is an imbalance in students' readiness. This imbalance is evident at various stages of the execution of tasks and projects, but it is most prevalent during the conceptualisation stages of a project, where students have to resolve a problem and develop a concept. Time is of the essence during this stage, and it is observed that students who have the ability to transform concepts into actual visual solutions have far greater confidence in completing projects within the required time period. These students succeed well in the first six months of the first year, and will usually complete the programme after three years, which is the minimum time period laid down for the completion of the National Diploma in Interior Design. Students without formal training at secondary school level in drawing and problem-solving must attain these skills, while at the same time keeping up with the completion of prescribed projects.

The imbalance in student readiness within the first year presents the following two questions:

- What factors impact on student readiness?
- What are the tactics that can be employed to address student readiness?

The research questions presented above were identified by the first-year lecturers after student readiness problems came to their attention. This paper aims to address these questions through employing the following methodology:

- Firstly, documentation of the observations and perceived factors presented by the first-year lecturers and Head of Department
- Secondly conduct of a student questionnaire to verify claims made within the observations
- Lastly consulting literature that could assist in developing strategies to address student readiness

Focus and Efforts of Design Education in Developing Student Readiness

Junginger [4], argues that:

> "Every student brings with him or her three essential tools for inquiry that, if they make use of them, allow them to succeed."

These three elements are identified by the author as heart, hand and mind. The heart represents a passion and love for participating in making and creating. The hand refers to the aspects of making, and finally the mind represents curiosity and the ability to generate ideas. Junginger [4] suggests that it is the task of educators to develop these three elements through the presentation of appropriate design methods and techniques.

One of the goals of design education as presented by Junginger is to get ideas out of the heads of students and onto paper. The author's study indicates that making skills should not be confused with artistic abilities, but rather with the ability to explore and discover novel solutions through introducing sketching and drawing methods to students which can be used as tools of inquiry.

Warner [9] agrees with Junginger when he states that:

> "Teaching design in the context of technology education must involve teaching students how to actively use both their minds and their hands in order to be creative, inventive problem solvers."

Ambile [1] further identifies that a student's attitude is derived from a variety of sources which includes friends, family, school, television and other forms of mass media, and local community. These sources mould the attitudes that affect the way in which a young student behaves.

Through these authors [1, 4, 9] it can therefore be identified that students enter a design programme with passion, skill and an attitude that needs to be developed throughout their study period. In their study on learning styles for Design and Technology education Poon and Joo [6] further indicate that education cannot neglect the problem-solving ability of students. They suggest that if this ability is lacking education must attempt to provide necessary curricula to correct the deficit. Education should therefore provide an equal opportunity to all students to develop their design skills and abilities.

Factors which Impact on Student Readiness

Varied Standards Delivered through Secondary Education

Student attitudes towards art and design are determined by their experience of secondary school art and design education or lack of it [Warner, 9]. In the first-year class students represent a variety of different educational backgrounds which range from private schools, government schools to technical schools. In these schools teachers emphasise different aspects of the nationally prescribed syllabus. Observation of individual portfolios presented at the first-year entrance assessment clearly reveals these differences in the approach of art teachers. This then results in the acceptance of students with widely varying results and approaches into the first year of study.

Taking Art as a High School Subject

Table 1 reports the outcomes of a questionnaire regarding the selection of Art as secondary school subject, completed by students from all three years of study in the department:

Table 1: Percentage of students that took Art as a high school subject

Study year	Secondary Education (SE) Art Grade 8-12	Art Grade 8-9	Other	Sub-total for SE	Art as extra-mural	No Art	Total
First years	47%	5%	7%	59%	7%	35%	100%
Second years	70%	5%	7%	82%	13%	5%	100%
Third years	55%	0%	10%	65%	10%	25%	100%
Total %	57%	4%	8%	69%	10%	21%	100%

The quantitative data presented in the table identifies that in the 2008 first-year group there is a decline in those that had Art as a high school subject. The table also indicates that the current second year students, described by lecturers as a strong design class, includes 70% who studied Art as a high school subject.

In addition, the qualitative data attained from the questionnaire aimed to identify the motivation for the choice of Art as a subject in secondary school. It became evident that the majority of students have a perceived passion for the subject. They also believed that they had a natural ability or talent which empowered them in this choice. Compared with other more academically orientated subjects, Art had the added value of enjoyment. A number of students saw Art as an opportunity for a career that involved creativity.

Lastly the questionnaire asked those students who did not study Art at school why this was. The majority of those responding indicated that it was not possible to take Art, because their high school did not offer the subject.

Change in Student Profile

The University of Johannesburg (UJ) is a comprehensive institution, and is the result of a merger that took place in January 2005 between the former Technikon Witwatersrand (TWR) and the Rand Afrikaans University (RAU). The Faculty of Art, Design and Architecture (FADA), and therefore the Department of Interior Design, formed part of the former TWR and offers programmes that are referred to as prior technikon type programmes. Technikon programmes are defined [3] as programmes that concentrate on the application of scientific principles to practical problems and to technology, thus preparing learners for the practice, promotion and transfer of technology within a particular vocation or industry.

With the advent of the merger, a change in the first-year entrance requirement occurred. A new set of criteria for entry-level prospective students was formulated. An M-Score for Interior Design was gradually introduced and since 2006 the applicants have had to attain a minimum M-Score of 12 to gain access to the entrance assessment. Table 2 shows the manner in which M-Scores are calculated through assigning numeric values to the symbols attained in Matric.

Table 2: Calculation of the M-Score

Subject Symbol	Higher Grade	Standard Grade
A	5	4
B	4	3
C	3	2
D	2	1
E	1	0

This increase in the M-Score has resulted in a different profile for Interior Design students. The current students perform well within theoretical modules and there has also been a greater increase in the number of female students. Students who are higher academic achievers stand a better chance of acceptance thus excluding more naturally talented applicants.

Ironically, it has been observed by the department that many of the previous top design achiever students who have excelled as Interior Designers in South Africa, and who qualified from the prior TWR, would not have been accepted under the present conditions as an M-Score was not an entrance acceptance requirement within the first year. Entrance was granted on the basis of a portfolio evaluation, completion of two- and three-dimensional exercises and an interview.

Termination of the Foundation Programme

The Faculty of Art, Design and Architecture had presented a centrally-offered Foundation Programme since 1987. Boucharenc [2] explains that the term Basic Design is often used internationally to describe this type of offering, and that this formed the basis of the pedagogy of the classical schools of design and architecture. Boucharenc [2] identifies that the offering of a Foundation Programme can often be enhanced by the curiosity and experiences of students rather than by the theoretical content of the subject matter.

In the Faculty this programme involved lecturers from the following departments; Fine Art, Interior Design, Graphic Design, Industrial Design and Ceramics. Lecturers from these departments presented the modules offered in the programme. The diversity introduced by inter-departmental involvement was significantly enriching to all first-year students. Mixed groups of students from the different programmes all received the same project outcomes, thus serving to provide a basic standard in educational approach for the faculty as a whole.

Sadly, FADA terminated the centrally-offered Foundation Programme in June 2007. The programme was terminated for the following reasons:

- Financial rationalisation per department within the faculty
- Implications of limited staff capacity and resources
- Industry demands that require an increase of focus on discipline knowledge and skills within programme curriculum

The termination of the Foundation Programme came at a time when it would offer a considerable advantage in assisting with student readiness and addressing the gaps resulting from the varied education backgrounds of students that currently wished to enrol at the institution.

Boucharenc's [2] international study on the offering of Basic Design programmes identifies that the past 20 years have witnessed a rebirth in the offering of Basic Design education due to many debates and pedagogical propositions presented by experts in the field. Internationally, therefore, design programmes are rethinking the offering and inclusion of these programmes.

Increase in First-year Student Numbers

An increase in student numbers is one of the financial viability indicators determined by the institution. The Faculty is required to indicate an on-going growth in the number of students accepted in undergraduate and postgraduate programmes. The demand for the increased number of students that must be accepted puts further pressure on the selection process. Greater scrutiny becomes necessary in the evaluation process. The first year is pivotal in establishing a successful throughput process which is required by the University, thus the readiness and personal and academic development of the student becomes crucial.

Furthermore, the increase in student numbers results in an increase in class sizes. This results in an increase in staff: student ratio which in turn impacts negatively on the contact time per student. In the report on student readiness, Lord [5] questions the size of classes and the impact that it has on student readiness.

Proposing Tactics to Address Student Readiness

The following tools and tactics were identified from existing teaching strategies and practices that are used in addressing student readiness.

Differentiated Instruction

Differentiated instruction is described by Tomlinson [8] as a philosophy of teaching which claims that a student learns best when a teacher effectively addresses variance in student readiness levels, interest and learning profile preferences. Tomlinson [8] continues to identify that the key goal of differentiated instruction is to maximise the learning potential of each student. One of the aims of differentiated learning is that the learning environment becomes a community of learning in which the student shares with the lecturer responsibility, optimum operation, and maximum individual growth. [8]

The principles of differentiation as identified by Tomlinson [8] are firstly that the students' attitude about learning and about themselves is of great importance. Secondly, differentiation must be an extension of a high quality curriculum, not a replacement for it. Thirdly, effective differentiation is not random and should be based on a clear teaching cycle.

In examining the strategies of differentiated instruction, as presented by Tomlinson [7], which can be appropriate to the Design curriculum, it is observed that the class should be divided into smaller groups. Grouping the class can assist the lecturer to create groups which attend to student learning differences. Group work should therefore be encouraged in projects that are presented by using differentiation strategies.

The following strategies as identified by Tomlinson [7] were considered to be of value for first years:

Compacting Students should be assessed before commencing a project or learning unit. It is important to attain what the students already know, what they do not know, and have a meaningful and challenging plan for students that already know much about the topic or skill. Tomlinson [7] states that: "Compacting begins with student readiness and ends with an emphasis on student interest."

Independent study Introduce independent study with the execution of projects. Independent study presents the student with the opportunity to develop talent and interest areas. The independent study should be presented at a level that will address the students at their current readiness and move them to greater independence with each project.

Compiling a portfolio Compiling a portfolio is inherent to the offering of a design curriculum. Tomlinson [7] identifies that this is excellent for helping students to set appropriate learning goals and evaluating their individual growth. Furthermore, this provides the lecturer and external examiners with a body of work which enables them to reflect on the student growth over a period of time. A portfolio can be integral to every part of instruction at every stage of the learning process.

Rapid Assessment

Yeh [10] suggests that: "Curriculum-embedded assessments which provide frequent, rapid feedback regarding student progress can improve teaching effectiveness". Yeh's studies identified that rapid assessment revealed gaps in learning and helped educators to attack those gaps by making immediate instructional adjustments. The focus of rapid assessment is on frequent and quick feedback.

In the studies Yeh presented [10] successful implementation of this assessment practice is dependent on an assessment software programme which can present individualised practice problems to each student. Students complete problems which are then immediately assessed by the lecturer. The lecturer has to identify areas in which the student needs help and present a new set of practice problems for the student. A new set of problems are introduced while current concepts in which the student remains weak are reviewed.

At the UJ, software programmes are available which enable on-line internet assessment and provide rapid assessment feedback to students. However these assessment programmes are more suited to theory-based modules, and would be problematic to the problem-solving environment where a solution cannot be described as either right or wrong.

However, what this teaching strategy does identify is the importance of incorporating effective and quick assessment of performance. This can result in identifying and addressing areas of student weakness quickly [10]. It is proposed that one-day projects, which can be executed during studio sessions, should be regularly introduced. This will enable lecturers constantly to monitor the design development and provide immediate feedback to students. The approach can be combined with strategies presented in differentiation instruction, which suggests that students should be divided into smaller groups to assist the lecturer in dealing with the learning difficulties that arise in each group.

Educational Support Systems

A report compiled by Lord [5] for the Southern Regional Educational Board aims to address problems relating to student readiness for Colleges in America. The report identifies a number of aspects that both parents and students need in order to prepare them for College. What was considered of value for this study were the requirements that were identified under a heading: Educational Support Systems. The following points are extracted from this area:

Introduction of academic safety nets: The report [5] suggests that academic safety nets which include a variety of activities should be made available to students entering tertiary education. The purpose of an academic safety net is to provide guidance in strengthening deficient knowledge and skills. The following suggestions are made; the inclusion of tutorial sessions, counseling and summer programmes.

It is therefore proposed that extra support should be provided to students who require more feedback. In lecturing design, additional consultation time can provide further feedback or focused individual attention to a student. The authors of the paper received suggestions from a first-year lecturer that students without prior art training should be given the opportunity to attend an introduction programme before they commence their studies. Although the introduction of such a programme would be of enormous value, it was noted that students would have to pay additional funds to attend the programme and that therefore the programme would not be compulsory.

Assistance for students to resolve personal barriers: The report [5] refers to personal barriers that students experience in attaining success in their academic achievements. At the UJ support systems such as Student Counselling and Learning Support are available. Students are referred to these units by lecturers, if they experience personal or learning and writing problems. It is proposed that these support units should be regularly consulted to assist the students to overcome personal barriers.

Conclusion

The paper describes the challenges that the Department of Interior Design at the UJ is experiencing regarding first-year student readiness. The challenges were identified by first-year lecturers through observation of student performance and identification of factors that impact on student readiness. This resulted in further research which included the completion of a questionnaire by students from all three years of study, and a relevant literature survey.

The paper identified five factors that impact on the imbalance that is experienced in first-year student readiness within the Department of Interior Design. These factors were identified as: varied standards delivered through secondary education; selection of Art as a high school subject; changing student profile; termination of the Foundation Programme; and, finally, the increase in first-year student numbers.

The investigation resulted in presenting proposed tactics that arose from existing teaching strategies and practices. The teaching strategies that were identified as appropriate to design education challenges at the UJ were: differentiated instruction; rapid assessment; and educational support systems.

References

[1] Ambile, T. *Creativity in Context.* 1989, Boulder, CO: Westview Press
[2] Boucharenc, C.G. Research on Basic Design Education: An International Survey. *International Journal of Technology and Design Education,* 2006, *16:1-30*
[3] Council on Higher Education. *A New Academic Policy for Programmes and Qualifications in Higher Education.* Available from: http://www.polity.org.za/html/govdocs/reports/education/universities/policy/foreword.html [Accessed on 2006 23 March], (2002)
[4] Junginger, S. Learning to design: giving purpose to heart, hand and mind. *Journal of Business Strategy*, 2007, 28(4), 59-65.
[5] Lord, J.M. (comp) *Student Readiness for Colleges: Connecting State Policies.* [PDF] Atlanta: Southern Regional Educational Board. Available from: http://www..sreb.org/main/HigherEd/readiness.pdf [Accessed on 2008, 5 April], (2002).
[6] Poon, J.T.F and Joo, N.T. Learning Styles: Implications for Design and Technology Education. *Management Research News,* 2001, 24(5) 24-37
[7] Tomlinson, C.A. *The differentiated classroom: responding to the needs of all learners*. 1999, Alexandria, VA: Association for Supervision and Curriculum Development.
[8] Tomlinson, C.A. Grading and Good Differentiation: Paradox or Good Practice? *Theory into Practice,2005*, 44(3), 262-269
[9] Warner, S.A. Teaching Design: Taking the First Steps. *The Technology Teacher.* 2003, 62(4): 7-10
[10] Yeh, S.S. High Stake Testing: Can Rapid Assessment Reduce the Pressure? *Teachers College Record.* 2006, 108(4)

Acknowledgement

We would like to acknowledge the valuable input that was made by Ms Lisa Titlestad who co-lectures in the offering of the first-year programme in the Department of Interior Design, University of Johannesburg

Ms Amanda BREYTENBACH
Faculty of Art, Design and Architecture
University of Johannesburg
PO Box 524
Auckland Park
Johannesburg
Republic of South Africa
2006
abreytenbach@uj.ac.za
+27 11 559 1120
+27 11 559 1120

Mr Ian Adair JOHNSTON
Department of Interior Design
University of Johannesburg
PO Box 524
Auckland Park
Johannesburg
Republic of South Africa
2006
ijohnston@uj.ac.za
+27 11 559 1114

Tactics of digitality and millennial generations

Andy MILLIGAN
DJCAD Duncan of Jordanstone College of Art and Design
University of Dundee

TACTICS OF DIGITALITY AND MILLENNIAL GENERATIONS – INTRODUCTION

In recent years researchers have identified new digital tools and tactics that are transforming interior design learning and practice. This brings new challenges which affect industry and higher education. The growth of social networking tactics, combined with smart phone educational 'apps' and continually evolving e-learning tools challenge how, where, when and in what manner interior design learning occurs.Central to these networking e-tactics are tools such as Building Information Modelling (BIM), and acknowledgment of the emergence of the Millennial generation – born between 1980 and 2000 – a group who

> "think differently from the rest of us. They develop hypertext minds. They leap around. It's as though their cognitive structures were parallel, not sequential." (Winn 2000).

In "BIM and I: How Advanced Modelling Technology Will Change Studio Learning", Jana Macalik suggests tactics to bridge the gap between the digital natives (Millennial learners) and the digital immigrants (academics). She describes the asynchronous learning habits of the Millennials and argues that learners' cognitive structures are parallel rather than sequential in nature, and increasingly at odds with the linear teaching tactics of universities and the time frames in which they operate. She draws parallels with this mosaic /millennial group and the parametric, non-linear and three dimensional modelling tools within Building Information Modelling.

Citing the impact of ubiquitous computing, social networking, and e-learning tools and the growth of a gaming culture as evolving a heightened digital aptitude in Millennial learners, she raises important concerns – particularly affecting North American interior education – about how a drive for BIM skills may lack a philosophical and theoretical dimension. Noting its potential for profound change in the design studio she suggests instead that BIM offers a virtual building that can be the central focus for the asynchronous habits of the Millennials, and thus the catalyst for the evolution of the design studio as we know it today.

This development also reflects a number of existing concepts such as a "play-station" concept describing MVRDV's Netherlands Pavilion in Hanover 2000 (Brooker), where spatial experience of a pavilion resembles a game culture through a sequence of levels that have to be encountered and absorbed before progressing to the next level. Equally virtual design education collaborations are on the rise (Milligan & Mohr 2007), that also bring more critical attitudes toward interior designs' exploration with digital tools and creative tactics. Creativity is also at the heart of Macalik's fascinating paper and expressions of this digital terrain is evident in Casson Mann's 'Digitopolis / Who Am I ?' exhibition in London. Macalik describes key targets to accommodate this type of asynchronous learner: extend design learning to every place that a student is at; capture more of their time and add value; contextualise dynamically; take information and assign greater meaning to it; individualise learning for the particular student. But are all learners uniformly Millennial and will they be so in the future? What is occurring in education is also evident in practice where BIM /Revit processes are enhancing collaboration as some speed altering the design process, challenge who now holds the creative edge in the workplace, and through BIM - offer a more positive and curious role for interior design graduates who may lack pragmatic understanding of 'real' practice, but who may eventually excel as digital BIM natives, (Beuhrle 2010).

In "Envisaging the Experiential", Peter Walker proposes tools and tactics that enable learners to envisage the qualitative characteristics of interior space through more objective mapping, research, analysis, distillation and communication tactics. In this study, Peter Walker echoes Jana Macalik's concern for the emotional disconnect students exhibit in their connected and networked lives. Similarly, Walker seeks to develop exciting tactics that will bring about and emotional and experiential 'connection' through new tools and toolkits. He describes a sketch modelling prototype entitled Alt-Space, devised as a tool for the creative exploration of the inter-disciplinary merging and morphing of concepts of space, a method for sketching internal space in order to appreciate the intangible – yet essential elements that combine to create a fuller environmental experience of lighting, scale, the movement of other people, ambient sound as a compliment and counterpoint to functional concerns and form, structure, texture and materiality. Acknowledging a need to rethink our attitudes toward digital skills, he describes the difficulties in communicating a sense of place to a client unfamiliar with the dynamics of three-dimensional thinking. He describes spatial mapping techniques such as semantic differential models (Lawson in "The Language of Space") – a tool normally used for measuring social norms and the socio-spatial behaviours we express, and these concerns are adapted to map retail spaces against opposing factors such as: warm/cold and friendly/unfriendly. Others include concept mapping matrices as experiential marketing devised by Schmitt, (Attract, Engage,

Affect, Relate), and Charny's use of museum-profiling methodology for the Holon in Israel. More expressive tools are explored, including the untapped potential of digital photomontage and occupancy narratives to drive and transform interior design thinking.

Walker describes an experiential method for communicating spatial proposals using digital sketch modelling tools that could offer designers a method for understanding user interaction more clearly than conventional design tactics, whilst touching on well established discourse on time:event and space:place theory. Touching on multi-modal thinking (Mair 2005), he explores methodologies using a matrix charting subjects against key concerns e.g. forms, atmosphere, colour, tone, texture and pattern and lighting to better convey design ideas,

> "The resultant 'palette' of references narrows the research material more precisely, eliminating superfluous images and provides a useful starting point for experimenting with ideas."

Gabrielle Knueppel's "Interspace: Spatial and Temporary Formation of Sensory Communities within Interior Environments", describes the multi-sensory, spatial and temporal design research installation "Kontakte" in Melbourne that aimed to reveal, amplify and produce multi-faceted connections between people by means of changing the spatial dynamics of the site context. Knueppel examines new paradigms of value to the interior community about how we engage and think about social connectivity, facilitated through tangible (material) as well as intangible (ephemeral) qualities. In this paper she applies digital tools to re-examine the tactics and relationship between personal and interpersonal space, offering a critical view of a controlling tendency of design to set limits that control to what extent the spatial composition encourages or limits social interaction. Suggesting alternatives to the familiar "tool-kit" of architectonic parts, (walls, floor and furniture) she explores intangible counterpoints that imply a more porous concept of space, boundary and limits. Touching on themes of an 'acoustic community', introduced by composer and academic Barry Truax, she describes

> "... how sound, in all its forms and functions, defines the relationship of the individual, the community, and, ultimately, a culture, to the environment and those within it."

Against this Knueppel investigates how materials determine our multi-modal experiences of space and place, suggesting that Pallasmaa's provocative critique of the ocular centric – rather than multi sensorial reality of spatial experience, "The Eyes of the Skin",dominates architectural design. Steven Holl also argues that

> "the way spaces feel, the sound and smell of these places, has equal weight to the way things look."

Knueppel cites events such as Sensoria Festival 2004 (Sensory Urbanism, the book, Sense of the City: An Alternate Approach to Urbanism), and Lars Spuybroek of NOX water pavilion as exemplars of a richer sensorial interaction where interior design needs to undergo the same sensorial revolution that has affected geography and anthropology. Quoting Zardini, he claims

> "Contemporary interiors – from hospitals to the communal spaces of shopping malls, theme parks, and places of entertainment and consumption – devote particular attention to differences in sensory perception, and many are conceived specifically as extensions of marketing strategies for consumer goods and experiences."

This is a claim that poses questions about the role and motivation of the professional practices of interior architecture/design.

In "Digital Ornament: new meanings and Skills", Annalisa Di Roma brings into sharp focus the relationship between the decorative artefact, rapid prototyping and digital processes. Her explorations into rapid prototyping, manufacture and decorative permutations remind us of a general neglect of the decorative that is now being rediscovered through digital experimentation. Di Roma describes the redefined role of the decorative as;

> "..the tangible representation of the aesthetic conception expressed by a designer and clearly explains the strong connection between art and technique, [and] ideas and construction methods."

Di Roma describes new and emerging relationships between designer and producer that reconnect previously separated processes of idea generation and production. New opportunities for CNC routing and milling, rapid prototyping and laser cutting offer interior design new ways of re-engaging with materiality, product experimentation of surface, object and decoration in a manufacturing and a critical context. Key to this may be a need to look beyond interior design and towards material experiments such as Droog's Dry Tech work with Delft TU.

Lisa DiRoma's research helps raise several important issues for interior design research. Whilst architectural theories, protocols and contexts have tended to dominate the content of many design programmes, there is an opportunity here to extend this to embrace new attitudes toward decoration, object making and [re]making and to bring a critical dimension to CAD CAM experimentation. Similarly, Gabrielle Knueppel's sonic studies expose critical auditory and kinaesthetic dimensions that frequently become a victim to the ocular bias of digital perspectives that permeate degree shows. However, there are also fascinating opportunities to innovate through digital tools such as Peter Walker's Alt SPACE toolkit and his attempts to envisage the experiential. Jana Macalik's examination of the Millennium generations potential to embrace BIM modelling software also suggests a new pedagogic tactic that is increasingly being seen as a viable method of engaging mosaic design thinkers asynchronously and parametrically.

Andy MILLIGAN
DJCAD Duncan of Jordanstone College of Art and Design
University of Dundee
Interior Environmental Design, Perth Road
Dundee, DD14HT
SCOTLAND
a.milligan@dundee.ac.uk
44 7929 136 580

Jana MACALIK
Ryerson University,

BIM AND I: HOW ADVANCED MODELLING TECHNOLOGY WILL CHANGE STUDIO LEARNING

Preface

...The group goes silent, as the projector hums into action. The first image of the presentation shows the hustle and bustle of a Turkish market. Quotes by Italo Calvino and Carlo Scarpa are interspersed throughout. Discussions of food as cultural identity evolve; theoretical elements are bantered around as catalysts for design interpretation and concept development. The professors are energised. The students are energised. Travel through time, interim reviews are in full swing and the discussions on progression, authenticity, experiential and sensory spaces have seemingly been forgotten as students present banal expressions of a plan for a restaurant; block zoning, circulation and furniture layout permeate the conversation, with limited three-dimensional spatial studies occurring. A student is asked why perspectives are not present. The response sends a cold chill down one professor's back, "I want the plan to be perfect before I extrude it." The professor turns to the rest of the group and asks if this is a common response. Many heads nod in agreement. The professor asks for volunteers to dispense oral descriptions of the site, the spaces that are being designed, and the experiences the students expect to develop. Silence. A few hands slowly rise and responses are thrown out as verbal bandages in a design emergency. It becomes clear that many students have only two-dimensional understanding of the spaces; extensive site visits are already forgotten and archived in their multi-tasking minds. Finally, one student stands up as the self-proclaimed advocate for the group… "Why would we do perspectives yet? We're just doing the schematic design, and all we need is the plan and elevations. We'll do

the perspectives at the end when we're done the design." The professor is stunned, confused, and left wondering...when did the world become flat?

The professor is me!

Process

The design academic in all of us expects the design studio to be a pedagogical demonstration of skills and knowledge evolving through the application of theoretical and programmatic attributes based in society and culture, technology and place making [1]. Designing, as expressed by Karl Aspelund, is a definable process; one that is sequential and recognisable in all design fields. The seven stages of design discussed by Aspelund are Inspiration, Identification, Conceptualisation, Exploration, Definition, Communication and Production. [2] These stages are constructed and expressed to be translatable to all design fields, spatial or otherwise. As a student, a practitioner and an educator, these stages are familiar and relevant to my experience in design and architecture. However, I am not the student of today; and therein lies the challenge.

The development of digital methods of entertainment (gaming) and design creation (CADD) in the 1980s have altered the way in which our students today relate and communicate with one another and to the world [3]. Their cognitive methodology has forever been altered by the ubiquitous usage and availability of technology (cell phones, MP3 players etc.), first and foremost here, the computer. The Millennials, those born between 1980 and 2000 [4], have been raised with the computer and thus

> "think differently from the rest of us. They develop hypertext minds. They leap around. It's as though their cognitive structures were parallel, not sequential."[5]

As is considered further in this paper, this explains their attraction and success with asynchronous learning and parametric design, and why Building Information Modelling (BIM)* as a means of creation and communication within design studio doctrine may amend our methodology of conveyance.

"Natives" vs. "Immigrants"

The realisation that the present day students are a completely different breed of student in comparison to all those who came before has recently been speculated upon in media and academic gatherings. There is a common impression, propagated by the media, that they are simply a generation of technologically savvy individuals who have been sheltered from the harshness of the world and now require a reality check upon entering undergraduate education [6]. Any (design) educator who begins their

---

*   Building Information Modelling is defined as a model-based design technology interlinked with a database of project attributes, information and fulfilling parametric requirements for design and building.

curriculum development with this simple interpretation may quickly become frustrated by their apparent inability to communicate or understand their projects. As expressed by Prensky [7], the description of the Millennial student as a "Digital Native" and the educator and a "Digital Immigrant" explains this experience as quite common. The students today are all "native speakers" of the digital language of computers, video games and the Internet. Designers and educators born before the time of integrated digital society, immigrants within this new culture, maintain methods and attitudes from before and have adopted the new language to maintain currency. As educators, to teach Millennials in a traditional pedagogical approach is similar to teaching in a foreign language. There will be misunderstandings, missed opportunities and inaccurate assumptions made by both parties. Success is fleeting.

The Millennials' public personality is that of a globally conscientious, technologically-adept, multi-tasking, overprotected youth; the reality is that they are, and that is ultimately the challenge for educators. The presumption that with additional schooling, they will function, interact and communicate as those who have come before is the fallacy [8].

> "Linear thought processes that dominate educational systems now can actually retard learning for brains developed through game and Web-surfing processes on the computer." [9]

For many Millennials, video games were the initial introduction to the computer. They interface spatially with the gaming technology, by manipulating objects on the screen with a mouse or a gaming controller, and do so individually or as a team; the Millennials have developed adaptive skills in which computers and digital technologies are central [10].

Communication

As an extension of the Millennials' aptitude for digital- and team-oriented activities, the proliferation of asynchronous learning within academia demonstrates the success and student satisfaction of learner-centric teaching [11]. An online course allows for self-directed learning, allows for self-directed time management and engagement, and has proven to provide greater engagement. To extrapolate the finding within the studies discussed in the SUNY Learning Network paper [12], one can contemplate that the asynchronous goals within the design process would be: to extend the design learning to every place that a student is at; to capture more of their time and add value; to contextualise dynamically; to take information and be able to assign greater meaning to it, but meaning that is individualised for the particular student.

Due to the Millennials' appreciation for visual over verbal learning dimensions and the use of technology within their personal and academic lives, the seamless integration of medium and context within a learning experience is only hindered by information being presented and knowledge development being expected in a linear controlled process [13]. The explosion of gaming and other online activities within their developmental years has enhanced their ability to recognise and find comfort within a virtual environment. For designers, the exposure to gaming and thus, repeated digital imagery of three-dimensional space, has improved the ability to read and understand these virtual environments and manoeuvre within them. This has led to improved visual understanding of spatial geometries, pattern recognition, multi-thread, multi-spatial monitoring and rapid resolution responses [14].

If one views the conjunction between the inherent thinking skills present in the Millennial generation, and the parametric requirements with a design studio project, the appropriate methodology and technology to be used would be Building Information Modelling (BIM). The tools presently utilised by thousands of design students are predominately representational tools – Sketch-Up, Rhino, and 3D Max – these all allow for the production of beautifully rendered views, with minimal demonstration of true spatial understanding. The standard elements, materials, finishes and lighting effects allow for even the weakest student to produce an enticing and realistic view of a space. Frequently, there is an emotional disconnect between the act of rendering and the act of design. Within the context of the design studio, there is a gap between the skills and the knowledge.

In the areas of industrial design and engineering, the act of design as a response to the parameters of a project has obvious advantages. In spatial design such as architecture and interior design, the parametric approach has limited examples. More recently, in the advent of environmentally responsible design, such elements as three-dimensional programming and energy-specific targets have driven many designers to forego formalistic responses to design problems, and allow for reactive design to occur. The use of BIM software such as Revit and ArchiCAD, with their inherent information gathering and dispensing, allows for this design approach to occur at the earliest stages of any design process and to be constantly revised as the design is developed.

As discussed by Schnabel in relation to the studio run at the University of Sydney, Faculty of Architecture, Design and Planning in 2006/7, the studio explored design by basing it on prescribed parameters. In order to build up a philosophy around parametric dependencies and relationships, the participants used digital tools which allowed them to create and express their designs. With these tools, users developed an expertise to engage creatively in design. Typically, designers employ such tools only for visualisations, or after the designs are completed, in order to feed them into the construction process [15]. The conclusion of the parametric design studio illustrated how non-linear design processes and the re-representation of ideas can lead to architectural expressions that differ from conventional approaches to design due to their different nature of design creation. The holistic exploration enhanced the understanding of spatial issues and led to meaningful and responsive architectural solutions [16].

To engage and communicate with Millennials, the layering of information in a non-linear methodology in order to allow for personal interpretation and implementation of the parameters requires the parametric software (BIM) to be as malleable and accessible as their minds and learning styles.

Correlation

The act of learning and associating with course content has been a primary focus of many educators within design or otherwise. Students learn through a variety of dimensions, each differing slightly from the next. As expressed by Richard Felder in 1988, and revised in 2002 [17], the learning styles of students have four primary dimensions – perception, input, processing and understanding. They are defined as the following [18]:

Perception

> *Sensing – Like learning facts; Solve problems by well-established methods and dislike complications*
>
> *Intuitive – Prefer discovering possibilities and relationships; Like innovation and dislike repetition*

Input

> *Visual – Remember best what they see – pictures, diagrams, flow charts, time lines, films, and demonstrations*
>
> *Verbal – Get more out of words – written and spoken explanations*

Processing

> *Active – Understand information best by doing something with it; Like group work*
>
> *Reflective – Understand information best by thinking about it quietly first; Prefer to work alone*

Understanding

> *Sequential – Gain understanding in linear steps; Follow logical stepwise paths in finding solutions*
>
> *Global – Learn in large jumps; Solve complex problems quickly once they have grasped the big picture*

Based upon the Millennial attributes discussed earlier in this paper, certain generalities may be extrapolated in terms of Millennials and their learning styles, in relation to those that enter the interior design field. Millennials are visual learners; Millennials are active learners; Millennials are global learners.

Based upon these statements, the following three descriptions [19] are assembled to review how BIM would contribute to the success of these students or be a hindrance.*

---

*   For this particular paper, the dimension of perception has been omitted due to the fact, from casual observation of Millennial students in design; this is the one learning style that has the least amount of consistency within the Millennial population. As with any generalisation, there are many students who do not adhere to the following statements.

1. Within the learning dimension of "input", the Millennials have proven to be visual learners. They respond more promptly to information presented visually as static examples (diagrams, charts, pictures) or dynamic examples (movies, animations, demonstrations). They also tend to retain information as a snapshot of time, place and experience, remembering context, details and environment. The use of BIM technology responds to and fulfils the needs of these learners by encompassing the following attributes and capabilities: the use of three dimensional modelling and 360° viewing; associative charts schedules; and integrated visualisation tools.

2. Within the learning dimension of "processing", Millennials are more responsive to active learning. Their appreciation for group work and discussion has allowed them to utilise their knowledge and learn from experimentation and repetition. The action of dissemination to others is one of the activities that acquires satisfaction from these students. Correlating BIM with these attributes, it grants these learners: the ability to maintain options within the model itself; the ability to share information with others such as detail development; the ability to develop detailed models from quick source files such as Sketch-Up; and finally, once again the associative schedules and information which assist in the explanation and dissemination of the building design.

3. Within the learning dimension of "understanding", holistic and non-linear approaches dominate the global learners. Without the comprehension of the "whole", the Millennial design student struggles to absorb material – at times, only by abstracting the overall concept can they see the connections between elements and aspects. Once the overall picture is made clear, they can address complex problems in unique and novel ways. They are able to create and understand outcomes and associations that others do not anticipate. However, they are known to have difficulties with their process and subsequent details. The benefits of BIM involve the ability to develop the model from rough conceptual models from other software such as Sketch-UP, and import and define attributes in a non-sequential manner. Ultimately, by working in three-dimensions at all times, the Millennial student has a holistic view of the project at all times. The parametric components and correlating attributes developed by the student allow for connections to be made quickly and interference to be flagged where occurring. The bidirectional associations within a program such as Revit ensures that all changes made are reflected throughout the project/model without the student being required to ensure the changes and concern themselves with omissions. These elements of flexibility and associativity are primary for the Millennial student to see the relevance of their design acts within the greater context.

Conclusion

Experiences are measured by their ability not only to meet the needs of the students on a functional and emotional level, but also to engage their different learning dimensions. Design studio is a pedagogical experience that requires holistic learning to occur within the confines of a mainly virtual world. The design process must evolve as a natural interplay between the parameters of the projects and the representation methods expected by educators, employers and accrediting associations. The Millennial student having been thrust into an undergraduate studio environment of self-expression, self-directed learning and critical thought has primarily two paths to choose from, linear or non-linear. Their cumulative learning prior to entering design school would more than likely have suggested a sequential approach, with their ability to succeed hampered by their inherent learning styles. Alternatively, the Millennial student should approach their project as an expression of components, assembled in an open variable method, allowing for the designs to evolve organically and as multi-thread compositions.

The hyper-adoption of BIM within the architectural and design industry as the next stage of project design and production indicates that the majority of our students will be entering the practice with the knowledge of the tool, but the misconstrued illusion that it is only a means to an end, rather than the road itself. During the 2008 Interior Design Educators Conference in Montreal, as a panel member on the teaching of BIM, I witnessed several educators talking about the instruction of the tool, but ignoring the alteration of the philosophy of design studio. The majority of the educators would have been deemed "Digital Immigrants" and thus would be adding BIM into their repertoire as an added skill or tool used only in the production of working or contract documents. The reality is that the Building Information Model is a virtual building that can be the central focus for the asynchronous habits of the Millennials, and thus be the catalyst for the evolution of design studio as we know it today.

Acknowledgements

The author gratefully acknowledges the participation and co-operation of John Peterson (Project Architect, KPMB Architects, Toronto, and Committee Member of the Ontario Revit Users Group), and the support of the Ryerson Faculty of Communication and Design SRC Committtee.

References

[1] Dutton, T.A. Design and Studio Pedagogy *Journal of Architectural Education* Vol.41, No.1 (Autumn, 1987), pp. 16-25
[2] Aspelund, K. *The Design Process* (Fairchild Publications, New York, 2006)
[3] Brannon, C,. Greenfield, P.M., and Lohr, D. Two-Dimensional Representation of Movement Through Three-Dimensional Space: The Role Of Video Game Expertise. *Journal of Applied Developmental Psychology* 15, 87-103 (1994)

[4] Howe, N., and Strauss, W. *Millennials Rising: The Next Great Generation.* (Vintage Books, New York, 2000).
[5] Winn, W., Director of the Learning Center, Human Interface Technology Laboratory, University of Washington, quoted in Moore, *Inferential Focus Briefing* (see 9), referenced in Prensky, M. Digital Natives, Digital Immigrants. *On the Horizon*, Vol. 9 No. 5 (NCB University Press, October 2001) (see 7)
[6] Neuborne, E. Generation Y. *Business Week*, February 15 (1999).
[7] Prensky, M. Digital Natives, Digital Immigrants: *On the Horizon*, Vol. 9 No. 5 (NCB University Press, October 2001)
[8] Wilson, M.E. Teaching, Learning, and Millennial Students. *New Directions for Student Services.* no. 106, Summer 2004, 59-71
[9] Moore, P. *Inferential Focus Briefing,* September 30, 1997. referenced in Prensky, M. Digital Natives, Digital Immigrants. *On the Horizon*, Vol. 9 No. 5 (NCB University Press, October 2001) (see 7)
[10] Brannon, C., Greenfield, P.M., and Lohr, D. Two-Dimensional Representation of Movement Through Three-Dimensional Space: The Role Of Video Game Expertise. *Journal of Applied Developmental Psychology* 15, 87-103 (1994)
[11] Dziuban, C., Moskal, P., Futch, L. and Shea, P. Student Satisfaction with Asynchronous Learning. *Journal of Asynchronous Learning Networks* 11(1): April 2007
[12] Shea, P., E. Fredericksen, A. Pickett and W. Pelz. Student satisfaction and reported learning in the SUNY Learning Network. In: T. Duffy and J. Kirkley, *Learner Centered Theory and Practice in Distance Education.* Mahwah, NJ: Lawrence Erlbaum, 2003.
[13] Prensky, M. Digital Natives, Digital Immigrants. *On the Horizon*, Vol. 9 No. 5 (NCB University Press, October 2001)
[14] Greenfield, P.M. *Mind and Media, the Effects of Television, Video Games and Computers.* (Harvard University Press, 1984)
[15] Schnabel, M.A. Parametric Designing in Architecture. In A Dong, A Vande Moere & Js Gero eds. *Caadfutures'07*, p.238. (Springer, Berlin, Germany, 2007)
[16] Schnabel, M.A. Parametric Designing in Architecture. In A Dong, A Vande Moere & Js Gero eds. *Caadfutures'07*, p.247. (Springer, Berlin, Germany, 2007)
[17] Felder, R.M. and Silverman, L.K, "Learning and Teaching Styles in Engineering Education," *Engr. Education, 78*(7), 674-681 (1988).
[18] http://chat.carleton.ca/~tblouin/Felder/felder.html
[19] http://www.ncsu.edu/felderpublic/Learning_Styles.html

Jana MACALIK
Ryerson University, School of Interior Design
350 Victoria Street
Toronto
Ontario
Canada M5B 2K3
jmacalik@ryerson.ca
1-416-979-5000 ext. 7627

Peter WATERS
University for the Creative Arts, Farnham

ENVISAGING THE EXPERIENTIAL

Introduction

"Architecture is not simply about space and form, but also about event, action, and what happens in space." [1]

Whether adopting an architectonic, programmatic or conceptual approach to interior design, the extent to which a designer considers the dynamics of user interaction within a space varies considerably.

Space created to accommodate human activities i.e. "containers for human behaviour" [2] gives a building meaning. A sense of place, defined by architectural form, can be realised through an event or a series of events.

The time:event / space:place theory is well established in spatial discourse and, though it is readily understood by most students, the implications for the design and communication process are less so.

Essential to this is an appreciation of how we perceive space. In "Sensory Design" Malnar and Vodvarka [3] explore how we experience space from both a physical and psychological perspective. This may range from sound-scapes and atmospheric considerations of warmth and humidity to memory, cultural signifiers and spatial conditions of compression and release or expansion.

"Architecture strengthens the existential experience, one's sense of being in the world, and this is essentially a strengthening experience of self." [4]

In this paper I will outline some of the design and communication tools with which we have experimented, or are seeking to experiment, to enable students to grasp this less tangible aspect of spatial design.

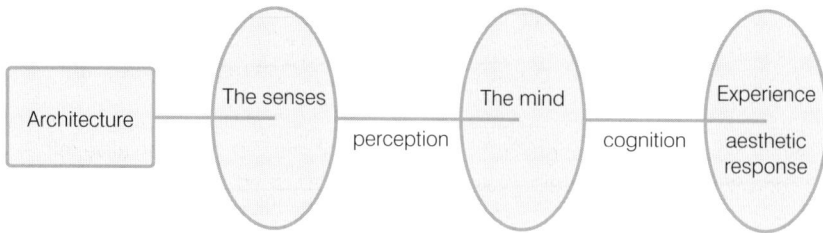

Figure 1: Experiential: the cognitive process

The process involves three key stages:

- **Enquiry:** determining the potential of the site and/or building structure relative to user requirements and the brief.
- **Experimentation:** with the possibilities for the space
- **Proposition:** the communication of a design leading to the implementation and the realisation of the concept

During the enquiry and experimentation phases, conventional "tools" such as mind maps, maquettes, sketches (line, shaded and coloured drawings), scale plans and sections and initial CAD models assist the student/designer to come to terms with the issues involved.

Often, the full implications of the design are not realised until the design is completed. Prior to this, a variety of mechanisms are employed to test and communicate an idea. These may be analytical in nature; programmatic considerations, organising methods and analysis models (e.g. the path of the sun) or part of a communication process that endeavours to impart a sense of the proposed solution. These methods are, often, purely symbolic and often singular in purpose:

- Models communicate space in a relative sense but to a scale significantly removed from human scale and do not convey the more ephemeral qualities of the space such as atmosphere or ambiance.
- A visual perspective (coloured, hand rendered or CAD generated) can communicate atmosphere (lighting, ambience etc) but fail to deal with the transitions from one space to another or a sequence of spaces.
- A fully-rendered CAD walk-through can convey progression through a series of spaces and their atmospheric qualities, but fails to communicate the technical issues involved.
- Technical drawings can explain how a design fits together but not the tactile qualities of the materials referred to.

- A material sample board enables the viewer to touch and appreciate the qualities of a range of materials but not the full implications of the material; noise underfoot, durability etc. For this yet more "devices" are required.

Conventionally, it is the triangulation of these metaphorical or representative references that convey the fullest possible experience of a proposed solution. The success or failure of these processes is subject to both the designer's ability to communicate (cross refer) and the viewer's ability to comprehend.

Well considered spatial design accentuates and exploits the possibilities of a site and building. It explores both the dramatic and subtle potential to accommodate the desires and aspirations of a client or user over and above the purely spatial and functional.

> "The ultimate meaning of any building is beyond architecture; it directs our consciousness back to the world and towards our sense of self and being." [5]

Envisaging space (exploring, recognising and communicating potential) is a task that bedevils both students (and often, therefore, tutors) and clients (and therefore designers).

For an inexperienced student, in particular, the difficulty can begin early on in the process. If they fail to employ the appropriate mechanisms they will struggle to comprehend fully the complex, holistic nature of the problems and possibilities available. Identifying the catalyst that defines these issues and unlocks the potential of a project will be the focus of this paper.

I will explore methods of analysis and communication that are beneficial or appropriate to both student/tutor and client/designer scenarios and relate some of the devices employed with our own students to explore the potential of these mechanisms in identifying, mapping and exploring aspects of the design process.

Enquiry

> "The role of the architect (or designer) is to interpret and synthesise the many different inputs. Knowledge is systematically gained and held up against present knowledge." [6]

Personal Construct Theory [7] relates to models of reality (constructs) that help us to understand and explain the world as we perceive it. These constructs are developed through a process of observation and experimentation. They initially emerge as unreliable assumptions in relation to the world which only become more precise as experience and evidence are acquired to corroborate a premise. Any tutor will recognise this process within a student group, through the gradual acquisition of understanding and the use of emerging methodologies which enable students to engage with design problems with increasing conviction.

Up to this point, a student's initial response to the conceptual stage of a project, particularly in the earlier years of study, may involve a high degree of frustration as they struggle to articulate their ideas. Raising awareness of a building's potential and the array of possibilities available is, of course, the first step in a student's education and a range of tools is available to assist with this.

In the "Language of Space" Bryan Lawson demonstrates the use of the semantic differential model to distinguish between a range of retail environments [8]. The semantic differential scale is a tool that is normally used for measuring social attitudes but is, here, effectively adapted to map retail spaces (butchers, greengrocers, newsagents etc) by degree against opposing factors such as; warm: cold, friendly: unfriendly and so on. In another example a range of descriptors map the characteristics of two bars in a suburban English public house. Basing the analysis on a polarised set of factors relating to a range of sensory considerations a "visual distance" is achieved that clearly differentiates one environment from another.

An undergraduate's perception of differing spatial qualities is enhanced through the interrogation of existing spaces, and this can be an effective technique to incorporate into initial analytical exercises.

Care is required when constructing the differential model however, through the considered adoption of suitable adjectives. Problems arise due to subjectivity and the

Figure 2: Determining "distance"

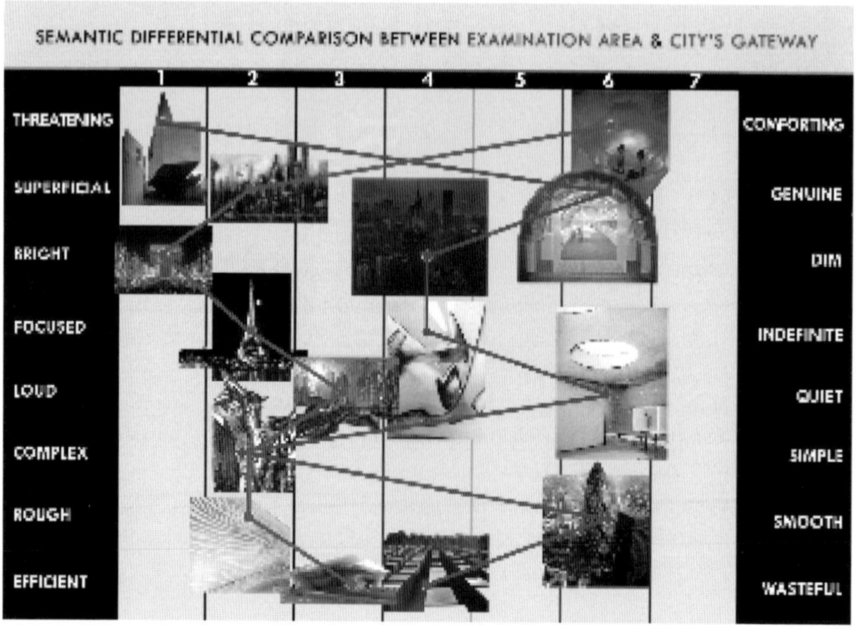

perception of the individual. This can be minimised through the design of the semantic differential scale (most likely by the tutor) by careful selection of adjectives in relation to the purpose of the research, subject and aims and objectives of the brief [9]. The paper by Jayne Al-Hindawe provides guidelines and issues for consideration, both to ensure the relevancy of the parameters selected and to determine the process as a genuine aid to designing.

Through exploring the subject area contained in a brief, students normally generate a text mind-map of related issues in conjunction with a series of "mood" boards. The danger is that this becomes a purely subjective juxtaposition of loosely related items which fail to determine a direction for the design. Unidentified images, plucked from the internet without rationale or reason, are often presented as (at best) a visual mind-map of vaguely related "research". Experience *can* make this a useful communication tool but a more strategic approach can be achieved through applying the semantic differential process to transform the study from a reactive to a proactive one.

By generating a visual representation of the factors deemed relevant to a particular design proposal, the images and references sourced can be differentiated by mapping them against the values represented by the scales. This is useful in early tutorials since it is easier for the tutor to comprehend what the student (especially an international student) perceives when considering a particular image. In the example in Figure 2, in relation to a Production Design focussed remake of the Wizard of Oz, a visual distance is determined between the "utopian" entrance to the Emerald City and the more sinister examination chamber. By careful selection a honed range of references (colour, tone, texture, pattern, atmosphere, structure, forms etc.) are acquired which act as a driver for the project.

The benefit gained from differing types of diagrammatical mapping devices in aiding the design process is clearly demonstrated through an example featured in Blueprint in recent years [10]. In striving to position a new design museum for Holon in Israel, David Charny developed a museum-profiling methodology which attempted to assess and map the key characteristics of leading design museums around the world. Each museum was mapped against contrasting affinities; industry/fine art and science/popular commercial culture.

Other mapping devices (a comparative diagram) positioned each institution relative to descriptors such as education: entertainment and museum: centre again, like the semantic differential tool, producing a visual representation of the "distance" between each museum. The next phase of the project was to "create a tool for building the identity of the new museum" relative to those analysed. Through this process the trend in museum design towards narrative environments (i.e. storytelling developed around a collection) was apparent (Figure 3).

Considering the comparative studies in conjunction with other relevant factors, such as location, collection and audience the resultant, desired outcome for the museum was identified as being closer to the entertainment/visitor centre category than a museum/educational institution.

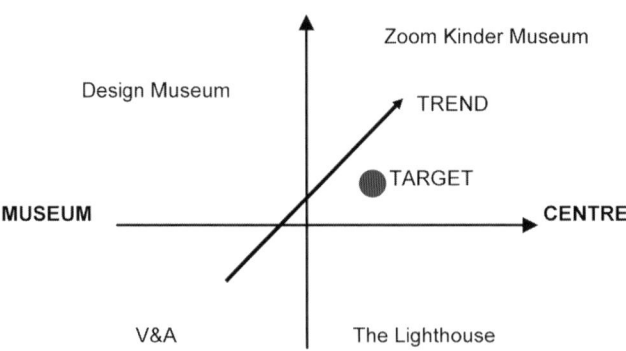

Figure 3: Defining the museum

Other devices that can help to define the scope of the brief include diagrammatical models which sum up key considerations. In Figure 4 the image conveys the critical concerns affecting ferry passengers: level of stress (during boarding, travel and disembarkation) relative to leisure and potential shopping time.

Figure 4: The selling window: the relationship between a stressed and relaxed state (more conducive to shopping) charted diagrammatically

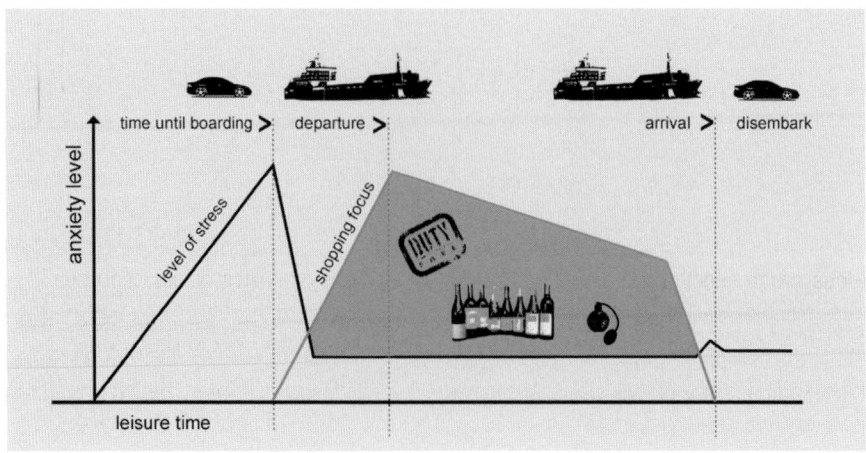

Applying models such as these to research tasks enables students to determine and "visualis" qualities which can form the basis of a more objective and fundamental design process.

Experimentation

"What is perceived first must be conceived first" [11]

A design methodology can be developed further through the use of a matrix charting issues against the main components (form, atmosphere, colour etc) in relation to the senses. The resultant "palett" of references narrows the research material more precisely, eliminating superfluous images and provides a useful starting point for experimenting with ideas.

In the example (Figure 5) ideas influenced by Schmitt (Experiential Marketing) [12] students were able to map a range of sensory considerations, physical characteristics and interactive processes relative to a promotional unit for a particular brand within an enclosed public space.

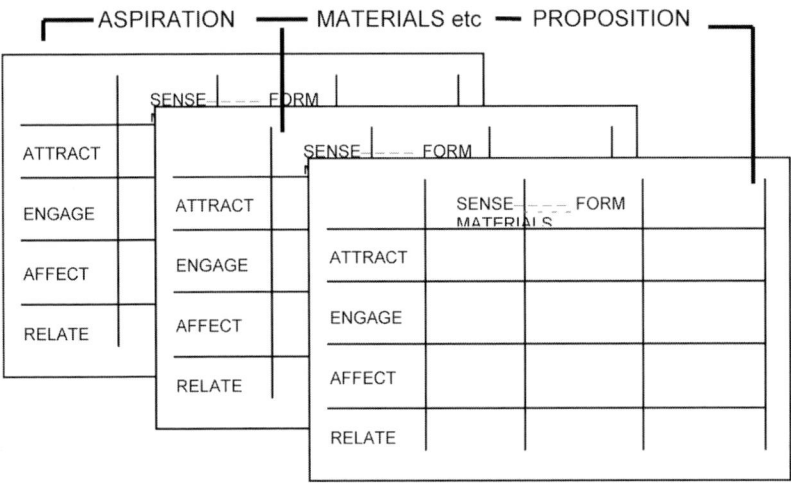

Figure 5: Attract / Engage / Affect / Relate matrices

Ideas progressed from generalised "aspiration" to the specifics of user engagement The resultant "palett" provided a framework for the next phase of the design (Figure 6) and helped with the translation of the project from the concept to proposal stage.

Through a postgraduate hotel-related project a sensory, spatial and material framework was arrived at through analysing the public to private transition from approach,

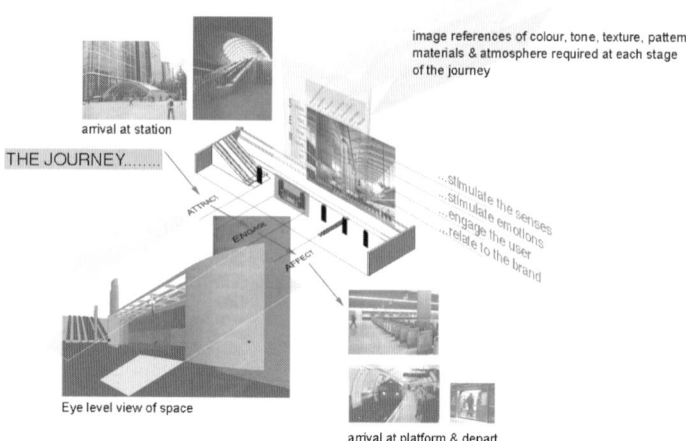

Figure 6: References mapped onto the space relative to experience and level of user engagement

Figure 7: Spatial and sensory inter-relationships mapped out and explored through illuminated maquettes

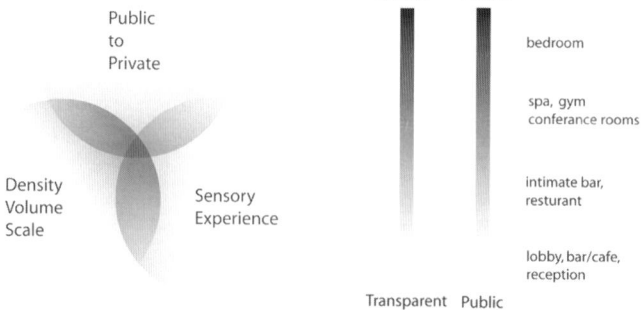

entrance and reception through to the semi-public spaces of the spa, gym and other facilities to the private bed and bathrooms. The aim of the project was to promote a more balanced approach to spatial design by re-appraising our environment through senses other than simply the visual.

By exploring the materiality of the interlinked spaces through transparency to opacity (denoting public to private) as well as density, volume and scale the student charted the relationship of each sense to the internal spaces to determine the essential characteristics of each area. By extrapolating the key concerns at each stage of the journey (public to private) a primary'"too"' for managing the complex, inter-related mix of spaces within a hotel was arrived at which could be applied or adapted for most situations.

Proposition

> '"There is no way to perform architecture in a book. Words and drawings can only produce paper space, not the experience of real space. By definition, paper space is imaginary: it is an image"'. [13]

Jaron Lanier pioneered and popularised the term'"virtual reality"'. In*'Riding the Giant Worm to Saturn: Post-Symbolic Communication in Virtual Reality'* he talks of a time when, through the application of virtual reality, we are, like Superman, able to'"fly around and pick up a building and turn it upside-dow"'. [14] In this way he envisages a time when architects (interior designers) can dispense with symbolic, metaphorical representations which require an orchestrated presentation to gain appreciation and acceptance of their designs, and turn to virtual reality to introduce a client to their building. Within this environment a client might say:

> "'Well, let's move this window over'" and simply moves it. That is post-symbolic communication. They are actually in the building, and no longer relying on models or animations or specifications or blue prints. They are dealing with a direct experience not a representation of an experience"'. [15]

In terms of engaging the senses some advanced haptic systems now include tactile feedback. Other developments have occurred that could help us to experience spaces in ways that go beyond the purely visual.

The (unfortunately named) iSmell or iSmell Personal Scent Synthesizer was a computer peripheral device developed by DigiScents in 2001. The prototype connected to a personal computer via a USB or serial port, and was designed to emit a smell when a user visited a certain web site or opened an email. The device contained a cartridge with 128 "primary odours"", which could be mixed to replicate natural and man-made odours [16]. DigiScents indexed thousands of common odours, which could then be coded, digitised, and embedded within digital products or environments. Presumably complications with the technology and/or the potential for unpleasant mishaps – analogous to the black running out on colour printers – caused the technology to fail and the company to fold.

Taking all of the above into consideration we could question whether this is indicative of where we are ultimately heading. An interior could be experienced in this way via this ability to probe and explore objects and data to a desired level but, apart from this being some way off, is this really how we would choose to explore space? Until the technology advances, we need to rely upon other tools.

3D CAD walkthroughs are fairly commonplace, where budgets permit, but tend to relate more to large-scale developments; office, residential and cultural projects, particularly where there are sensitive planning issues. Development in this area however is often driven by technical, program related know-how rather than by filmic or narrative qualities. A typical walk-through tends to depict a'"true to life"' experience of the proposed design relative to the existing site. It often incorporates a fly-through technique (to add dynamism) and may convey day- or night-time scenarios, sun path analyses or pathways through the building.

An enhanced form of walk-through sequence is suggested in'"Narrative Structured Walk-Through Scenario"' where a

> '"narrative engine…for generating new ideas for exploiting potentially positive interactions and responding to observed potentialities"'

This would provide'"occupancy narrative"' [17]. It seems unlikely that students (or practising designers) would readily warm to this terminology and, as a degree of embedded programming would be required, this would not be viable within a typical interiors company or project. Perhaps a more impressionistic, less algorithmic approach would be more applicable for creative designers borrowing storytelling techniques from the worlds of film and animation [18].

Heather Puttock in *'Vsevolod Pudovkin and the Theory of Montage'* [19] explores the possibilities provided by montage in early Soviet film making to transform existing contexts into new propagandist formats. This was achieved through the appropriation of old, bourgeois film sequences – a necessity due to the shortage of film – reworked and merged to create an entirely new work.

> "…Inherent in a single piece of edited film were two strengths: its own and that found in its relationship to other pieces of film'"

Montage was a meticulous construction of interdependent pre-planning that sought to resolve the raw material into its constituent elements long before the film was assembled [20].

While the strivings of students can hardly compare with the social manoeuvrings taking place during those tumultuous times, the process is very familiar in this multi-media age. Utilising readily available multi-media sources should provide a rich variety of considerations which enables students to generate ideas.

A body of work which brings together disparate elements; architectural images, graphics, materials, examples of light (natural or artificial) and so forth is in essence

Figure 8: Alt-Space: Scale can be manipulated in a relative sense by increasing or decreasing the figure in the foreground

Figure 9: An interactive, modifiable scenario that conveys the character of the operation (the brand) as a whole

creating new associations, new possibilities and greater comprehension for the designer and the client. Differing strategies or tactics are sometimes required to unlock the potential of a project, to create new associations that are not immediately revealed through normal conventions.

> '"…new types of representation are emerging such as 'IKEA planning' where cut out elements of their products are pushed around a piece of gridded paper and…'Get the Look' images harvested from glossy magazines.
>
> Rather than be threatened by these developments, the interior architect or designer should look to these emergent and easily accessible method'". [21]

At Computers in Art & Design Education (CADE 2003, Malmo / Copenhagen) we presented a sketch-modelling prototype entitled Alt-Space [22]. This could not provide the flexibility of SketchUp but it included a similarly intuitive interface and audio-visual, interactive experience which featured moving images and sound attenuation. It was devised as a tool for the creative exploration of the inter-disciplinary merging of concepts of space.

The aim of the project was to enable a student to'"sketch'" internal space Figure 4) and begin to appreciate the less tangible elements which help to create our overall impression of place: lighting, scale, the movement of people, ambient sound/echo as well as the more traditional concerns such as the physical design: form, structure, texture, materiality and overall character of a building.

The project was conceived with interactive designers Squid Soup to explore, in particular, the more sensory aspects of spatial design – particularly appropriate where audio-visual material is used extensively such as in museums, visitor centres, branded environments or themed entertainment venues. The software had the potential to create space, populate it, navigate through and explore and experience it in a way that had not been possible before. It would have required considerable funding to develop it as a stable, commercial product but was a useful prototype that helped to further thinking along these lines.

The Flash animation driven website (Figure 9) representing Sketch Restaurant and Gallery in London's Piccadilly [23] offers an interesting approach. With its eclectic photomontage of contemporary, retro and traditional forms and spaces, scene setting (music, mood and lighting) and wit, it offers an insight into other possibilities to explore ideas and envisage an experience.

Conclusion

There are many well-established, conventional techniques for developing and testing ideas at each stage of the design process but we should be open to opportunities provided by inter-disciplinary collaboration and technological advances if we are to create new spatial paradigms or more engaging communication. The methods referred to in this paper are a natural development for an increasingly visually-literate generation whose approach to research and analysis is significantly different.

If we consider that only 25 years ago students would graduate from courses using watercolours and drawing boards (computer aided design did not fully emerge until the mid-eighties), the paperless office was only a dream (!) and we were (blissfully) ignorant of the digital revolution which would turn all of this on its head. Today we benefit from new tools with which to explore the design process with ever more complex and specific software developing year by year.

We are now moving into new dimensions with resources such as the semantic web, which will further inform our research by making intelligent links between data, enabling us to refine searches for specific and/or inter-related knowledge and improve understanding of historical precedents. Possibilities are constantly unfolding as new facilities become available to explore creative options, enhance the design process and, perhaps most importantly, formulate new opinions.

References

[1] Tschumi, B., *Manhattan Transcripts*, Bernard Tschumi Architects. Available: http://www.tschumi.com
[2] Postiglione, G., Lupo E., 'The Architecture of Interiors as Re-writing Space: Centrality of Gesture', *Thinking Inside the Box: A Reader in Interiors for the 21st Century* (Middlesex University Press now Libri Publishing, 2007) pp. 145-154
[3] Malnar, J., and Vodvarka, F., *'Sensory Design'* (Minneapolis: University of Minnesota Press 2004)
[4] Pallasmaa, J., 'The eyes of the skin: Architecture through the senses', (London: Wiley-Academy 2005)
[5] ibid
[6] Beim, A., 'Defining strategic design processes among practicing architects', *Emerging Research and Design* (ARCC 2007)
[7] 'The Personal Construct Theory', *Changing Minds*, Available: http://changingminds.org/explanations/theories/personal_construct.htm
[8] Lawson, B., *The Language of Space*. (Oxford: Architectural Press 2001)
[9] Al-Hindawe, Jayne, 'Considerations when constructing a semantic differential scale'. Available: http://www.latrobe.edu.au/linguistics/LaTrobePapersinLinguistics/Vol%2009/Contents.htm (Victoria, Australia: La Trobe Papers in Linguistics Vol 9,1996)
[10] Charny, D., *Collection of thoughts*, Blueprint no.226 December 2004 / January 2005 pp46-50
[11] Bihanic, D., Interview with Régine Charvet-Pello, *CADI Journal*, 2007, pp10-11. Available: http://www.lecoledeedesign.com/english/rubrique.php3?id_rubrique=43
[12] Schmitt, B. Experiential Marketing: How to get Customers to Sense, Feel, Think, Act and Relate to Your Company and Brands. New York: Free Press, 1999
[13] Tschumi, B., *Advertising in Architecture*, Bernard Tschumi Architects. Available: http://www.tschumi.com
[14] Russell, M. Riding the Giant Worm to Saturn: Post-Symbolic Communication in Virtual Reality. *Druckery, T ed. ARS Electronica: Facing the Future*, (MIT Press 1999) pp. 242-243,

[15] ibid
[16] Martin, J., 'Sniff that website', *PC World*. Available: http://www.pcworld.com/article/id,13263-page,1/article.html
[17] McCartney, Kevin, 'Design Procedures in the Interactive Age', *Emerging Research and Design* (ARCC 2007)
[18] Engeli, M. Digital Stories: The Poetics of Communication, (Birkhauser 2001)
[19] Puttock, H., Vsevolod Pudovkin and the Theory of Montage. *Fear, B ed, Architecture + Film II* (London: Wiley-Academy 2000) pp. 9-15
[20] ibid
[21] Spankie, R., 'Thinking through drawing', *Thinking Inside the Box: A Reader in Interiors for the 21st Century* (Middlesex University Press now Libri Publishing, 2007) pp. 241-252
[22] Waters, P., and Rowe, A., 'Alt-space: Audiovisual interactive software for developing narrative environments', *Proceedings of Computers in Art and Design Education Conference* (CADE 2004).
[23] Sketch Gallery and Restaurant. Available: http://www.sketch.uk.com/#

List of Illustrations

[1] Meade, T, (2007) *The Sensory Hotel,* MA submission, UCA Farnham
[2] Borg, V, (2008) *The Wizard of Oz,* BA submission, UCA Farnham
[3] Charny, D, (2005) *Holon Museum,* Blueprint
[4] Cripps, M., (2008) *Retail in Transit,* Lecture, UCA Farnham
[5] Waters, P., (2008) Design *Matrices,* Lecture, UCA Farnham
[6] Cripps, M., (2008) Space *Mapping,* Lecture, UCA Farnham
[7] Meade, T, (2007) *The Sensory Hotel,* MA submission, UCA Farnham
[8] Rowe, A, & Waters, P, (2004). *Alt-Space,* Conference Paper and publication, CADE
[9] Sketch Gallery and Restaurant

Acknowledgements

The author gratefully acknowledges the participation of Tracey Meade, Taehee Kim, Vanessa Borg, Neil Pace O'Shea, Anthony Rowe (Squid Soup), Sketch Restaurant, Matt Cripps and Michael Thomas.

Peter WATERS
University for the Creative Arts
Falkner Road
Farnham
Surrey
GU9 7DS
pwaters@ucreative.ac.uk
01252 892759

Gabriele KNUEPPEL

RMIT University

INTERSPACE: SPATIAL AND TEMPORARY FORMATION OF SENSORY COMMUNITIES WITHIN INTERIOR ENVIRONMENTS

Spatial Concepts of Social, Sensory and Temporal Design

One of the key issues in interior architecture and interior design projects often is the relationship between personal and interpersonal space. Designers control to what extent the spatial composition encourages or limits social interaction. The tools used to allocate areas for shared or individual activities are commonly physical elements, such as walls and furniture. These elements establish tangible boundaries and can serve to either impede certain views or maintain a visual connection. Open plan offices, for example, encourage interaction between employees through a spatial design that sustains a visual relationship between people even over longer distances. The space may be divided up by workstations, but the fundamental idea is not to separate people through floor-to-ceiling partitions. Naturally, the model of an open-plan office also has other sensory implications, such as unimpeded sound transmission. This means that every individual in the space is not only connected visually but also aurally as one "acoustic community" [1]. Composer and academic Barry Truax introduced the term acoustic community to describe

> "how sound, in all its forms and functions, defines the relationship of the individual, the community, and, ultimately, a culture, to the environment and those within it". [2]

Material selection and application have a crucial part in interior architectural design. Some materials, such as timber or plasterboard, act as spatial as well as visual dividers, whereas glass for example, segregates areas physically, but not visually. As a design tool the use of materials also has strong consequences for the acoustic environment:

> "Because visual and aural boundaries are independent means of enclosing a space, our visual and aural experience of size, the space between boundaries, may not be consistent. For example, glass is an auditory partition but not a visual one, and black curtain is a visual partition, but not an aural one". [3]

Interior architects are generally well-trained designers of the visual realm, including compositions of shapes, materials, textures, colours and lighting. In direct relation to this, tactile qualities usually get some consideration in the material selection. Other intangible conditions, such as sound and acoustics, however, have in the past been given significantly less attention within interior architectural design. Even though these sensory qualities are equally related to physical and visual design decisions, in many cases they seem to end up as a mere by-product of spatial compositions that have been conceived predominantly through visual means. This is not surprising as interior architecture and interior design education and practice in Western industrialised countries have only recently realised or re-discovered the potential of multi-sensory design considerations beyond the visual and tactile. Similarly, practitioners, researchers and academics from closely related areas of spatial design, such as architecture, landscape architecture, digital and interaction design have begun to explore multi-modal tools and techniques.

In architecture, since the 1990s the most prominent advocate of a new integrated approach to sensory design has been the Finnish architect Juhani Pallasmaa. His book publication *The Eyes of the Skin* introduced an argument

> "for the crucial phenomenological dimensions of the human experience in architecture". [4]

In this text Pallasmaa strongly critiques a hegemony of vision in architectural design and calls for an architecture that addresses "all the senses simultaneously." [5] American architect and academic Steven Holl supports Pallasmaa's claim in the preface to the publication and argues,

> "the way spaces feel, the sound and smell of these places, has equal weight to the way things look". [6]

Dutch architect and artist Lars Spuybroek of NOX uses computing tools and technology to design interactive sensory structures. The architecture of his water pavilion*

> "was developed simultaneously with a highly innovative interactive interior that fully involves all the senses in the visitor's experience...Collectively visitors can make enormous waves of sound and light and completely alter the atmosphere and emotionality of the interior." [7]

---

*   NOX. H2O Expo. The Netherlands, 1994-97

This is achieved

> "through a series of interactive systems controlled by sensors distributed throughout the pavilion. Visitors can manipulate the sensors to transform their environment through light, colour, projection and sound." [8]

There has been a range of publications and conferences discussing the significance of multi-sensory design in built environments in the last decade. *Sensory Urbanism* was an international conference held at the beginning of 2008. Papers from multiple disciplines were invited to respond to the issue of the:

> "whole sensory experience of the urban environment". [9]

The book publication *Sense of the City: An Alternate Approach to Urbanism* presents essays on different physical and ephemeral conditions of urban environments, such as sound, surface, thermal qualities, darkness and the seasons [10]. In the introduction the editor Mirko Zardini argues that human bodily sensation has recently been a topic of interest also in areas outside of architecture and design. In his opinion

> "the human and social sciences, from anthropology to geography, have undergone a 'sensorial revolution' in which the 'senses' constitute not so much a new field of study as a fundamental shift in the mode and media we employ to observe and define our own fields of study." [11]

Later on, Zardini elaborates:

> "Contemporary interiors–from hospitals to the communal spaces of shopping malls, theme parks, and places of entertainment and consumption–devote particular attention to differences in sensory perception, and many are conceived specifically as extensions of marketing strategies for consumer goods and experiences." [12]

The Sensoria Festival of Design Education, hosted by the Interior Design Program at RMIT University in 2004, aimed to inspire discourse related to the "contemporary fascination with the 'sensuous intellect.'" [13] The conference stream *phenomena* explored "contemporary art and design practice ... between sensation and thought," [14] which

> "has brought a renewed interest in the mechanisms of perception, and new models both scientific and intuitive". [15]

Installation artists have explored multi-sensory spatial compositions in relation to social connectivity for some time. Specifically, works of Dan Graham, Bruce Nauman, Susan Hiller and Bernhard Leitner have been important influences in my research.

Video and spatial artist Dan Graham is

> "interested in inter-subjectivity, exploring how a person, in a precise and given moment, perceives him/herself while at the same time watching other people who in turn are watching him/her". [16]

He understands the public realm as a space "for social performance purposes." [17] His spatial works use concepts of transparency and reflection that shift the relationships between viewers.

Multimedia artist and sculptor Bruce Nauman uses a variety of practices in the production of his works. His *Going Around the Corner Piece* (1970) and *Live-Taped Video Corridor* (1969-70) have been particularly inspiring to me in that they again raise questions about relationships to others as well as to the self. In these installations the viewer is video-recorded whilst moving through or around a built structure. At an early stage of his career Nauman's

> "art became more of an activity and less of a product". [18]

The point was "no longer to 'entice' or 'captivate' the viewer but to activate him, to make him the ultimate object of the work." [19]

At the Sydney Biennale in 2000 UK-based multimedia artist Susan Hiller exhibited a sound installation called "Witness". Visitors walked through 70–80 suspended earphones that played back voices speaking in different languages. In this work, Hiller was interested in the tension between

> "an overall kind of fable effect of all the voices talking at once" [and] "a close relationship with all the people telling their stories" [20],

depending on the listener's position within the space.

The sound works of Bernhard Leitner, who graduated with a degree in architecture, explore spatial experiences of acoustic environments. His work

> "shows the potentials of sensual experience that we are barely conscious of because they are either lost or have remained unknown as possibilities." [21]

The issue of sound introduces another important dimension to the discussion: Time. Critical theorist Brian Massumi has explored concepts of bodily movement, change and "qualitative transformation" [22] in relation to the human body and sensation. His work has has inspired a new way of thinking about encounters, flows and forces within interior environments, distinct from the dominant phenomenological view of experiential architecture and design. Massumi argues that

> "we are stopping the world in thought and 'thinking away its dynamic unity, the continuity of its movements', when we think of a space as 'extensive', as being measurable, divisible and composed of points plotting possible positions that objects may occupy."

It would be

> "looking at only one dimension of reality". [23]

This notion challenges the tools of traditional spatial design practices, for which techniques of measuring and representational drawing are so prevalent. It provokes the question of whether the tools currently used in interior architectural design are appropriate and what might be new tools to work with dynamic spatial relations.

The above practices and theories suggest diverse tactics and tools for an engagement with multi-faceted sensory qualities of environments in relation to human occupation and connections. This sets up the following key question for investigation in this paper:

What are new tools and techniques for working with multi-sensory, spatial and temporal conditions of site in the context of interior architectural design?

Case Study: *KONTAKTE*

An investigation of the issues introduced above is demonstrated through the case study of my design project called *Kontakte* (English: Contacts). The title of this project was inspired by an electronic music piece composed by Karlheinz Stockhausen in 1958–60. In the context of my work it alludes to the notion of temporary connections and dynamic networks between people and multi-faceted sensory relations within a site. *Kontakte* aimed to further explore ideas that I had developed through previous project works, studies of related creative pieces, literature reviews and conversations with my supervisors and colleagues.

Research Methods

The applied strategy was to undertake research "through design" rather than "about design" [24]. Architecture academic Peter Downton developed these concepts to claim that designing is a "way of inquiring", "producing knowing and knowledge" and a "way of researching." [25] Accordingly, artist and academic Paul Carter argues that

> "because of the lack of credibility given to the vital processes of design and creativity... scholarship and research in these fields, where it does occur, is "about" them, rather than "of" them." [27]

Research through design is an investigation undertaken by a practitioner, and is distinct from that of a theoretician or historian. It opens up a possibility of unknown findings and unpredictable results because

> "designing is not normally intended to produce a fully pre-conceived outcome, rather it is expected to produce change in the existing situation and hopefully offer fresh surprise and delight". [28]

Carter's notion of a "material thinking" supports a research approach through project work as "creative research": "If research implies finding something that was not there before, it ought to be obvious that it involves imagination. If it is claimed that what is found was always there (and merely lost), still an act of creative remembering occurs. As a method of materialising ideas, research is unavoidably creative." [29]

Project Incentive

My research evolves around issues of temporal, spatial and multi-sensory qualities of interior architectural environments in relation to concepts of interpersonal and intrapersonal connections. With *Kontakte* my main objectives were to analyse multi-sensory qualities as well as various flows and forces of a site in order to shift the spatial dynamics through design.

My selection criteria for the project site stipulated a publicly-accessible space with rich sensory stimuli, indeterminate numbers and types of users, high frequency of motion and movement as well as continuous change. I believed that such site conditions would highlight how a variety of tangible and intangible sensory qualities within an interior architectural environment shape human occupation and interaction. The kinds of user groups in the space were not given any particular relevance in the site selection because I wanted them to be varied and not fully controlled. This allowed me to develop my design independently of specific requests and programmatic considerations.

Site Selection and Documentation

The site that I eventually chose for my research project is an access space to RMIT University's Building 14 in the inner city of Melbourne, Australia [Figure 1].

Figure 1: The Kontakte project site RMIT Building 14 in Melbourne, Australia

The access space is located on a main street and near a major traffic crossing. Besides the street traffic, there is a high frequency of pedestrian traffic past the site along Swanston Street. The space opens onto the street and is easily accessible during business hours. Numerous people use the space as an entry to or exit from the campus. The site contains a staircase providing access to four levels of Building 14. It leads to key facilities, which connect to other university buildings such as the student service hub. The staircase opens to the outside at street level as well as on the level above. After hours a perforated roller door closes the site off to public access, but still allows for unobstructed air movement and views into the space from the outside. The space's strong relationships between the architectural inside and outside are its key features. Inside the staircase, the solid structures all have hard and acoustically reflective surfaces, such as exposed brick, concrete and glass.

Investigations of the multi-sensory conditions in and around the existing project site were the starting point for developing my design response. These site visits and various recordings happened between February and July 2008. I approached the investigations through observations, conversations and documentation, using video and stereo sound recording, photography, mapping and note taking as my main media. Each of these media revealed distinct qualities about the spatial relationships and ephemeral conditions of the site context. The video recordings enabled me to analyse the flows of people and change over time visually and aurally. Photographs captured particular moments and views visually, such as light, shadow and reflections. The sound recordings amplified the dominance of mechanical and low frequency sounds in the site. Furthermore they drew attention to repetitive sound marks, the level of noise caused by an air duct and they auralised the strong draught through the space. The media used for this site documentation revealed very particular sensory qualities about the site context. The most notable of these qualities were the lively soundscape[*] with a distinct keynote sound caused by an air vent within the space, changing lighting conditions throughout the day, the strong wind penetrating the staircase as well as continuous flows of people and traffic through and past the site. These sensory forces and flows continuously enter into the space from the street and resonate within it. As to the openness of the circulation space, it is directly exposed to changes in weather. Strong wind, rain and variations in air temperature all contribute to the sensory site conditions and relationships changing significantly.

Project Design

Based on these site investigations I developed a design response that aimed to reveal, amplify and produce connections between the spatiotemporal environment and human occupation by means of shifting the multi-faceted sensory dynamics of the site. The main tools used to realise my design concept were sound, air movement, the changing lighting conditions and reflection of light, and the flow of traffic past the site as well as human activities.

---

*   The term *soundscape* was coined by author, composer and environmentalist R. Murray Schafer in the 1970s.

Figure 2: Kontakte installed in the site

My final design was a kinetic screen made from over 1000 suspended pieces of aluminium sheet and was installed in the access space for two weeks [Figure 2].

Its matt reflective surface was designed to blend into the background of the site. It was activated through wind lights and colours reflected from the street (natural light, passing motor vehicles, people, signage and shop fronts). Air currents of varying strength caused undulations on the surface of the screen, which produced a metallic high-frequency sound. Depending on the force of the wind the sound varied from soft to rather assertive.

Recording and Documentation Methods of Kontakte

For my documentation of *Kontakte* I used obtrusive as well as unobtrusive methods of recording in order to collect a variety of research data. For most of the time I carried out unobtrusive observations of activities in and around the project site. I had direct interaction with people in the space only when a meeting had been specifically arranged or when I was approached spontaneously. Most of the information gathered was qualitative material. I used the following research tools and techniques for the documentation and evaluation of my project in situ:

- Video recordings
- Photographs
- Stereo sound recordings [Figure 3]
- Recordings of dB(A) levels in different locations of the site
- Mappings and notes of daily observations

- Poster, postcards and a feedback box inviting people to comment on the project
- Email correspondence and minutes from meetings with Property Services staff
- Arranged conversations with individual design practitioners and academics
- A talk to a group of designers and academics
- Conversations with university maintenance staff and construction workers that arose from project related tasks
- Spontaneous encounters and conversations with university staff, students, visitors and passers-by

Figure 3: Stereo sound recording of Kontakte

All of the above means of recording and documenting the project have been useful to my project evaluations. Each of them captured different aspects of a variety of information about multi-sensory, spatiotemporal and social dynamics of the site with Kontakte installed. The still frames of photography have emphasised specific situations purely visually, while the sound recordings eliminated any visual distractions and have allowed me to focus on the acoustic environment. They have furthermore allowed me to analyse flows of movement and change over time. The video recordings brought together visual, kinetic, temporal as well as aural aspects of the installation and highlighted their interconnections. The measured dB (A) levels in the site showed data that was consistent with my notes and mappings of perceived noise levels.

Some of the comments I received from the feedback postcards were merely stating whether or not the person liked the installation. However, the more interesting ones described the way in which Kontakte picked up on the sensory qualities of the site context and indicated notions of the installation as an auditory and visual landmark. The stereo sound recordings revealed specific cues about the altered soundscape of the site context during my project installation

The kinetic screen added a high frequency sound to the existing keynote drone, which was caused mainly by passing traffic and the air vent. Interestingly, this introduced

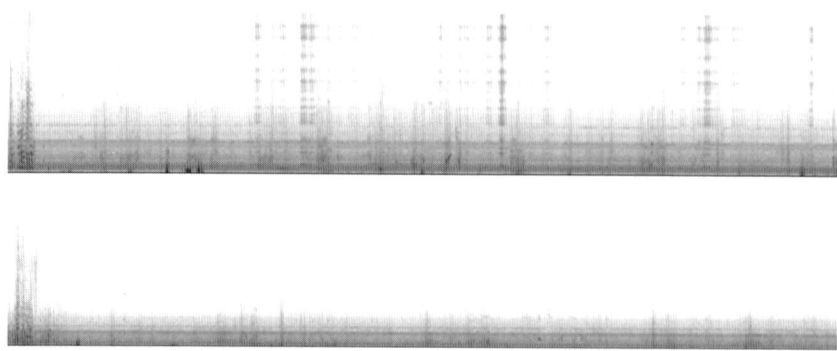

Figure 4: Excerpts from sonograms of the Kontakte site before (bottom) and during the project installation (top); x-axis = time, y-axis = sound frequency content

sound seemed to draw specific attention to the low frequency sound sources within the space, rather than masking them. Depending on the social context and the intensity of air movement, people tended to either get irritated by the sound environment or enjoy the auditory transformation. In one-to-one meetings right next to the installation, it acted as a pleasant aural backdrop for most of the time.

Once in a while the conversations were interrupted by a strong wind that activated the screen and made it rather difficult to hear the other person speaking. This was not much of an issue because it was possible to shift the attention quickly between the person and the installation. Social interaction proved to be more difficult in a talk that I gave to a group of about ten designers and academics within the project site. The wind, and hence the sound produced by the screen, required the audience to listen to my words carefully and required me to make an extra effort of speaking loudly and clearly for the whole time. This experience turned out to be a rather tiring task for all of the participants. In these examples the acoustic environment strongly influenced the manner in which people occupied the site and interacted within it at different times.

Conclusion

As a project experiment, *Kontakte* highlighted the significance and potential of multi-sensory qualities in spatial design. By shifting the sensory and spatiotemporal relations in the site I was able to introduce new modes of occupation without changing the physical configuration of the passageway. The sensory qualities, and in some cases the sound qualities, affected how people acted or interacted. I found that my installation created a sense of place within the site context and offered a pause in a highly transitional space that is characterised by movement and constant change.

The project site had previously been a functional circulation space that did not actively invite passers-by to stop. My installation encouraged a number of individuals and groups to spend more time in the space than they normally would have. For example, when I arrived at the site one day, an RMIT staff member had brought a chair into the space and was eating his lunch next to the screen. He explained how he enjoyed listening to the sound of the installation and that it seemed like a good location to spend his break. Furthermore, *Kontakte* introduced dynamic sensory zones, which became a visual or aural landmark to some people. These zones were not wholly defined through physical (built) interior and exterior conditions, but through the fluid movement of light, sound and air in and out of the site. These ever-changing sensory qualities continuously produced new spatial, temporal and social interrelations within the site context.

My approach to exploring a variety of recording methods and devices in the site investigations initially revealed certain sensory flows and forces, upon which I was then able to act. As such, I derived the design of my *Kontakte* installation from a combination of dynamic visual and auditory mappings of the site context as described in my preceding discussion. I believe that my design response would not have drawn on the multiplicity of intangible temporal qualities within the site if I had merely taken photos of the architectural space and produced a set of orthographic drawings based on site measurements, as is common practice in interior architectural design projects. The range of tools and techniques I used shaped my understanding of the site conditions and design of *Kontakte*. For interior architecture and interior design practices concerned with multi-sensory, spatial and temporal qualities it is therefore useful to experiment with such diverse media and methods in the different stages of a design process, as this may offer up new ways of designing environments for human occupation and interaction.

References

[1]   Truax, B. *Acoustic Communication*. Ablex Publishing, 2000.
[2]   Truax, B. *Acoustic Communication*. Ablex Publishing, 2000, 4.
[3]   Blesser, B. and Salter, L.R. *Spaces Speak, Are You Listening?*. Cloth, 2006, 21.
[4]   Holl, S. in Pallasmaa, J. *The Eyes of the Skin: Architecture and the Senses*. John Wiley & Sons, 1996, 7.
[5]   Pallasmaa, J. *The Eyes of the Skin: Architecture and the Senses*. John Wiley & Sons, 1996, 11.
[6]   Holl, S. in Pallasmaa, J. *The Eyes of the Skin: Architecture and the Senses*. John Wiley & Sons, 1996, 7.
[7]   NOX. Available: http://www.noxarch.com/flash_content/flash_content.html [Accessed on 2008, 04 May]
[8]   Van Cleef, Connie. Water Worlds (design and construction of an exhibition pavilion in Neeltje Jans, the Netherlands). *The Architectural Review*, 1998.
[9]   *Sensory Urbanism*. Document of Conference Abstracts. 2008
[10] Zardini, Mirko (editor). *Sense of the City: an alternate approach to urbanism*. Lars Mueller Publishers, 2005.

[11] Zardini, Mirko (editor). *Sense of the City: an alternate approach to urbanism.* Lars Mueller Publishers, 2005, 22.
[12] Zardini, Mirko (editor). *Sense of the City: an alternate approach to urbanism.* Lars Mueller Publishers, 2005, 22-23.
[13] McLeod, Ross (editor). *The Sensuous Intellect.* RMIT University Press, 2006, 7.
[14] McLeod, Ross (editor). *The Sensuous Intellect.* RMIT University Press, 2006, 8.
[15] McLeod, Ross (editor). *The Sensuous Intellect.* RMIT University Press, 2006, 8.
[16] Valle, P. Interview with Dan Graham. Artland. Available: http://architettura.supereva.com/artland/20020515/index_en.htm [Accessed on 2008, 04 May], (2002).
[17] Valle, P. Interview with Dan Graham. Artland. Available: http://architettura.supereva.com/artland/20020515/index_en.htm [Accessed on 2008, 04 May], (2002).
[18] PBS. Quote Bruce Nauman. Art21. Biography. Available: http://www.pbs.org/art21/artists/nauman/ [Accessed on 2008, 04 May].
[19] Criqui, J.P. Bruce Nauman. (Kunstmuseum Wolfsburg). Artforum International. Available: http://www.encyclopedia.com/doc/1G1-20381893.html [Accessed on 2008, 04 May], (1997).
[20] Copeland, J. Interview with Susan Hiller. (From the edited transcript of Radio National's Sunday Morning program originally broadcast on 26/5/02). Available: http://www.abc.net.au/arts/visual/stories/s597706.htm [Accessed on 2008, 04 May].
[21] Pichler, C. Website Bernhard Leitner. Available: http://www.bernhardleitner.at/en/index_2.html [Accessed on 2008, 04 May].
[22] Massumi, B. Parables fro the Virtual: Movement, Affect, Sensation. Duke University Press, 2002.
[23] Massumi, B. Parables fro the Virtual: Movement, Affect, Sensation. Duke University Press, 2002, 6.
[24] Downton, P. *Design Research.* RMIT University Press, 2003, 2.
[25] Downton, P. *Design Research.* RMIT University Press, 2003, 1.
[26] Downton, P. *Design Research.* RMIT University Press, 2003, 2.
[27] Carter, P. *Material Thinking: The Theory and Practice of Creative Research.* Melbourne University Publishing, 2004, 7-8.
[28] Downton, P. *Design Research.* RMIT University Press, 2003, 5.
[29] Carter, P. *Material Thinking: The Theory and Practice of Creative Research.* Melbourne University Publishing, 2004, 7.

Gabriele KNUEPPEL
RMIT University
77 Barnett St
Kensington
Victoria 3031
Australia
gabriele.knueppel@rmit.edu.au
0061-3-93726967

Annalisa DI ROMA

Polytechnic of Bari

DIGITAL ORNAMENT: NEW MEANINGS AND SKILLS

Introduction

"The history of production techniques presents two major phases: the handicrafts one and the industrial one. The fact that the modern age is characterised by the industrial development, which is so rapid and expansive to provoke a so deep and probably definitive crisis of the artisan, lets us think that the two cycles are successive. Really two methods were, for a long time, strictly connected [...]. Handicraft technique is devoted to the production of objects made singularly or for a small series; the industrial technique is devoted to large serial production: in the first one quality researches prevail, in the second quantitative research. In the modern age, with the growth of mechanical instruments, industrial techniques are shown to be able to achieve qualitative results superior to those of the craftsmanship methods."

This quote from the Italian Historian of Art, G. C. Argan, summarises the heart of this paper, focusing his attention on the role of production methods in the aesthetic conception of industrial design production. From here the choice of the theme of architectural decoration allows a theoretical and a practical reflection on the role of Tools and Tactics for Interior design growth.

The presupposition of industrial production tools introduces the matter of "technical reproduction" and how it changes the sense of the art conception. A process of exact replicas of the original piece is the origin of large scale production.

Given this premise, the circle of historical investigation around the industrial product continues. The debate concerning the characteristics of serial repetition started during the industrial revolution. It centred around the perception that mass production has an absence of traditional artistic input and craftsmanship.

Particularly in the field of building and in the great works of engineering that occurred following the development of principal European capitals, there is evidence of the passage from traditional construction to industrial production, particularly in the elements of house building.

The materials that properly allowed this passage toward the birth of industrialisation of the processes of production were mainly *cast iron* and *iron*.

The New Aesthetical Paradigm

At the beginning of the 19th century architects took inspiration from classical ornament without wondering if the ornament was proper for industrial civilisation.

In 1851 the question if the ornament had to be used or not on buildings and on in interior design had not instigated moral passions yet, but after the Great Exhibition the products of the artistic industry collected in the Crystal Palace of Joseph Paxton showed the dawning complexity of the new relationship of project and production of the objects destined to the fruition of a large number of custom. Ability to use the ornament in correct and grammatical ways had to distinguish the architect from the mere builder and to qualify him as an artist. To copy trends and engraved ornaments constituted the introduction of industrial design. Such education was institutionalised throughout France, Germany and England in the Schools for *Kunstindustry*.

At the end of the 19th century eclecticism was substituted with a new architectural language and the movements of art applied to industry; the ornament, from a universal way of unification of architectural language that was, became a vehicle through which an architect and a designer could express their own individuality. Since then the history of ornamental art follows the complex articulation of the single poetic expression of the movements of applied art and the new architectural languages of art nouveau. Industrialism had changed deeply the meat and bones of architecture and it demanded a linguistic form that expressed fully the role that the industry was given.

The synthetic nature of the project of ornament with the actual digital models and prototyping with CNC machines

Practical knowledge in building and architecture is currently undergoing massive change due to computer graphics and construction management software. These reflections are the starting point for the hypothesis of updating ornament design and production process through the use of the actual technology for digital design and virtual realisation. Digitals instruments, for the first time, allow us to draw the complex project of the ancient architectural order and its decorative apparatus in three-dimensional space, creating an experimental phase of research on the true form of the classical ornament.

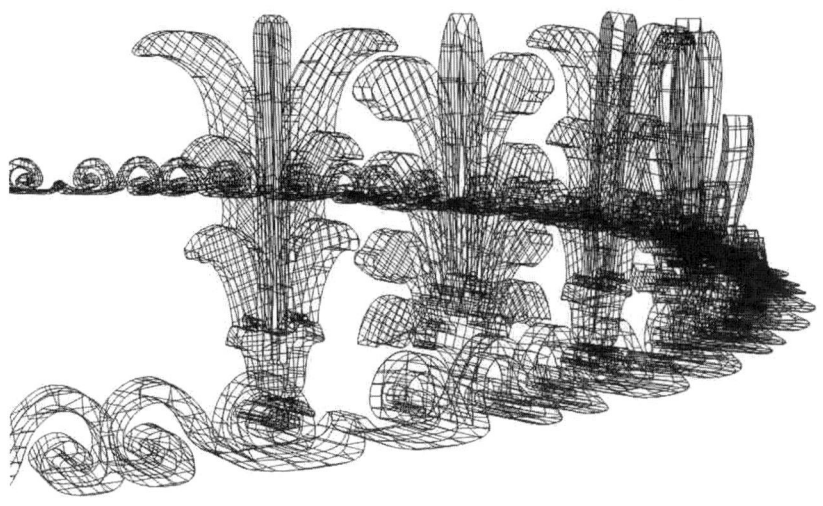

Figure 1: Digital ornament: three-dimensional model of Palmettes and flowers made by the author

This hypothesis of updating the methods and the technique for architectural design is subtended by the question on the possibility that computer technologies have not only transformed the tools of the project, but also the project itself.

How did digital design change from a planning instrument to an expressive technique for the production of architectural models?

"The digital system revolution" arrived when the whole disciplinary corpus of architecture was put into relationship with digital systems, comparing the specificity of each discipline with the potentialities of development of the various softwares (among them, CAD models, software for graphics and animation, software for structural building calculations and informatics systems for GIS).

The actual digital systems give the design discipline the possibility to manage the three dimensions of Cartesian space immediately and directly. In any kind of three-d modelling software logics (solid modelling, nurbs modelling, mesh modelling, parametric and variable modelling) the planner has the tools to try and explain geometrically complex forms.

In the case of decorative architectural apparatus, as it already happens for the industrial design objects, this new form of project is characterised by the direct process from the design as pure representation, sketch, to reality, prototype. Virtual models represent a hybrid among these two extremes; a new form of the sketch as method and as tool of the architectural project. It describes synthetically the complexity of the geometric constructive matrix of the architectural organism and its elements.

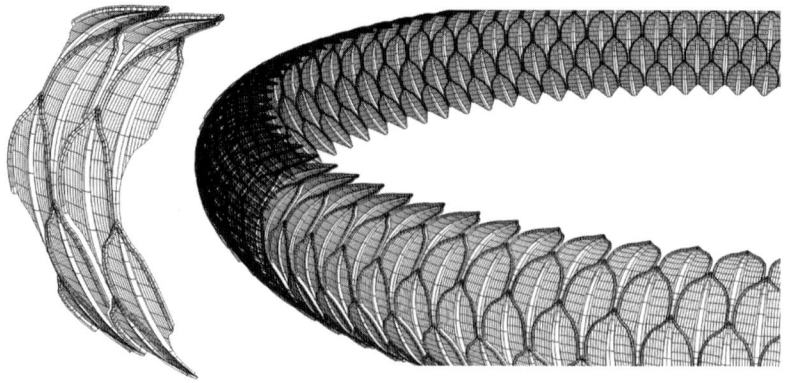

Figure 2: Digital ornament: three-dimensional model of Imbricate leaves decoration made by the author

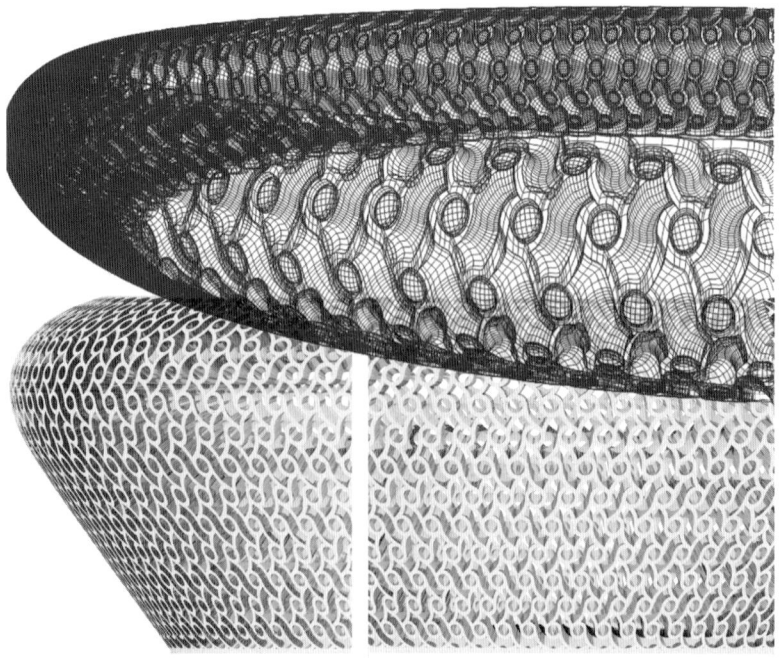

Figure 3: Digital ornament: three-dimensional model of interlaced band decoration and an application made by the author

Figure 4: Digital ornament: three-dimensional frame made by the author.

The use of the mechanical systems for the actual productive methods and ancient handicrafts methods

The question of tools and the techniques of rough-shaping and finishing are important to any research project that intends to recover the expressive nature of stone, since certain plastic outcomes of the period (from the working of the drum to the undercut, from abacus to echinus) are to be evaluated as the result of the tools which were used for boring.

The study of the artisan ornamental techniques permits a comparison of the similarities and differences between a manual production system and a mechanical system using numerical controlled machines.

In ancient building the constructions of finished elements necessitated a series of work phases (often performed by different specialists) analogous with mechanised systems in which the number of jobs to do depended on the nature of the object to construct and on the type of ornament.

A decorated surface would be subject to at least three work phases, which would increase in relation to the morphological characteristics and to the number and type of tools necessary to the job. In the ancient period the production of different blocks was often the responsibility of various workers and the result was a slight difference between the pieces. The production of a series of elements entirely produced with mechanical processes, on the contrary, guarantees absolute similarity.

In the ancient period the first work phase after the squaring of the block was the redesigning of the orthogonal surface of the moulding. The pattern was accomplished using templates and boring tools. The templates were generally made in wood and appear as the negative of the mouldings, they permitted control of the required shape during the sculpting process. The circulation of templates and pattern cards throughout building sites was associated with the mobility of artisans and allowed for the rapid execution of similar elements. Only in the final surface finishing phase were abrasive tools used.

The mechanised processes employed by computerised numerically controlled machines use mills and rotating drums which need materials with different characteristics to those required by boring tools. Certain processes (including 'bush hammering', which is typical of the surfaces between the blocks and the drums) do not appear to be reproducible with off-cut techniques. Thus it is necessary to establish a priori both the type of tools necessary to create the desired effect and the right type of operation (wholly mechanical, partially manual etc.). This problem is more complex in the study of decorative pieces, in which the finished product reveals both intaglio and, sometimes, fretwork.

Cad-Cam project phases of the study case

The three-dimensional models realised through the use of specific CAD software constitute the first level of a direct approach to the planning of the ornament and they allow us to develop a critical reflection on analogies and differences in the methods of ancient and contemporary production.

The ornament themes used as study case for this paper are chosen as an example of the complexity in the planning process. Particularly, the decoration *interlacement band* and the *meander* (fret band) will be used to point out the process for the realisation of the *prototype*.

The project of the ornament starts with the drawing of the bi-dimensional decorative pattern through the geometric definition of the pattern, the identification of the axes and the centre for the symmetry, the rotation, the translation, which are the fundamental entities and geometrical relationships used to achieve a different configuration of

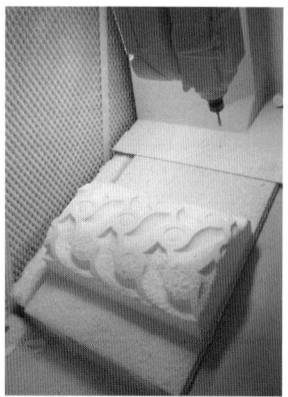
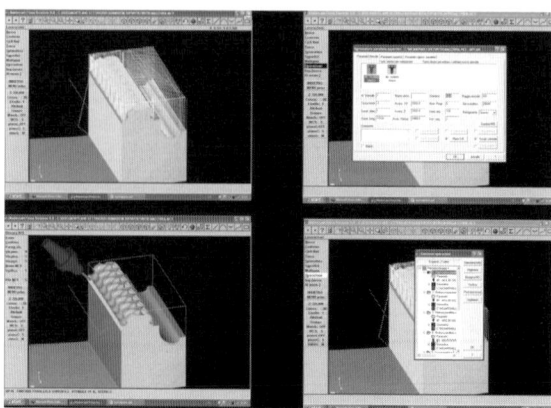

Figure 5: Prototyping: prototype of the interlaced band decoration made by the author using a cn machine and Cam project

the decorative themes. The second step is to put the decorative theme into the correct relationship with the moulding surface developed. In the case of the tours radial surface, we know that this kind of surfaces is not achievable; so the surfaces approximates to a space grid made by the parallels and the meridian, and these will be the guide line for the transformation of the decorative pattern, from bi-dimensional to three-dimensional. Using nurbs modelling software it is possible to apply the planar curves to surface, and then all the CAD process for the 3D model can be set.

The second phase is the CAM project that allows the passage from the three-dimensional virtual model to the final prototypes. This process will transform the mathematical model, elaborated according to the logic of the nurbs modelling software, into an ISO normalised post script file CN, containing all the instruction on operations and tools that will manage the phase of mechanical production of the object using a numerically controlled machine or a fast prototyping machine.

The first operation in the CAM project is to import the file of the 3D model. The model will be moved into the Cartesian space of the software using the x, y, z co-ordinates, from the ideal position to that one corresponding to zero (origin of the axis) of the machines. Each mechanical operation will start from this point, which is the new origin point for the model. On the basis of the morphological property of the model it will be defined as the box limit representing the row block. Generally the block is parallel-piped as it was in the ancient building yard, as close as possible to the geometry of the prototype. The box limit operation will represent in the virtual space of the software the row block. When the absolute and relative coordinates for the prototype and the tools are fixed, the planning of the operation, and the tools to use, can start.

The operations are generally divided in two main groups: the row shaping and the finishing. The first is performed into a virtual pocket of maximum dimension and will approximate the row block to the general morphological characteristics of the model. The finishing jobs will be used to create the exact final configuration of the architectural details.

Associated with the different job-cycles is the tools library. Tools will be chosen on the basis of the cutter shapes. Then the tool parameter will be fixed, such as pilot diameter, speed and feed on the base of the characteristic of the material. The last phase in CAM project is the creation of the NC file. The software creates both a binary and a text version of the NCI as part of NC program generation. The binary NCI remains with the specific software file. It is updated when you regenerate toolpaths so that it reflects changes you make to geometry and toolpath parameters.

The last operations in order to make the prototype are performed using the numerically controlled machine that, thanks to its calculator, elaborates the NC file in those mechanical movement of the tools.

References

[1] Arte e tecnica nella produzione industriale, Argan G. C., "Introduzione: Tecnica e Arte" in: *Dizionario Universale dell'Arte De Agostini, voce Tecnica*, Vol XIII pp. 686-691.
[2] AAVV., *Aus Einem Guß, Einsenguß in Kunst und Technik*, Museum für Verkehr und Technik Berlin Nicolai, 1988 Berlin
[3] AAVV., *History of Industrial Design: 1750-1850 The Age of the Industrial Revolution*, Electa, Milano, 1990
[4] Benjamin W., *L'opera d'arte nell'epoca della sua riproduzione tecnica*, Einaudi, Torino, 1991.
[5] Ceccarelli N., *Progettare nell'era del digitale*, Marsilio, Milano 2000.
[6] Di Roma A., *La produzione in serie dell'ornato architettonico: dall'industria artistica ellenistica alla protoi*
[6] Meyer F. S., *Handbook of Ornament*, Dover Publications, Inc., New York, 1956.
[7] Obiectile, "Le décoratif entre mythe, géométrie et rhétorique" in: *L'architecture d'aujourd'hui* n° 333, Marzo – Aprile 2001
[8] Riegl A., *Stilgrafen. Grundlegung zu einer Geschichte der Ornament, Berlin* 1893 (trad. it. a cura di Mario Pacor *Problemi di Stile. Fondamenti di una storia dell'arte ornamentale*, Milano 1963).
[9] Riegl A., *Spätrömische Kunstindustrie, nach der Funden in Österreich-Ungarn*, Wien 1901 (*Industria artistica Tardoromana,* Venezia 1953; e col titolo *Arte Tardoromana*, Torino 1959, passim).
[10] Semper G., *Der Stil in der technischen und tektonischen Künsten oder praktische Astethik*, München 1860 (trad. it. a cura di A.R. Burelli, C. Cresti, B. Gravagnuolo, F. Tentori, Prefazione di V. Gregotti, Editori Laterza, 1992).
[11] Vitta M., *Il progetto della bellezza*, Torino, Einaudi 2000.

RU Annalisa DI ROMA
School of Architecture
Politecnico di Bari
St. Orabona 4
70125
Bari IT
adiroma@poliba.it
Tel +39 080 5963893
Mob +39 339 7400607
Fax +39 080 5963823

Tactics in the workplace

Drew PLUNKETT
formerly of Glasgow School of Art

TACTICS IN THE WORKPLACE – INTRODUCTION

The experience of those taking part in the session and the examples offered were all drawn from within the United Kingdom.

Initial discussion centred on the motivation of further and higher educational institutions to accept fundamental changes in the way staff teach and students learn. There was a consensus that, while change has been significantly driven by digital technologies offering viable options for staff and student interaction, there is an economic imperative to recruit greater numbers of students, particularly high fee payers from "overseas" and glamorous socialised learning spaces are recruiting tools.

Predictions for new learning provision, if based on analysis of current use patterns and preferences, are suspect because there are limited precedents to draw on and it is difficult to quantify productive learning within superficially unstructured digital environments. Antonia Cairns of DEGW described the intensity of interaction amongst *ad hoc* student groups in the "White Space" at Abertay University, which also incorporates staff work areas, breaking down barriers between staff and students while clearly signalling that it is primarily a work place.

The logic of academic staff repetitiously delivering formal lectures, which could otherwise be offered digitally at times to suit individual students, was questioned. Formal and semi-formal individual and group tutorials were cited as mechanisms to consolidate understanding of digitally dispersed information and to structure the pace of learning. Different disciplines have different requirements.

The importance of a "bottom-up" contribution to the briefing process was recognised and Val Clugston and Scott Mason of Nomad spoke about their experience in developing appropriate methodologies for gathering information from student users. Having tried conventional observation and interview techniques they experimented with social websites and were satisfied that these allowed wider interaction with interested and opinionated potential users and a longer period for opinions to evolve. Their initial suspicion was that online postings were predictable and more complex and considered opinions could only be drawn out in a structured interview. Within a short time however they found that online discussions would ignite spontaneously, with articulation of more subtle and resolved conclusions, which were unlikely to have evolved in the necessarily limited time span of a structured interview. They spoke about concerns of staff members within institutions, usually librarians, who felt that the initiative was passing from them and that the quality of their own working environments and effectiveness would be sacrificed to satisfy, possibly transient and naive, student whims.

Systematic and objectively conducted research into student needs and preferences also has value for the commissioning institute in the competition for funding, where there is a strategic advantage in offering convincing evidence of a serious attempt to identify and quantify demand.

While the area of independent student learning remains comparatively uncharted there is emerging evidence that new learning environments do offer more popular and productive solutions that are more than expedient responses to a funding crisis. The digital technologies that provide students' working tools also make further analytical information, about demand and work patterns, easier to collate and may also reveal work patterns off campus.

Hugh ANDERSON
haa design limited

DYNAMIC (SPACE) BUDGETS FOR DYNAMIC (WORKING) ENVIRONMENTS

Introduction

Developing a space budget might not be every designer's idea of fun, but get the space budget wrong and the total project is likely to be wrong. It will either be too extravagant and thereby wasteful and debilitating in terms of working the financial budget, or too mean and thereby debilitating in terms of any sort of growth or change. Most importantly, optimum sized spaces are likely to be lively places, naturally policed, loved and well maintained.

Getting the space right has always been contentious, and the methodologies to date popular only because they depersonalise or simplify what is a difficult or dreary process. The methodologies, for the most part, also are hit and miss, taking little account of the current complex manner in which space is used. Thus a traditional space budget based upon multiplying a space standard by a number of persons and then adding for ancillary or support space does not take account of shared space or the dynamic use of space over time. Of course, adjustments can be made to reflect utilisation but this does not take account of the desirability of one space over another or the value for money it might represent to the organisation in terms of improving the performance of the "workforce" in any way.

Creating space budgets in this way falls into the trap which so much of building assessment tends to do, of favouring that which is measurable over that which is difficult to measure, of focussing on *quantity* rather than *quality*. In moving forward there is a need therefore to find methodologies which better reflect the complex way in which we currently use space and notion of *effectiveness* rather than *efficiency*.

Figure 1

Ironically, developing space budgets for educational buildings is more sophisticated just now than the generally more sophisticated office sector, possibly because speculative new build is driven by the economic imperative to maximise on plot ratio, and occupier space calculation is perplexed by the increasing unpredictability of business growth (when it is not being swayed by dubious agents keen to achieve a sale and always finding it simpler to justify the purchase of too much space rather than too little). Educational projects by contrast normally have to be answerable to central funding and the constant drive to reduce costs, and cannot therefore concentrate on the alternative strategy of generating business benefit.

Educational projects (within England and Wales and Scotland) call for stringent assessments of space utilisation in the face of such budget constraints. This takes the form of a survey of observed room and seat utilisation over specifically directed periods of time. The process is accurate and a useful indicator of existing and projected occupancy patterns but, once again, goes only so far in helping to develop a space budget which properly reflects current space usage and value in terms of space allocation. The translation of these utilisation statistics into this same space allocation is at best unclear.

However, working with the current (English and Welsh) system of educational space budgeting is a useful way into what might be an improved system for Scotland and may have pointers as to what could be appropriate for general space budgeting purposes. This paper examines therefore the way in which educational space budgeting is currently undertaken in England and Wales (Scotland currently takes its lead from the LSC – the Learning & Skills Council in England and Wales – with some modifications), and hypothesises on how this might be improved to better reflect the issues that characterise the way in which students (and others) work.

Major change is currently working its way through educational institutions, at all levels, as a result of the impact of new technology. In simple terms there is a move from *teaching*, as a form of dispersing information, to *learning*, where information is freely available via the internet and other electronic means, and the emphasis can now be in the digestion and understanding of this information and a more informal, more interactive relationship between teacher and learner. As a result various new forms of space use have started to come into being. First there were ICT suites, rooms with banks of computers available for student use in their own time. These then began to migrate towards libraries, where self-directed learning via computers as well as more traditional access to books became increasingly popular, combined with the notion of group work and greater interaction between students. This has in turn led to the acceptance of more informality in these work settings, the introduction of soft seating, working clusters, and in those particularly daring institutions prepared to challenge the conventional ethos of work, the previously unheard of notion of food and drink in these areas. In most HE and FE institutions nowadays we will therefore find spaces variously entitled "learning hubs", "learning streets" or "social learning spaces". Frequently they are combined with a central atrium (providing that now obligatory "wow" factor) or deliberately loosely-defined circulation spaces, where the real living of the institution tends to take place. What was therefore deemed, in funding terms, "unusable" space is now seen as being intensely "usable" and is recognised as such in determining a space budget, albeit in an ad-hoc manner.

In England and Wales therefore (and by adoption in Scotland) the current space calculation process allows for "teaching spaces" (based on various space standards), a percentage allocation for "learning spaces" to which are added support spaces and balance areas, and then a welcome but slightly arbitrary 10% for "atrium spaces". All of this goes a considerable distance towards recognising the notion that the nature of space use is changing, and that what was previously ignored or victimised should be recognised and valuable within the broader educational objective of supporting learning. However, the space allocation process is somewhat arbitrary, and it does not have a coherent link with that other initiative, previously mentioned, namely the workman-like exercise of calculating the utilisation of teaching spaces.

Significantly, the process of observing and calculating space utilisation does not currently extend to the various forms of "self-directed learning space" referred to above, the spaces which increasingly constitute the life of a college or university and

Figure 2

which (by strong anecdotal evidence at least) are proving most valuable within the student experience. The reason for this presumably relates to the simple fact that recording the use of these spaces is more difficult, with constant and informal comings and goings and with the academic difficulty of deciding what at any moment in time constitutes "learning" as opposed to "socialising", something which until now has been put in a discrete space calculation and funding box. The truth of the matter however is that it is in these awkward categories of overlap between work and non-work that greatest interaction now occurs, where truly "blended learning" occurs with a constant oscillation between conversation and information gathering and where the increasing value to the organisation lies.

To try to capture some of this variety and quality therefore the following proposal for a modified form of space calculation is put forward, relating to educational use but, by analogy, being relevant to other forms of working spaces also. However, before exploring this, there is a further brief diversion, as we look at the current practice of space calculation.

In England and Wales there is the concept of the "guided learning hour", the time when students are in formal contact with their tutors and presumably benefiting from this staff-student contact. The measurement is obligatory for all institutions and is at the basis of the contract between institution and state in constituting the obligation of the institution to undertake a required amount of prescribed activity in return for its state subsidy.

Built on this therefore, and used in calculating an overall space requirement, there is a simple process of relating these guided learning hours to the amount of time within the academic year to numbers of students using the following formulae:

MNW (minimum number of workplaces) = **GLH (guided learning hours)** / **annual hours**

followed by;

MNW x (between **11.5 m²** and **14.5m²**) + **1,500m m²** + **10%** = **College Gross Internal Area**

As a shorthand to understanding a space requirement this is a convenient guide and, on the face of it, bears some relationship to the valuable use of the institution's resources. However, it falls short of this in various ways. These are worth disentangling, bearing in mind the desire to recognise the emerging different forms of learning and teaching and the notion that value should be recognised in different forms of space use, not just teacher/student contact.

Firstly the notion of a "guided learning hour" has embedded within it the idea that learning equates to formal teaching, to those timetabled hours when staff have to present material, or conduct teaching sessions, to assembled groups of students, generally in specialised teaching rooms. While all institutions (staff and students alike) would argue to some extent for the value and necessity of formal teaching, they would also be bound to admit to the diminishing value of this as a learning norm or, in other words, that the use of the lecture theatre as the primary vehicle for inculcating knowledge in many institutions is a concept from the past. By contrast of course guided learning via seminars or "workshops" might be on a related rise, but this is not necessarily undertaken within the timetabled conditions of a classroom.

Secondly there is the dislocation of this limited but nevertheless useful statistic with the recorded information relating to utilisation. The information relating to guided learning hours is used within the "top-down" calculation for determining a total space requirement, whereas the information relating to utilisation is used within the "bottom-up" calculation for determining department sizes and the allocation of the total space budget, with some fairly arbitrary juggling between the two so they can be made to match. As can be seen this process is neither logically consistent nor particularly accurate in reflecting how space is currently used, nor does it take account of where value lies within the learning process.

Building on these concepts the following might therefore be a way of developing a more consistent process:

- The process must first of all be conceived from the bottom-up. (A shorthand process from the top down can also be available for purposes of speed and

Figure 3

convenience but derived *after* a more accurate bottom-up process has been developed and in order to reflect this calculation, not to pre-empt it.)

- The process must then be built on, not just for generalised allocations of space standards, but as an understanding of working, learning or teaching *modes*, the bedrock of understanding space usage, and that which reflects the way in which learning, teaching and working is increasingly varied over time, reflecting the needs of the moment. Thus a classification requires to be drawn up of a range of space use types/learning modes, ranging from formal instruction in large groups, through blended learning/ seminar type situations, to that ambiguous and still sometimes academically suspect mode of working called "social learning". For each of these modes, by dividing the particular space by the number of persons able to be accommodated, a clearly defined *"space per person"* or *"space standard"* can be derived, (which, incidentally, can be modified in the light of new or different work modes that a particular institution might wish to justify.)

- Next in line is the *occupancy factor* which, as previously suggested, might be modified from present use to incorporate non-formal learning/teaching spaces. A more complex but not impossible form of observation can be derived to cover those social learning and circulation spaces now relevant to the working/ learning day. The notion of an *occupancy factor* already carries within it the notion of *value*, insofar as that which is deemed valuable by students who tend to support that which they find useful and ignore that which they deem a waste of time. To this extent FE institutions are annoyingly but usefully democratic. Students tend to vote with their feet.

- Possibly to counteract this or to recognise that there is a value beyond what might be appreciated by the sloppy student, there is then a need for a compensating measure. This might be termed a "*quality weighting*". This would be an unashamedly subjective weighting, possibly determined from "on high" in terms of what was deemed by the Funding Body necessary for the preservation of certain types of knowledge and understanding. Being subjective however it could be a measure which once again gave room for argument or the justification by an institution for a somewhat different form of treatment in its particular circumstances. Thus in one particular situation, formal instruction via a professor in a poorly utilised lecture theatre may be considered essential, in another situation, not. In another college, by contrast, it might be argued that social learning space had a higher educational value than formal teaching and in addition had the utilisation to match this.

- Next is the number of students, a number to be determined by department or by whatever social grouping is most relevant eventually to give rise to a particular lump of space likely to be accommodated in a particular area. Issues immediately arise here in the use of the deliberately shared/overlap spaces described above, where their allocation might still be on a departmental basis or could be (like genuinely common resources such as cafeterias) dealt with on the basis of shared "support" space. In either case their space calculation might still be determined on the basis of observed occupation/utilisation and required space per person.

- Added to all the above would then still be the allocation of ancillary and support spaces necessary for making up the total compliment of a learning institution, similarly identified as either centrally located or locally distributed.

This then might be summarised in the following formula:

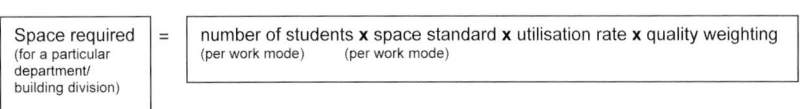

Space required (for a particular department/ building division) = number of students **x** space standard **x** utilisation rate **x** quality weighting
(per work mode)   (per work mode)

As the above suggests, the formula would result in totals for "identifiable working areas" to which would require to be added allowances for other ancillary/ support/ balance areas, as defined, to produce a set of sub-totals adding up to a total amount of *usable space*; to which in turn would require to be added allowances for primary circulation (i.e. spaces usable only as such) and building structure and core, to come to an area of total *gross space*, as normal. The above might form the basis of a detailed space-by-space calculation of a total space budget. It will still be necessary however to have some form of "ready reckoner" to give an indication at an early stage of what might be required.

As has been suggested, the current LSC formula for calculating gross space based on guided learning hours is simple and convenient and one which may even bear some correlation to the current "bottom-up" approach used for understanding departmental sizes and used for the purpose of allocation. Based on the more sophisticated bottom-up approach, as suggested above, it might therefore be similarly possible to find a correlation with some other readily available statistic to give a similar simple indication of total space.

At present this simplification is based on "Guided Learning Hours" which statistic, measured in hours, does not translate directly into metres squared, but nevertheless appears to have a spacial correlation.

To improve upon this system in the light of the "qualitative" comments made above therefore, but using its general approach, it is suggested that there might be a unit called a *"quality learning hour"*, based on guided learning hours but measured not just in terms of timetabled events (i.e. identifiable staff/student contact times) but in terms of these hours modified by the type and number of other spaces within the college where other types of contact might be deemed to take place. This might grade the guided learning hours either up or down and give recognition to the increasingly relevant non-didactic teaching modes.

This modified rule of thumb calculation in order to generate a minimum number of workplaces (MNW) might therefore be summarised as:

$$\text{MNW} = \frac{\text{quality learning hours}}{\text{annual hours}}$$

The minimum number of workplaces might then still be converted into an approximate gross internal area using the formula:

$$\text{MNW} \times (\text{between } 11.5 \text{ m}^2 \text{ and } 14.5\text{m}^2) + 1{,}500\text{m m}^2 + 10\% = \text{College Gross Internal Area}$$

To arrive at what specifically might be the multipliers and weightings to be used in both the full and the simplified calculations above requires considerably further thought and statistical analysis, but might nevertheless indicate a possible way forward. What is certain is that the formulae currently available do not give sufficient emphasis on the changing situation we currently find ourselves in.

Hugh ANDERSON
Hugh@haadesign.co.uk

Val CLUGSTON
NOMAD Design Associates

SPACES FOR LEARNING

Nomad is a research-led design practice which specialises in the design of public spaces. Our particular expertise lies in learning and healing environments and through the course of our practice we have been testing and developing methods that help us to gather and understand complex information about the infrastructure and culture of our clients' environments.

Developing the Brief

Until recently, Nomad worked almost exclusively within the field of education, developing learning environments that are uniquely relevant to the student body therein. The abolition of the student grant, and subsequent introduction of fees in the late 1990s, mean that students are now consumers who are in the market for the most valuable "student experience". As a consequence, institutions are competing for the custom of local students as well as for the more lucrative overseas markets.

This has triggered a wealth of improvements in the estates of universities across the UK, and often the greatest focus is placed on creating new learning facilities that will enhance this "student experience."

This concept of "student experience" has put a distinctly human emphasis on the design of these projects and this, coupled with the popularisation of concepts about individual learning styles (first proposed in the 1970s but only really popular in recent years), has opened the door to interior specialists in these areas.

Why Is a New Methodology Required?

Education and Healthcare are new areas for interior design, which is itself a relatively young discipline. Until recently, interior design has been most commonly associated with domestic, leisure or retail spaces. These environments are often specifically targeted at particular groups, and this gives the designer a solid reference helping them to understand the users.

Unlike the users of these typical spaces, the patrons of learning environments, students and academics, cannot be characterised into personas with which the designer can then empathise. Learners are often of differing age groups, cultures, religions, languages and learning abilities. We cannot relate to them intuitively and therefore our ability to find suitable references is disabled. To complicate matters further, the clients in this area are new to the process of commissioning design and are not yet experienced in developing useful briefs for designers.

The complexity of these issues and the competing requirements means that a degree of research and/or consultation is essential for the designer fully to understand both client and user needs.

Exploring Methods

The common factor which joins these complex and competing issues is people. Each problem revolves around the relationship of a person to their environment or a group to another group. The solution demands a people-centric approach, and our team were naturally drawn to anthropology as a starting point for gathering useful methods. As a result initial projects utilised all or some of the following methods:

    Interviews

    Questionnaires

    Observational techniques

    Mapping

    Cultural Probes

This early package of methods helped us to gain insights into real, rather than perceived, problems with the space, student working practice, student identity and culture. Inevitably the process of undertaking these studies highlighted some shortcomings. They were;

1. This type of field study does not explore staff relationships with the space. Designers must understand how to harness the valuable knowledge of these participants.

2. Field time: collating, analysing and processing data is both time-consuming and expensive.

3. The process is open to criticism. To run a truly robust study it could be argued that a minimum of one year is necessary to allow for all variables.

Examples

Our response to these problems was to adopt a participatory approach to the design process, and combine this with techniques learned in field projects. The following examples illustrate a range of experiments with these methods:

1. Glasgow University Fraser Building (Figure 1)

The Fraser Building is a four-floor student services centre located at the heart of the University of Glasgow. The building houses four of the University's busiest services and Nomad was commissioned to work with these services to design a student-centric space.

At the outset of the project one month was spent on site observing the current operations and interviewing key personnel. This generated valuable logistical data while helping designers to understand the identity of the University.

The movement of services from individual town houses to an open plan office represented a significant shift in culture and status for many of the staff members. To help staff understand the new space and feel comfortable with the move a series of participatory workshops were organised. These workshops would aid designers with understanding the fears and desires of the staff group, access detailed information, and assist the University with managing change.

An early experiment from the participatory phase demonstrates the usefulness of this approach. In the planning stages, designers ran a one-day planning workshop for the service teams (60+ people). The aim was to design a footprint for each of the spaces that would then be agreed with all participants. In the morning session the groups were presented with a draft plan. The group criticised this and their comments were carefully recorded. In the afternoon session, groups were presented with blank plans for the space along with a brief, which comprised the most basic requirements only. The teams were then given two hours to design the plan and satisfy the brief. Once complete, the group reviewed the plans from all teams and voted on the most successful. This winning plan bears a striking similarity to the plan original presented in the morning session (see Figures 2 and 3). This workshop helped staff groups to understand why difficult design decisions were made and built trust between the staff groups and designers.

Figure 1

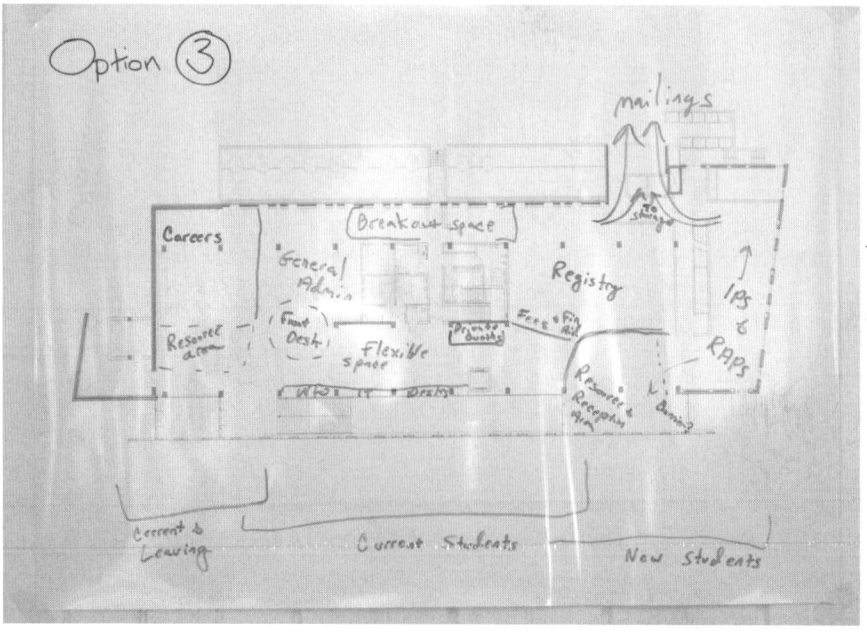

Figure 2

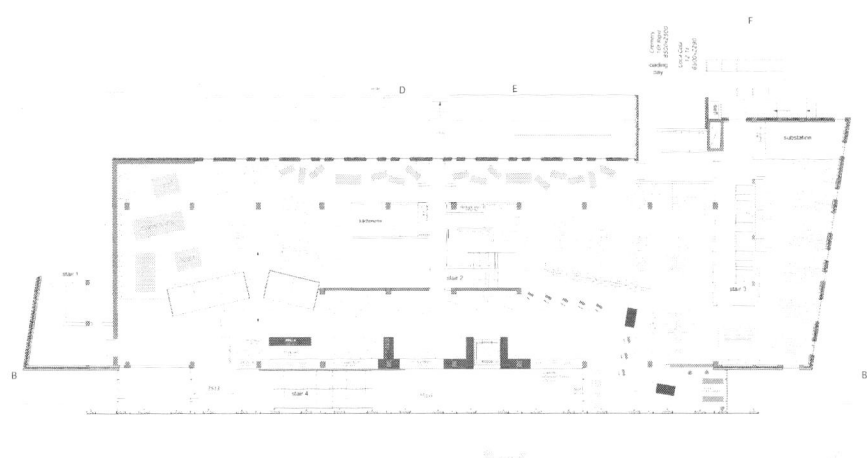

Figure 3

2. TLC@Bedford (Figure 4)

TLC@Bedford is a social learning space created in the Ground Floor of the Bedford Library at Royal Holloway, University of London.

The brief asked for an exciting social learning space that responded to the views of the University's student body. The project had a relatively small budget and time frame. This meant that a protracted period of fieldwork was not possible and alternatives had to be considered.

Social media presented itself as an alternative method for interacting with the student body. The selection of the social media site was critical. The platform selected must reflect those popular with the student body. In this instance Facebook was agreed to be the preferred platform. Advertising was also critical, and our team saturated the campus with paper and electronic posters (Figure 5).

The group was an immediate success, 243 members joining within the first three days. Designers were able to gain insights into the ways in which students work, their spatial requirements and desires, and gauge aesthetic tastes via discussion boards and galleries.

In this example the strength of student opinion expressed via discussion boards within the Facebook group influenced the change of a key management decision. This in turn released funds into the spatial budget.

This experiment with social media proved that designers could interact with a large sample of students at little or no cost or inconvenience to the client. Furthermore we

Figure 4

Figure 5

found that we could interact with an even larger sample of students than would be possible over the same time frame using more traditional methods. Most interestingly students were naturally comfortable with this medium and would express opinions and ideas that we rarely accessed using other methods such as interviews.

1. University of Bristol (Figure 6)

Nomad has worked with the University of Bristol for a number of years. During that time we have authored a Design Guide and designed and implemented four library spaces. All of this work is underpinned by a period of initial fieldwork in which we observed, mapped and interviewed students. This was accompanied by a series of participatory design workshops with a volunteer group of staff members.

The most recent commission is the refurbishment of the upper levels of the Arts and Social Sciences Library. In this project a social media platform was used in conjunction with an onsite presence.

Two site visits were planned, each lasting three days. In the first visit researchers engaged students in informal interviews. A total of 150 students participated in these interviews. In the second visit an exhibition of consultation results along with plans and designs was installed. In this instance, a difficult design decision had to be made. This second visit was used as an opportunity for students to vote (Figure 7). The researcher/designer was available to provide detailed explanations and engage in discussion. The information gathered during this visit would later form the basis of the client's decision. These visits were supported by a project blog, www.uobassl.wordpress.com. Over the course of the design phase (one month) the blog received 892 visits, seven comments and 274 students took part in polls.

Combining an onsite presence with a social media strategy enabled our team to communicate with over 1,300 students and staff members in a little over one month. The project was carried out at little cost to the client and the onsite presence of a researcher encouraged both staff and students to interact with our team and engage in discussion.

As our work with the University of Bristol now spans several years we have been presented with the unique opportunity to assess and evaluate our work. The information gathered in this most recent study is strikingly similar to information gathered in earlier projects for the University and in studies we have carried out in institutions across the UK. We are therefore positive that the methods that we employ provide a realistic snapshot of campus life and culture

Our Methodology (Figure 8)

The methods that we have tested and refined over the last five years of practice have helped us to arrive at a unique methodology for examining spaces and the people who inhabit them.

This methodology can be summarised as a four-stage process,

1. **People** We have compiled a kit of tested methods which enable us to interact with the people who use each space. These methods include detailed fieldwork which exposes the subtleties of culture and identity of each place; participatory workshops which aid designers to gather detailed information while also supporting participants through the process of change; and finally social media platforms that are convenient, economical and open to all.
2. **Profile** Each project is supported by documented evidence submitted in the form of a report. This report will then form the basis of the design brief.
3. **Plan** Using the information gathered in steps 1 & 2, a strategy is generated that is based on real, rather than perceived, uses of the space.
4. **Implement** Designers undertake the usual project stages, always referring to and reflecting upon the information gathered in steps 1–3.

We are confident that the model that we have developed to enrich our clients' briefs is both conceptually- and economically valid. Furthermore, our recent work within the Healthcare Sector indicates that this methodology is flexible enough to be adapted to a broad range of public spaces.

Val CLUGSTON
val@nomad-rdc.com

Figure 6

Figure 7

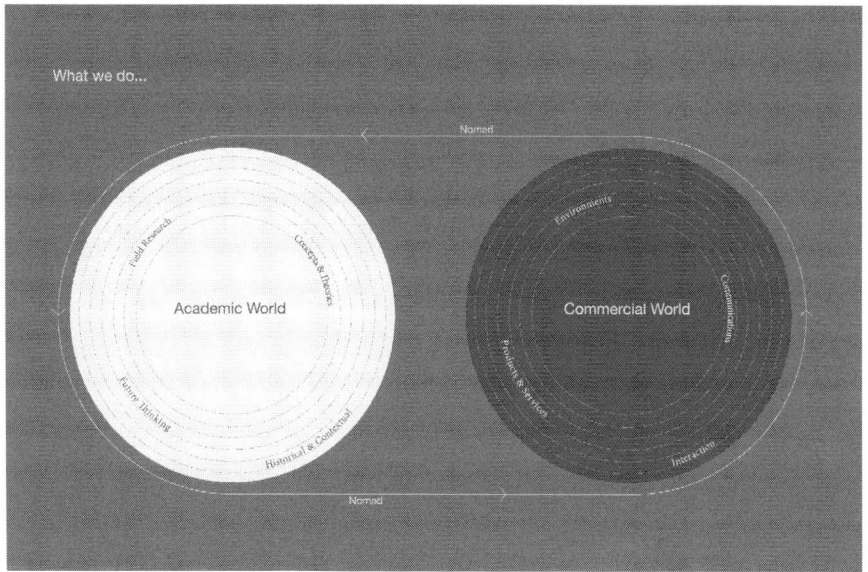

Figure 8

Spaces for Learning 121

Lynn CHALMERS
University of Manitoba

TACTICS AT WORK

Introduction

"the miniscule loose spaces that certain silent and subtle tactics "insinuate" …within the imposed order" Michel de Certeau, 1998, ppxxii. [1]

"He arranged his days so that they were a harmonious succession of little joys, and the absence of the least of these joys threatened the whole edifice. A cup of coffee a slice of bread and butter, a dish of bright green peas, reading the paper beside the fire, a maidservant standing on a pair of steps and washing a window, a thousand quiet pleasures that were waiting for him at every turning of life, which he had foreseen and looked forward to, were as necessary to him as the air he breathed, and it was thanks to them that he was incapable of feeling any real suffering."

Old Desire living in Liege from Pedigree by George Simenon. [2]

I propose theorising the workplace beginning from Michel de Certeau's optimistic thesis of the practice of everyday life. A former Jesuit priest, historian and cultural anthropologist, Michel de Certeau celebrated the notion that the everyday person retains some vestige of control over their environment.

Certeau patiently develops a research methodology, derived from sociology, anthropology and narrative research, to uncover these slippages, and subtle practices. In *The Practice of Everyday Life* Certeau and his circle of young graduates study the city and its inhabitants to understand the cultural practices of the everyday, practices such as cooking, reading, and walking the city. The two texts published in 1984 and 1998 respectively were the result of research and cultural analysis undertaken between 1974 and 1977 with the intention of uncovering the actions, and subtle practices of everyday

French citizens. Certeau moves beyond the usual depiction of the mindless masses [4, 5] to closely analyse the everyday practices of personal consumption. He is most interested in the purposes to which consumed objects are put – searching for small practices of resistance. In the street it might be the path taken home that delights in small diversions; in everyday life it might be the role of a café or bar in the satisfaction of an individual's need for community or escape from family expectations.

Why Workplace?

If home is, as Bachelard [6] suggests, "human beings' first world" before we are cast into the larger external world, then the workplace is our second world, in a busy and often alienating city – his or her "corner of the world" which performs as a site of constructed identity. These spaces of our possession in the workplace broadcast to co-workers many significant details about our values and culture, education, work ethic, social status and personal taste allowing them to be evaluated as signifiers of the constructed self.

The early development of the office in the twentieth century was characterised by spatial serialisation. As the office grew in size and complexity, so the classification and ranking structure developed to reward diligence and productivity, social position and knowledge. Modernity served to further rationalise the spatial design and systems of power of the office, entrenching hierarchies. Entitlements to office size, location, view and furnishings were determined and defined by rank and title. The clerical work area became an even larger open space thanks to the advent of the speculative office tower that had become the preferred template for office space in North America. The invisible structural grid of the building now determined the location and orientation of walls, ceiling systems, doors, and office cubicles. The spatial diagram of the office signified it as the perfectly efficient machine [7, 8].

With the introduction of computers into the workplace of the late 1960s and early 1970s, and desktop computers in the early 1980s, a period of radical transformation of the instruments and institutions of work commenced. New media and modes of reproduction changed the nature of communication. Social theorists debated the benefits and threats inherent in a knowledge-based society [9, 10]. Despite the knowledge revolution of the 70s and 80s and the subsequent dramatic streamlining of organisational management structures in the 90s the physical form of the workplace has demonstrated very little lasting innovation in the past 20 years.

During the 1960s Robert L. Propst and George Nelson at Herman Miller, strongly influenced by the democratic ideals of *burolandschaft**, recognized the dramatic

---

* In 1969 Frank Duffy wrote *Office Landscaping*, examining a European management approach that co-located workers based on functional need rather than office hierarchy. It was derived from *burolandschaft* developed by the Quickborner Team, in Hamburg, in the 1950s. Burolandschaft was the first attempt to design a truly democratic spatial template with organic open office planning based on landscaping principles.

change that was occurring in office work and produced the first contemporary text on office design in North America, *The Office: a Facility Based on Change* [11]. Propst's research led to the design of the first panel-based furniture system in North America, "Action Office"; developed to suit the needs of the new generation of computerised office workers, systems analysts and programmers. Action Office defined the furniture that accommodated the emerging class of knowledge workers.[*]

The nature and job description of office workers located in open space has changed substantially since the seventies when bullpens[†] accommodated mainly clerical staff. Steelcase research data [12] suggests that in 2006 approximately 58% of all North American office workers were working in office systems furniture in open planned areas. These workers include some managers, but the vast majority are data processors and knowledge workers.

The new theories of office management that flourished in the 1980s and 90s generated various experiments in office planning and design: clubs and dens, bullpens and cellular offices, caves and commons, hot desking and hotelling (Duffy 1997)[‡]. Despite these innovations in the manipulation of office space, office design remains largely determined by standardised furniture and partition systems in large open areas; rational furniture systems that provide limited and generic responses to the provision of the place of work.

Counter to the intrinsically static nature of office systems furniture the language of flexibility and multifunctionalism are embedded in the literature on office systems furniture:

> "In today's business environment, change occurs rapidly. This is a time of transition, of experimentation, and of new competitive forces. Customers need products that support a broad spectrum of planning strategies and undefined future requirements." [13]

The prevailing media representations of the office workplace show a place of imposed order with management structures and hierarchies represented by gridded and impersonal office planning. The individual is subservient to organisational need. Often passively hostile environments, offices are places where the need for individuation becomes critical and the achievement of individuality is remarkable.

Individual practices of resistance in the workplace are celebrated in the media, subversive tactics are an expected and much lampooned aspect of workplace environments. They are the subject of cartoons (Dilbert), films (*Playtime* by Jacques Tati) and TV series (*The Office*) but have not been yet received critical attention by

---

[*] The term knowledge worker, first coined by Peter Drucker, applies to workers whose work deals primarily with information. Knowledge workers work alone, or as part of collaborative teams that are often multidisciplinary.

[†] Bullpens are unscreened open areas with rows of desks.

[‡] Refer to Frank Duffy's *The New Workplace* for detailed descriptions of these typologies.

designers. The tactics of subversion in the work environment demonstrate the inherent creativity of individuals and their need to assert independence from the corporate machine that structures their daily lives.

> "Things extra and **other** (details and excesses coming from elsewhere) insert themselves into the excepted framework, the imposed order. One thus has the very relationship between spatial practices and the constructed order." [14]

De Certeau's "practitioners of space" seem uncertain and alienated by the ways in which the organisation controls space to contain them. Small acts of subversion suggest a refusal to repress the messy fragmented trajectories of subjectivity in the face of constant uncertainty and change. Lebbeus Wood, co-founder of the Research Institute for Experimental Architecture, considers the relationship between uncertainty and flexibility to be evident in the impact of commodity fetishism on the design of space itself:

> "Space of the more mundane sort, that which is designed by architects for everyday use, seems as full as ever of human presence, but it is so in precisely the same way that everyday life, in its increasing consumption is more full than ever, yet at the same time more empty. Office buildings, hotels, condominiums, schools, airports, cinemas, spas, private houses and shopping centres are bristling with human activity, but the purpose of this activity, its 'meaning', is becoming less and less certain. Increasingly the design of space today is spoken of in terms of 'flexibility'. Even spaces in existing buildings must be considered for their possible 'adaptive reuse'. … Flexibility and multi-functionalism are euphemisms for uncertainty." [15]

Office workers are expected to adapt to constant and externally imposed change in the form of reconfiguration of workstation components to accommodate expansion and contraction of organisations; or relocation to create new work teams and departments.

Anxiety and Alienation in the Workplace

Since 9/11 and the destruction of the Twin Towers in New York a pervasive and permanent sense of unease has marked Western urban society; challenging the capacity of the authorities and the built environment to protect everyday citizens from the anxiety of *unknown threats*. This sense of insecurity is reinforced every time we enter an airport, train station or public building, turn on the television or the radio, or read the newspaper. Terry Meade suggests that for urban city dwellers

> "survival requires vigilance, adaptability and creativity" [16]

in situations of every-day existence. We need to assert the capacity for creativity to continue to thrive.

Anxiety infiltrates the workplace and it is compounded with the inevitable alienation of workers in Neo-liberal societies where many are unable to feel intimately and significantly connected to their work and find themselves working unwillingly to satisfy a compulsion for material goods rather than to satisfy real needs*.

We have known since the mid-1980s through the work of Eric Sundstrom and Michael Brill that individuals in the office environment require a degree of autonomy [17,18]. Office workers complain about the lack of privacy, the need for quiet places to work, and the lack of control over personal space. Workstations need to provide a sense of identity, control and purpose.

Space and Being

Bachelard depicts our need for privacy as a response to our need for immobility – he describes the corner as a signifier of self. The corner provides the physical boundaries that allow for territorial marking:

> "Consciousness of being at peace in one's corner produces a sense of immobility, and this in turn, radiates immobility. An imaginary room rises up around our bodies, which think that they are well hidden when we take refuge in a corner. Already the shadows are walls, a piece of furniture constitutes a barrier, hangings are a roof. But all of these images are over-imagined. So we have to designate the space of our immobility by making it the space of our being." [19]

The imagery of the corner is powerfully descriptive of the typical office cubicle. One of the inherent problems of workstation systems are their inability to signal when the occupant wishes to remain undisturbed. The office door has been the signifier for North Americans of the desire to communicate or to be left alone, and with the removal of the office walls this signifier has vanished too. The co-location of workers creates problems where one worker is engaged in intense activity and others are relaxing and enjoying a personal conversation or noisier collaborative working. Co-workers default to using personal sound systems to create a private corner for retreat; some use discrete ear buds, while others choose to wear full headphones, providing a visual clue to others that they wish not to be disturbed.

Auditory Privacy

Re-appropriation of space is not only occurring physically; new and mobile media technologies have the capacity to create a *non-spatialised conceptual space* or a subjective aural *private bubble*. Simmel may have been the first sociologist to write about the creation of mobile bubbles, his concern was with sensory overload in the urban environment and the need for citizens to create a private aural retreat [20]. Michael Bull analyses this phenomena from the perspective of the mobile user:

> "...as geographic notions of personal space become harder to substantiate and negotiate in some urban environments, the construction of a privatised conceptual

---

*   *Reason and Revolution* Herbert Marcuse 1955

> space becomes a common strategy for personal stereo users… [they] appear to achieve a subjective sense of public invisibility. The users essentially 'disappear' as interacting subjects withdrawing into various states of the purely subjective." [21]

These tactics address issues of territoriality and privacy for the knowledge worker whose work requires intense, quiet, individual work, in addition to collaboration and team working.

Territoriality

> "Everyday practice patiently and tenaciously restores a space for play, an interval of freedom, a resistance to what is imposed (from a model, a system, or an order). To be able to do something is to establish distance, to defend the autonomy of what comes from one's own personality." [22]

In the workplace it is an accepted practice to co-opt fragments from other parts of our lives to create an identity, to claim territory and to personalise our assigned workstation or office space.

Office workers are notorious curators of collections of tkotches*, inspirational and humorous quotations, sporting fixtures, kids' artwork and photographs of family and pets. But there are other tactics the office worker uses to individualise and subvert the intended use of their assigned space.

Tactics might take the form of the co-option of furniture from an absent co-workers workspace, or they might involve the re-arrangement of those elements of a furniture system into a unique and satisfying perversion of the system designer's intention. Office supplies and archive boxes are useful for providing ad hoc screening devices and I suspect that the quality of team work may be measured from studying these in conjunction with the orientation of individual desk chairs. †

From my observations the desire to define the boundaries between workspaces seems to be the source of most tactical operations. Office workers need to anchor the edge boundary between their workspace and another and will employ random objects used as totems or identity markers. They may be a visitor's chair with a jacket slung over it, or a filing cabinet face given over to impromptu display.

De Certeau depicts the street as it is subjectively experienced in his essay "Walking in the City" [23]. He sees it conforming to a new order, a sieve-order, torn open and leaking. The messy, complex and practised experience is vastly different from the Gods-eye view of the diagram or signified plan, and so it is with the office furniture systems and the workers that people them. Systems furniture brochures represent workspace as tidy, empty and devoid of personalia. The accumulation of paper or coffee mugs jostling tkotches, messages stuck to computer screens, and additional

---

*   Believed to be an Ukrainian term for figurines.
†   Case study carried out in 2006 in Toronto design office.

display are not encouraged – the desk surface – if the images of ideal workspaces are consumed and believed, should be ordered, sequential and calm. There are no hooks to hang keys from, no prominent vertical surfaces for post-it notes, no picture frames or vases that suggest it is permissible to inhabit this space in an alternative way that might seem pleasing or necessary to the user.

As designers we do not pay sufficient attention to tactics of possession and authorship. We are dismissive of such subtle acts of creativity and the messages they might give us about the occupants of office space. My project here is to suggest the significance of these tactics of subversion as a tool, a cultural barometer that may provide an honest reading of corporate culture in an organisation. I propose these tactics could be the canary in the mineshaft that tells us the real story about the toxic environments that workplaces can be.

References

[1] De Certeau, M. *The Practice of Everyday Life: Volume 1* (Berkeley: University of California Press, 1988)
[2] De Certeau, M. Giard, L. and Mayol, P. *The Practice of Everyday Life: Volume 2 Living and Cooking* (Minneapolis: University of Minnesota Press, 1998) p.4.
[3] Bachelard, G. *The Poetics of Space* (Boston: Beacon Press. 1994 ed.)
[4] Lefebvre, H. *The Production of Space* Trans. Nicholson-Smith (London: Blackwell Publishing, 1991)
[5] Marx, K. *Capital: a critical analysis of capitalist production* trans. Moore and Aveling ed. by Engels. (Moscow: Foreign Languages Publishing House, 1956-1963)
[6] Bachelard, op.cit. p10.
[7] Foucault, M. *Discipline and Punish: the birth of the prison* Trans. Sheridan (New York: Random House, 1995 ed.)
[8] Lefebvre, op. cit.
[9] Toffler, A. *Future Shock* (New York: Random House. 1970)
[10] Drucker, P. *The Age of Discontinuity* (London: Business Books.1968)
[11] Propst, R. *The Office: a Facility Based on Change* (Michigan: Herman Miller. 1968).
[12] Unknown. The State of the Cubicle: What's now and what's next *360 Steelcase Magazine*, January. (Michigan: Steelcase 2006)
[13] http://www.teknion.com
[14] Certeau1988, op. cit. p160
[15] Wood, L. The Question of Space in *Technoscience and Cyberculture* Eds. Aronowitz, Martinsons and Menser. (New York: Routledge.1996) p.284
[16] Meade, T. Thinking Inside the Box – Anxieties of Containment in *Thinking Inside the Box: a reader for interiors in the 21st century.* Eds. Gigli, Hay, Hollis, Milligan, Milton and Plunkett (London: Middlesex University Press now Libri Publishing, 2007)
[17] Sundstrom, E. *Work Places* (New York: Cambridge University Press, 1986)
[18] Brill, M. (ed.) *Using Office Design to Increase Productivity* (New York: Workplace Design and Productivity Inc.1984, 1985)

[19] Bachelard, op.cit. p.137.
[20] Simmel, G.The Metropolis and Mental Life, in *Simmel on Culture* Eds, Frisby and Featherstone,(London: Sage. 1997)
[21] Bull, M. To Each Their Own Bubble: Mobile Spaces of Sound in the City in *MediaSpace* Eds. Couldry and McCarthy (London: Routledge. 2004) pp.284–5.
[22] Certeau 1998, op. cit. p.255

Lynn CHALMERS
University of Manitoba
Department of Interior Design
200 Lenore Street
Winnipeg
MB R3G 2C5
CANADA
Chalmers@cc.umanitoba.ca
204 774 9560

Sharn LIM

Studio Daminato, Singapore
RMIT, Melbourne, Australia

TACTICS OF THE PERIPATETIC: ON VENDORS' MAKING AN INTERIOR OF THE STREET

Introduction

On the Parisians' technique of *inhabiting* their streets:

> "Returning by the Rue Saint-Honoré, we met with an eloquent example of that Parisian street industry which can make use of anything. Men were at work repairing the pavement and laying pipeline, and, as a result, in the middle of the street there was an area which was blocked off but which was embanked and covered with stones. On this spot street vendors had immediately installed themselves, and five or six were selling writing implements and notebooks, cutlery, lampshades, garters, embroidered collars, and all sorts of trinkets. Even a dealer in secondhand goods had opened a branch office here and was displaying on the stones his bric-à-brac of old cups, plates, glasses, and so forth, so that business was profiting, instead of suffering from the brief disturbance. They are simply wizards at making a virtue of necessity."
>
> Adolf Stahr, *Nach fünf Jahren* (Oldenburg, 1857), vol.1, p.29

Seventy years later, I had the same experience at the corner of the Boulevard Saint-Germain and the Boulevard Raspail. Parisians make the street an interior. [1]

The starting point for this paper is the seemingly random appearance of street bazaars within street space.

The various *pasar malam* of my childhood have long been a source of fascination for me with their irregular appearances. In Malay, *pasar* means "market" while *malam* refers to "night"; operating in the evenings, a *pasar malam* is a travelling night market of sorts in Southeast Asian countries such as Malaysia, Singapore and Indonesia. They are comprised of stalls where, amongst themselves, traders pick a location for their stalls, creating varying permutations each evening. Families – from that estate and neighbouring ones – attend the *pasar malam* and enjoy an evening out.

Heralded by the smells of freshly cooked street fare, this random juxtaposition of makeshift stalls selling anything from food to accessories, from furniture to live pets and clothing, renders the street impassable to vehicular traffic. Consequently, the street is transformed into a pedestrian mall for the evening.

A "Y", the Sumerian ideogram for market, Mumford writes, indicates perhaps that the idea of a market to handle local barter at the juncture of traffic routes was already recognized.[2] Preceding the two classic forms of the market - the open or covered bazaar and the booth-lined street which had developed by 2000 BC at latest, an even more ancient form of the market existed within the temple precinct. It was within the controlled totalitarian economy of the temple grounds that the first vending booths possibly appeared, within a "trading estate" where goods were to be stored and then distributed.

The history of street vending has had its roots in a noble, ancient trade in everyone's service. The travelling vendor was an everyday sight in sixteenth to seventeenth century Paris, as shown from the engravings of Nicolas Larmessin II (1638–94). As a form of portable display, their wares were attached to their bodies as they roamed the streets crying their services or products they had for sale. These vendors inhabited the practices of the street, and seized on opportunities to invite participation in order to perform their tasks.

Figure 1: The garb of a traveling vendor selling perfume. 17th-century engraving by N. Larmessin II

In *The Arcades Project*, German writer and philosopher Walter Benjamin noted makeshift arrangements for the use of space. Quoting a passage that described vendors "profiting instead of suffering from the brief disturbance" caused by workers repairing and laying pipeline, Benjamin pronounced them "wizards at making a virtue of necessity" as they *made an interior of* the street. Today, a century later, street vendors are still very much peripatetic agents of the street. Their adaptive practices involve temporary arrangements to invite other street users' participation into the spaces they produce.

Vendors' recurrent appropriation of space raises some important questions for interior designers. How and where do vendors set up their mobile stalls within street space? What sorts of interiors are unfolded from their actions? What are the tactics used to invite participation from other street users, and how is this expressed through the implements deployed? Are these street vendors spatial designers of sorts – are there similarities between both practices? By analysing vendors' seemingly immediate, occasionally contradictory practices, I hope to illustrate the role of tactics – i.e. as a means of operating and how – and their implications for the production of interiors.

As moments that invite the crossing of a boundary, a threshold, the practice of vendors interiorises the street on two scales: one being a temporal scale, the other on an intimate and personal level. Vendors operate in relation to what is being offered *at that instant* in terms of space and time, to produce sites for encounters and pause amidst movement. Four tactics are presented as a framework to inform an interior practice: *poaching*, *inviting pauses*, *practicing in variations*, and *being mobile*. These tactics enable vendors to *make* interiors in response to the changing conditions of the street and the various opportunities offered. By considering the role of tactics in an interior practice, I conclude by reflecting on the tactics by which space could be interiorised.

The Street: Conditions for Interior, and Interior Conditions

> "Interiority is temporal because changes in its variables (boundary, performance, intimacy, between-ness, enclosure) can cause the dissolution or the materialization of interiorities." [3]

With spaces that seem designated for specific purposes, its variant uses are often much more intriguing: office workers sitting on the steps of the Library during lunchtime, or a procession for some festival down the main thoroughfare of a city, for instance. The open-ended outcome is a curious condition: providing the user with various possibilities to work from, and enabling various sorts of spatial connections to be generated as a result of temporary inhabitation.

Twentieth century French sociologist and philosopher Henri Lefebvre observed,

> "the diversion and reappropriation of space are of great significance, for they teach us about the production of new spaces". [4]

Street vendors' practices engage with space: rearranging to produce new connections between themselves, other street users, and the resultant interiors created. As different arrangements from their wares are generated each time they are laid out from their respective containers, they provide diversions by inviting engagement between the practitioner, viewer, time and space; they become implicated as participants in the production of "new spaces".

Abercrombie describes our encounter with an interior to be

"a result of an entrant into it, a movement from outside to inside".[5]

As peripatetic agents of the street, the ephemeral nature of the interiors produced by vendors address various spatial contexts. Serving as layers added to space, these tactical operations imbue space with different meanings, inviting users inside to engage.

Vendors' arrangements are transient: they need to be packed up, moved off, and set up again. This fleeting condition of interiors is observed by Interior Design educator Christine McCarthy to be

"[...] temporal, because changes in its variables [...] can cause the dissolution or the materialisation of interiorities". [6]

The new spaces that are produced and subsequently re-produced provide renewed suggestions of fresh connections between and *through* layers of hierarchies.

In their collection of essays titled *Spatial Practices*, urban planners and theorists Helen Liggett and David Perry approached the city as an entity transformed over time. Following sociologist Henri Lefebvre's notion of social space as a social product, Liggett and Perry situate spatial practices as a generative approach, positioning urban space as a mode of social production rather than as a social product.[7] Liggett defines spatial practices as processes that

"have to do with the everyday social/spatial patterns of people in particular places". [8]

This addresses immediate concerns from the perspectives of *users*, and has been particularly useful in framing an understanding of the ephemeral nature of interiors. Interior is a fleeting condition; it is a set of constantly shifting relationships between space and its user/s.

The street vendor recognises and exploits the tension existing between *intended* and *eventual* use of street space: this is a tension whose resolution can only last for a short period of time; there is a necessary coexistence between the rules made by authority, and responses that work *around* those rules imposed. Negotiations need to be made between these two extremes in order to occupy street space, contributing to the necessarily ephemeral nature of interiors produced within the street. As such, the interiors created by the peripatetic vendor undergo an ongoing process of negotiating a series of shifting boundaries, between the acceptable and tolerable, various time scales, or an elaborate set-up versus one that can be rapidly dismantled.

Methodology

> "Only by measurement of distance and angle, by repeated triangulation and traverse, can a picture of the topography of the region be built up ... It is thus precisely through ... active involvement with the landscape that an accurate mapping is made." [9]

To study the tactics of vendors operating in the street, I observed and documented the vendors encountered in the streets over two periods of eight weeks between 2006 and 2007. Interviews were not strictly conducted, as many vendors – especially those operating illegally, to whose practice I was particularly drawn – tended to be suspicious of the nature of research and any questioning. However, much could be gleaned through nuances during informal chats, made by way of purchasing an item from the vendor to get started.

The research method adopted in order to carry out observation and documentation involved much *walking* and *noticing*.

Walking Twentieth-century French philosopher Michel de Certeau describes walking as an elementary form of experiencing the city [10]. Indeed, walking establishes mobility at a suitable pace for noticing; many of the encounters within my research have resulted from walking. The most salient trait of walking comes to mind: its pace – it is neither a run, during which details of the surroundings may be foregone in favour of speed, nor is it a crawl where movement is both strenuous and laboriously slow. Walking also permits pausing and re-turning. A walk might be brisk, or leisurely: both promoting noticing that is less dependent on the speed of the walk than, perhaps, the "open-ness" of the walker to distractions. These distractions may have the potential to punctuate the experience of the walker as they are encountered and noticed. Walking can also be understood in contrast to vehicular procession, where passing through a street at motorised velocity discourages physical engagement with surrounding spaces.

Noticing How does one notice? When walking in the street, my attention is often drawn to the activities of other users of the street, especially if they are stationary. Their temporary immobility makes apparent the various ongoing activities within the street, highlighting different possibilities within a single context. Mathematician and educator John Mason describes the discipline of noticing as "an act of attention", involving an exercise of re-calling and seeking threads for multiple interpretations, rather than detailed explanation [11]. It increases an awareness of the range of "things" offered by making

> "a distinction, to create foreground and background, to distinguish some 'thing' from its surroundings." [12]

Distinguishing ongoing practices from their surroundings makes apparent the aspects that have made them different. In this case, though the practice of peripatetic vendors is very much a part of the street, it is easily noticed for its temporary immobility amongst movement.

Figure 2: A candy vendor situating herself on a busy footpath outside a bank, Singapore

A candy seller – an elderly woman, sits hunched against a pillar by the steps at a bank's entrance. Setting up her makeshift stall, she removes from a large striped plastic bag an impressively simple arsenal of implements. The red plastic stool she sits on is the first to be taken out of the bag. She positions it against the wall. She sits, and proceeds to remove the rest of the contents: two containers, a pot of syrup, and a sheet of paper in a scratched plastic covering bearing the words "old fashioned candy" is placed at her feet. This candy is served on a stick like a malleable lollypop. The vendor can prepare the viscous syrup beforehand at home. The containers – one mineral water bottle with its top cut off and the other a tin can – hold, respectively, sticks for stirring the candy and serving sticks for the candy. These containers are attached to the pot with steel wire. She is only slightly obscured from the flow of pedestrians because she aligns herself along the wall with a key-maker who operates from a similarly sparse set-up.

To apply Mason's discipline of noticing as "an act of attention", the candy seller is noticed by the way she arranges herself to be encountered. She is stationary against the movement occurring on the footpath before her; the location she has chosen (at the entrance to a bank), and her position in relation to other vendors (such as the key-maker) contribute to distinguish the vendor from her surroundings. How might a vendor's practice be spatially engaging? While a vendor's motivations for getting noticed by other pedestrians becomes a way for the vendor to engage others, their tactics interposition changes in scale, movement, and degrees between concealment and open-ness. As an immediate response to spatial context, noticing is a way of distinguishing interiors from their surroundings, highlighting situations which could be utilised to invite engagement. Noticing then becomes a starting point from which other connections could be made.

Walking and noticing have played central roles in my research of vendors' spatial practices. Repeated triangulation and traverse has led to an understanding of how vendors' practices might produce interiors through adaptive tactics, seizing on opportunities to inhabit a space. The spatial implications of vendors' practices are less about unchanging control than they are about constantly adapting and responding to changing spatial relationships. Theirs is a practice involving an ongoing making, dissolving, and remaking of interiors, set against a short timeframe.

Agents' Tactics for Operating within the Street

While vendors' practices appear to be fairly straightforward in their attempts to make use of space to sell their wares, I suggest their methods not only vary from one vendor to the next, but also are trickier than they seem because of their need to constantly negotiate between control of and dependence on various spatial conditions. While vendors employ tactics to make themselves noticed such as arranging their goods or positioning of their stalls, an interior practitioner may learn from the ways of vendors by exploring their tactics as means to engage with, inhabit, and invite inhabitation into a space.

In addressing tactics as a manner of operating which is differentiated from strategy, de Certeau described the tactic as an "art of the weak" [13]. While street vendors – especially those operating illegally – have little or no authority over the state of movement and circulation within the street and might be perceived as the "weak" within the street, their actions certainly have an effect on the outlook of a street. A lively thoroughfare that attracts pedestrians will correspondingly draw vendors to operate there; subsequently, it is apparent that the robustness of street conditions depends on vendors who seize the opportunities offered *at that given moment* to make engaging interiors. Thus, the edge the "weak" has above the overarching rules set by those in power lies in its ability to operate tactically, through a series of small, rapidly executed actions to carry out an objective [14].

The following distinguish four elements as part of vendors' practices to make an interior of the street. *Poaching*, relating to ways of operating in an opportunistic manner, thereby foregrounding issues of adaptability; *inviting pauses*, focusing on means of engaging and drawing attention to an interior that has been created; and *being mobile*, referring to the nature of a practice that hinges on the fleeting aspect of interiors. These four properties express a process that makes an interior of the street; the decisions, deliberations, and systems of operation employed by vendors as peripatetic agents of the street.

Poaching: Seizing on Opportunities within the Street

As a method of operating, poaching denotes making use of the space of the street without permission – to steal, per se – for one's own use. Vendors poach on street space by devising ways to insinuate themselves into this space. This suggests the vendor's ability to inhabit spaces instantaneously. By poaching spaces in which to insinuate itself, *vendoring* suggests a method of practicing to inhabit spaces instantaneously. The process of making interiors – through vendors' practices – poaches on space by adapting its arrangements readily to suit various spatial conditions.

Figure 3: Karaoke vendor with audiovisual equipment operating out of a van in a car park, Taipei

A vendor, with a markedly different arrangement from the candy seller discussed earlier, is encountered in a small car park beside the main road. The vendor steps out of his van with some plastic chairs and proceeds to unfold four fibreglass tables to face the van. Meanwhile, various popular melodies can be heard issuing from the speakers, attracting attention to his makeshift business. He rolls up the tarpaulin and unlatches the side of the van to reveal a hand-painted price list: a combination of songs and drinks (alcoholic and otherwise). Above this, a television set sits atop a karaoke machine; two speakers are located on either side, and there is a shelf to the right. From the shelf, he removes two black box files containing lists of the songs from his collection of karaoke discs in plastic sleeves. He sets these on two of the nearest tables, along with pads and pencils, awaiting his first customers of the evening. The karaoke vendor adapts to various situations by varying his arrangement in relation to the conditions offered by the site (i.e. lighting, circulation, visibility, etc.).

Poaching also denotes the lack of a "proper" place; as a system of adaptive arrangements, vendors operate opportunistically within spaces to produce interiors that are – though constantly renewed, dissolved and re-made – necessarily short lived.

Inviting Pauses: Engaging Others within the Street

Variant uses of space are frequently more intriguing than intended ones because of the possibilities for the unexpected to attract attention, or to distract from attention. In temporarily inhabiting spaces, vendors have arranged themselves, their wares, and the position of their stalls in relation to a larger spatial context, to attract others street users' notice. It can be said the vendor's success depends on his/her ability to create the need to pause within the movement evident within the street. In their variant uses of space, the practice of vendors generates invitations for others to pause; this is not only a way for the vendor to engage with space, their arrangements invite others' engagement with the interiors they have produced as well.

Figure 4: Fairy lights set up by the side of a beverage vendor's van invite others to pause, and invites their participation. Taipei

With his van doubling up as a mobile stall, a beverage-vendor sets up his stall at a car park in Taipei. His arrangement of fairy lights and portable seating embellishes the space: an expression of the kinds of engagement he wishes to invite. Within the car park, this vendor has produced a space with interior qualities; by transforming it, he draws others to the space he has temporarily occupied.

As unintended or unexpected spatial arrangements, the variant interiors produced by vendors engage spaces *through* the pauses they invite.

Being Mobile: Producing Interiors within the Street

The practice of vendors is dependent on implements allowing them to engage (and disengage) instantaneously with space. de Certeau described a tactical operation to depend on opportunities, giving the space of the tactic

> "a mobility that must accept [...] and seize on the wing the possibilities that offer themselves at any given moment". [15]

Indian sociologist and educator Sharit Bhowmik notes the lack of "permanent built up structure from which to sell" renders vendors as nomads; mobility not only provides a means for the vendor to operate anywhere, it also allows them expedience in moving off. [16] The aspect of mobility offers an immediate, temporal quality to the interiors produced. The interiors produced in this manner, as with those of the *pasar malam*, have a sense of temporality; various spatial qualities such as materiality, circulation,

Figure 5: A vendor with an array of brooms, encountered at a street junction

lighting, spaciousness and the effect of the surrounding can be made apparent with each temporary arrangement within space.

The array of brooms, feather dusters, mops, scrubs and other cleaning paraphernalia appears to be more visible than the vendor peddling in front. His street-cry precedes his appearance. Witnessing a mobile exhibition of cleaning implements has a strange incongruity against the mix of residences and small shops selling a range of food and beauty products. The elderly gentleman dismounts to re-arrange some of his goods that may have become dislodged during the journey; the street-cries stop correspondingly. The vendor's mobility allows him to operate opportunistically, seizing the possibilities offered at any given moment.

Being mobile is perhaps the greatest strength *and* tactic of the peripatetic.

Conclusion

Tactics are a means of manoeuvring in order to achieve a desired end.

This paper has observed the practices of vendors that defy any ability to be planned for – sometimes even resisting spatial and social hierarchies. As a process of creating very transient interiors, vendors' practices depend on making immediate use of space: it cannot be planned for, but is to be discovered and engaged with. Vendors undertake a spatial practice through small actions rather than large, overarching plans. This produces arrangements that inspire curiosity precisely because they are improvised responses, dependent on each situation. This paper has focused on ongoing tactics to re-present space (with an emphasis on the "**re-**").

Rather than to be taken as a given state, interiors are understood to be *made* – produced through everyday spatial practices such as vendors' tactics of making an interior of the street. The tactics of vendors offers to the discipline of Interior Design a range of opportunity-dependent ways of engaging space by *poaching, inviting pauses,* and *being mobile*. As such, these tactics can be contextualised within an interior practice as a method of *production* – to produce interiors from which new meanings could be made and re-made. This enables adaptive arrangements for noticing, translating, interpreting and re-reading meanings into space, thereby offering different ways to inhabit space.

What can interior design practitioners learn from observing the repertoire of tactics employed by street vendors? In exploring the interiors produced by peripatetic agents, we need to take into account the opportunity-dependent practices that affirm and challenge our understanding of interiors; at the same time, interior practitioners need to reflect on the ways in which varying opportunities call into question the means by which we engage with space.

Acknowledgements
Thanks to Suzie Attiwill and Mick Douglas for conversations and advice; Serena Pang for support and sharing insights; and to the numerous anonymous street vendors I have encountered along the way, who have made me notice.

References
[1] Benjamin, Walter. Eiland, Howards trans. *The Arcades Project*. Cambridge: Belknap Press, 1999. p. 421
[2] Mumford, Lewis. *The City in History*. U.K.: Penguin Books, 1961. p. 89
[3] McCarthy, Christine (ed) "interiorities", theme issue "Space and Culture". *International Journal of Social Space*, vol.8, issue 2, may 2005, p.120
[4] Lefebvre, Henri. *The Production of Space*. Trans. Nicholson-Smith, Donald. UK: Blackwell Publishing, 1991. p.167
[5] Abercrombie, Stanley. *A Philosophy of Interior Design*. New York: Harper & Row, 1990. p. 5
[6] McCarthy, p. 120
[7] Liggett, Helen & Perry, David (eds.) *Spatial Practices. Critical Explorations in Social/Spatial Theory*. Thousand Oaks: SAGE Publications, 1995, p. viii
[8] Liggett, p. 249
[9] Malpas, J. E. *Place and experience. a philosophical topography*. Cambridge: Cambridge University Press, 1999. p. 40
[10] de Certeau, Michel. *The Practice of Everyday Life*. Trans. Randall, Steven. New York: University of California Press, 2003, p. 37

[11] Mason, John. *Researching Your Own Practice. The Discipline of Noticing.* London: Routledge, 2001. pp. 61–88
[12] Mason. p. 33
[13] de Certeau, p. 37
[14] ibid.
[15] de Certeau, p. 37
[16] Bhowmik, Sharit K. "Street Vendors in Asia: A Review". in *Economic and Political Weekly,* vol. 40, no. 22, May 28–June 4, 2005, p. 2256

Ms Sharn LIM
RMIT, Melbourne, Australia
11 Medway Drive
S556507
Singapore
sharnster@gmail.com
+65 975 77 319

Andy MILLIGAN
DJCAD Duncan of Jordanstone College of Art and Design
University of Dundee

TOOLS FOR MODELLING AND MAKING – INTRODUCTION

In contrast to themes of digitality and immateriality, this chapter re-evaluates critical strands of modelling, representation and the relationship and role of the observer within the spatial experience. In Suzie Attiwill's provocative paper, "Between Representation and the Mirror: Tactics for Interiorisation", the author challenges the concept of the framed and contained definition of interior design and suggests wider perspectives and deeper processes of "interiorisation". In this she expands thinking from the interior as enclosure bound to building and offers a linguistic and theoretical shift from "the interior" as a thing contained to one of "an interior" composed not with space, programme and function, but focused upon surfaces, illusion, allegory and immersion – each set within time and experience. The latter suggests a multiplicity of interior terrains where the observer is not "inserted" but moves freely. Both interpretations act as modes of *interiorisation*.

Focusing on three early 20th century experimental exhibitions spaces that shift the centrality of the viewer and the surface, (as implied in Ro Spankie and Ana Aruajo's "Modelling the Domestic: revisiting the Doll's House"), Suzie Attiwill's evocative paper also offers a close examination of the work of Alexander Dorner's atmosphere rooms, El Lissitski's abstract cabinet and Frederik Kiesler's Surrealist Gallery. Each defines a shift in thinking from sequential historical period rooms to one of atmosphere rooms where movement, transformation and multiple readings of the spatial experience are "designed" quite distinct from the positioning and identification of artefacts within more didactic and linear exhibitions.

The relationship of the observer to the space continues in Spankie and Aruajo's "Modelling the Domestic: revisiting the Doll's House". Describing the interior as a fluid field that also exposes gaps in architectural and interior thinking. Whilst architectural tools adeptly describe built matter, the authors argue that they are less successful in describing the interior space which is particularly true of the model. Whereas architectural models strip surfaces of detail and celebrate volume and light, the authors retrieve the dolls house from the toy cupboard and re-examine its suitability as a tool to aid spatial interpretation of surfaces and objects.

The role of the model, often bypassed by digital tools, is critically analysed and describes how fabrication methods may mirror those of practice. This brings in ludic design thinking and play ethic attitudes into interior processes but suggests tensions in interpreting scale and the authors describe how you make affects what you think. Here the dolls house provides a tool that privileges objects and surfaces over form and volume; a process that invokes user engagement, repositioning and imagined living-in. The dolls house, like a *wunderkrammer* operates as an historical artefact and as an image based representation, reflecting what Rice calls a phenomenon of *doubleness* in *The Emergence of the Interior*.

Rather than a maligned and childlike toy this is a tool that offers equal access for designer and client. Again a concern for surfaces (Di Roma), in effect, 'resurfaces' as a significant concern themselves resurface; the flattening of pattern, textures are affected by scaling down but also reintroduces historical legacies where such "houses" projected significant status in society and acted as instructional tools to teach young girls their domestic duties.

In "Word, Image, and the Space Between: A Pragmatic Approach to Literary Theory and Artistic Practice", Illustrator Brigid Collins (DJCAD) and Word and Image scholar Valerie Robillard from the university of Groningen re-examine the role language plays in enriching interior design thinking. Using emotive modelling techniques which depict conceptual and poetic territory between words, spaces and images, the paper echoes the work of Forty's key text *Words and Buildings* and the mental spaces envisaged in Italo Calvino's *Invisible Cities*. The paper describes interactions between writers, artists and designers concerned with the process of *making* and expressing spaces through other art forms. Developed from an initiative between Interiors at DJCAD / University of Dundee and word and image research from the University of Groningen, it describes the term ekphrasis, a term revived from early Greek rhetorical practice in which scholars were expected to describe an object or artwork as clearly as possible in order to bring it vividly before the inner eye of the listener (in other words, to create "enargeia"). Focussing on Interior Environmental Design workshops that explored conceptual links between poetry, the authors describe the process of "translation" from text to interior spaces. Ekphrasis, like drawing or modelling, is an act of mediation: the introduction of poetry served as a starting point for the design of interior architectural spaces.

This process developed through the creations of full scale poetic (emotive) objects, site visits and construction workshops, installations and finally, design proposals for a House for a Poet in Residence. Taken further, the creation of "Poem Houses", based on the poems of Seamus Heaney, applies a number of ekphrastic operations at work. If we consider this artwork in the context of the Differential Model, we see that the Poem

House made in response to this poem (fig. 2), addresses the text *dialogically*, and in the "associative" nature of the work – which largely informs its final structure – is not based on what the poet puts on paper, but on the subjective response of the designer to the text – a subjectivity reflected also in the tactics of *experience prototyping* pioneered by the design group IDEO. Similarly, through developing spatial responses to "flattened" text, the authors also describe the term *Intermediality* – the confluence and interaction between design or artforms and other fields offers a useful metaphor for the radical changes and blurring of boundaries between design disciplines.

Andrea Mina's paper on "Manual Modelling: a Pedagogical Tool", offers a counterpoint to the dominance of digital modelling methods and celebrates the tactility and visceral act of making to explore connections between modelling of ideas, such as isolation, home or the rituals of a dining experience. Describing emotive modelling and making processes linked to the author's three year research project "Homo Faber", this paper focuses on a student workshop "Manual Ideas", where metaphors, small-scale making and group working reflect the work of Collins and Robillard. Mina highlights some of the drawbacks of architectural drawing, its exclusivity and abstraction in contrast to making at palm-sized scale. Mina also describes how 3D objects alter how groups interact during presentation and discusses how through using unfamiliar materials drives new thinking and attitudes. In some ways this low fidelity making, however framed, touches upon making methods used in co-designing workshops but also suggests deeper research potential for object making processes in interior education. Equally important here amongst these papers are themes of physical immersion, differing scale relationships, modes of meaning and representation and ludic and thoughtful making at the fuzzy front end of the design process. Cristina Fiordimela offers another insightful paper that reexamines the idea of the model as a full scale narrative device set within the contexts of museums spaces. Here the interiors programme and function are subverted and subsumed through museological conversion. Once active interiors undergo a cultural and curatorial metamorphosis from private living space to public museum diorama or fabrication - to build and to lie. Fiordimela's research reinforces the relationships between the interior and the exhibition and describes the recreation of Le Corbs designs made real..

Andy MILLIGAN
DJCAD Duncan of Jordanstone College of Art and Design
University of Dundee
Interior Environmental Design
Perth Road
Dundee
DD14HT
SCOTLAND
a.milligan@dundee.ac.uk
44 7929 136 580

Ana ARAUJO

University of the Arts

Ro SPANKIE

University of Westminster

MODELLING THE DOMESTIC: REVISITING THE DOLL'S HOUSE

Introduction

Conventionally thought of as a children's toy, the doll's house can also be understood as a miniaturised or scaled reproduction of interior domestic space. This paper will attempt to understand the doll's house as a possible means of representation for interiors, looking at how it might function both as an analytical and then productive tool, and finally investigating how it might open up new forms of thinking about and practicing interiors.

The first section will ask what a doll's house is, discussing the way that, unlike the architectural model, it privileges a lifelike representation of objects, surfaces and characters, accounting for their material and scenographic qualities and thereby dealing with aspects that are specific to the practice of interiors. We will also investigate how the doll's house operates as both an artefact and a representation being understood and experienced as both a spatial- and an image-based condition – which, as discussed in Charles Rice's *The Emergence of the Interior,* is equally true for interior design. [2] The second section will look at the fabrication of doll's houses and at ways of making intrinsic to its practice, such as flattening, scaling down and using found objects. These ways of making can work as a source of inspiration for architecture and interior design and potentially stimulate renewed pedagogical approaches for teaching these disciplines.

The Doll's House as an Analytical Tool

Object and Arrangement Rather Than Form and Space

Over time the doll's house – or baby house as it was also known – has played many roles. Originally furnishing the world of the adult, it served as a status symbol for the wealthy and a cabinet of curiosities or "wunderkamer" of the miniature. By the seventeenth century, it was used as a visual tool for practical instruction to teach young girls their household duties. More recently, its mass production as a toy resulted in its relegation to the children's nursery. Throughout all these transformations the doll's house has continuously operated as a pattern book or microcosm of the domestic environment, rather than as a model of the architecture that contains it. [3]

What do we mean by this? Although they refer to the architectural styles of the day, doll's houses are usually more concerned with domestic arrangements and details of family life. The house is viewed from one side only and makes no attempt to show more architectural elements such as a staircase or any circulation. The rooms provide empty boxes, or backdrops for a scenographic representation of objects, surfaces and characters. As John Berger has articulated:

> "Home is represented not by a house, but by a set of practices. Everyone has his own". [4]

By privileging objects and arrangement over form and space, the doll's house, it could be argued, privileges occupation over architecture.

Both Artifact and Representation

The doll's house occupies the curious position of being both an object and a scaled-down representation of something: an artefact and a model. This doubleness interferes in its relationship with its context.

A doll's house is an artefact in the same sense that a piece of furniture is and, as such, it has a mobile relationship to its immediate physical context. Unlike the building to which it alludes, a doll's house may be moved many times during its lifetime and has no control of the room in which it is placed – of its exterior context, so to speak. The context to which the doll's house responds is therefore more generic and alludes to the wider cultural position of the interior. As with the practice of interiors, this context refers to issues of style, taste and culture as much as physical context. The doll's house can be said to privilege the interior over the exterior.

The architectural model, on the other hand, understands itself first and foremost as a representation, and the design is often driven by the desire to refer to its physical context and to the buildings that will surround the final building. The architectural model, it could be claimed, privileges the exterior over the interior.

Figure 1: User enters in. Photo by Ro Spankie

Used Over Time and Invites Participation

Architectural models are often finely crafted and delicate. Although often populated with mobile elements such as plastic figures or furniture, these tend be fixed and there is an understanding that they should not be touched. The architectural model refers to a single moment in time. The dolls house, on the contrary, because of its status as a toy, invites play not just by its creator during the design phase but also by the client or user. This has two consequences. First, in order to satisfy its status as an artefact it must be much more robust than the average model. Second, it is never finished in the way an architectural model is: things can be added and taken away over time, as happens in the domestic interior to which it refers.

In this digital era, there is a great deal of discussion about dynamic modelling, evolutionary techniques and user interaction. Yet, often these techniques are so complex that the client/user feels unable to interact. The familiarity of the doll's house as an artefact makes it a highly accessible representational tool understood by everyone. This means that if the doll's house is used as a tool for spatial design, the authorship is shared between the user and the designer. [6] It also opens up questions of originality and the role of the designer, which are relevant not only to discussions of the model but to interiors as a practice.

Thinking Interiority

The doll's house is a miniaturised reproduction of an interior domestic space. The world of the doll's house is one of interiority, literally as well as metaphorically, and this in itself indicates its peculiar affinity with the practice of interior design. If, as argued by Philip Tabor in *"Striking Home: the Telematic Assault on Identity"*, architecture may be thought to articulate a conflict between interiority and exteriority, the doll's house, as Stewart claims,

> "represents the tension between two modes of interiority" [7]

> "Existing often within an enclosed domestic space, it articulates a condition of a 'centre within a centre, within within within'" [8]

Because of this enclosed condition the interior is challenging to model: one is designing inside a box, inside the architectural envelope. In order to allow an audience a view *into* an interior-design proposal there are a variety of conventions such as lifting the lid or taking away a wall. The doll's house provides recognisable strategies to which to refer, such as the hinged front façade.

Referring essentially to interiority, but also alluding to other aspects of spatial design, the doll's house promises concurrently to take into account the specificity of interiors and to interrogate, if obliquely, prevailing routines in architectural practice. Its role therefore is, on the one hand, productive and analytical and, on the other hand, critical, insofar as it may question, and potentially even transform, architectural procedures. As such, the dolls house may flip the prevailing hierarchy that commonly assigns to interiors a secondary position in relation to architecture: consisting of an interior-specific tool that may interfere in architecture's mode of practice, it implies that architecture might be transformed and redefined by the practice of interiors.

The Doll's House as a Productive tool

Designing with Found Objects – On Altering and Reuse

> "Our transcendent viewpoint makes us perceive the miniature as object and this has a double effect. First, the object in its perfect stasis nevertheless suggests use, implementation, and contextualisation. And second, the representative quality of the miniature makes that contextualisation an allusive one; the miniature becomes a stage on which we project, by means of association or intertextuality, a deliberately framed series of actions ... That the world of things can open itself to reveal a secret life – indeed to reveal a set of actions and hence a narrativity and history outside the given field of perception – is a constant daydream that the miniature presents This is the daydream of the microscope: the daydream of life inside life, of significance multiplied infinitely within significance." [9]

The Secret House, originated as a design studio brief run by Ro Spankie and Alan Sylvester, explored techniques relevant to the interior practice of operating in an

Figure 2: Secret House. Mami Sayo & Helen Warren. Interior. Photo by authors

existing building and reinventing found objects. Students Mami Sayo and Helen Warren investigated the childhood desire to construct fantasy worlds, hidden houses and camps. Starting with an old carriage clock, this domestic interior was carefully constructed without disturbing the existing clock mechanism. From the front, there is no hint to the occupation, except for the light shining from the shaft where the clock can be wound up. On opening the back, a fairy tale world shines out. Referring both to the domestic – through the use of wallpaper and typical furnishings – and to the fantastical – as the heavy brass pendulum swings amongst matchstick chairs – its appeal lies not only in discovering a secret but also in the strange juxtapositions of scale. It could be said to bridge the traditional and the innovative, the everyday and the dreamlike, in a way that the architectural model rarely achieves.

The Secret House could also be seen to operate in the same way as the surrealist technique of collage, which allows a fragment to be read as part of a new whole while still referring to its former self, stimulating the imagination, revealing unexpected readings. The inhabitation of the found object and the practice of altering and reuse can all be seen as creative acts where the everyday is considered with fresh eyes and the bizarre looks possible, while also challenging conventions of style, taste and correctness-to-scale demanded by the conventional model.

By firing the imagination, the doll's house connects us to the world of childhood. Childhood, as Stewart argues, is for adults spatially and temporally miniaturised. Spatially, it speaks of a scaled-down dimension no longer accessible to our grown up bodies: the secretive spaces under tables and stairs, the overlooked gaps on the floor or the wall, the internal rooms of a clock machine. Temporally, it glimpses on a remote period of our lives, visualised, in Susan Stewart's words, as if "on the other end of a tunnel – distanced, diminutive and clearly framed". [9] Our vision of childhood is both remote and intimate, impregnating the spaces, objects and memoirs we identify with it with a similarly evocative, nostalgic feeling. The doll's house operates in this register of remoteness, nostalgia and intimacy, communicating, in Stewart's words, an "exaggeration of interiority": an interiority which is not only physical but also emotional. The Secret House alludes to this intimate and nostalgic territory by building an interior within an old object. Often, interior design practice does precisely the same, and for this reason, like the Secret House, it invokes the routine as well as the dreamlike.

Designing as Craft-making

While design-based practices are generally motivated by a desire to innovate and be creative, the doll's house conveys instead a predilection for the traditional and the customary. As it perpetuates an idea of domesticity that relies on familiarity and identification, the doll's house privileges what is recognisable, unoriginal. Contrary to the notion of inventive production with which design-based processes are usually associated, the doll's houses connect with repetitive reproduction.

Figure 3: Knitted house, by Ana Araujo, Pooja Asher, Erica Calogero, Ana Matic, Sagit Yakutiel and Jenny Wyness. Photo by authors

Constructed like a gigantic doll's house, the Knitted House looks at processes of making, and at how those influence the practice of design. In *On Longing*, Stewart notices that not only doll's houses but also other miniatures, however based on reproduction, often rely on a specific, craft-based method of fabrication that makes them rather unique. [10]

Stewart's observation implies that innovation might be connected not to the creation of something new but rather with the reconstruction of the same employing a new technique. The Knitted House reconstructed a typical London townhouse using the technique of hand knitting and in doing so it generated a unique artefact. Such an engagement with making and matter, rather than with forms and ideas, might, we believe, prove deeply insightful for spatial design practices such as architecture and interiors.

Designing as Reproducing

The Silhouette Dining Box, designed by Ana Araujo, consists of an interior design project based on the practice of reproduction. Inspired by the model of the doll's house, this project recreates a traditional dining set by reconstructing its silhouette profile.

Silhouette profiling, a pre-photographic form of portraiture, was a favourite domestic pastime in Europe and the United States around the mid-eighteenth century.

Figure 4: Silhouette Dining Box, by Ana Araujo. Photo by author

It constituted a cheaper and more democratic version of the cameo profile, a miniaturised bust carved in marble to represent a human profile. Both the white marble bust and the black silhouette were considered mysterious and fascinating for their ability to convey a sense of vividness and distinctiveness in a totally austere and static art form. This was attributed to their process of imprinting shadows, which to some meant the same as imprinting souls. In the eighteenth and the nineteenth century Silhouettes were often used for diagnosing characters, being connected to other superstitious practices such as phrenology and palmistry. As Marina Warner observes in *Phantasmagoria*:

> "A shadow, preserved on paper, acted as an epitome of the subject's character. For all their schematic stillness, silhouettes can present the liveliest studies of family groups and friends [...] The blackness, emptiness, and simplicity demand work, but as if by miracle, the shadow figures appear to possess clear features: the shade summons the person." [11]

Like the silhouette, the doll's house is a miniaturised, still, imperfect form of reproduction. Although minutely modelled either in 1:12 or in 1:24, the actual dimensions of the dolls' houses' furnishings are rarely consistent with such scales. As these little objects are often produced with the same materials as the ones used in full-scaled domestic settings, in a doll's house, the fabric of the curtain is bound to look stiffer than normal, the chandelier is prone to appear oversized and the veins of the timber are unlikely to fit the tiny floor of the living room. Instead of corroborating with the doll's-house desired lifelike effect, these over-detailed fabrications end by sabotaging its aspiration to realism. Yet, as Warner suggests in relation to the profile, it is precisely this condition of imperfection that makes an artefact meaningful. *"The very absences and inadequacies",* she writes, create *"psychological space".* [12]

The Silhouette Dining Box constituted an attempt to incorporate the idea of incompleteness that is inherent in reproducing practices to the process of design. Accordingly, in the doll's house in which the design is represented, only one quarter of the space is real: the rest is mirror reflection, illusion. In Warner's understanding, silhouettes have a spectral condition in that they evoke absence through the presence of a double. In doing so, she states, they communicate a sense of mystery, affection, and intimacy. Doll's houses have a similar effect. As such, we believe, they might incite the production of mysterious, affectionate, intimate interiors.

Conclusion

In its diminutive scale as well as in its representational status, the dolls house resembles architectural drawings and models: the entities that for some, if not all, designers constitute the very essence of architectural practice. As Carlo Scarpa writes:

> "My architecture is done with the architect's medium which is drawings and drawings only". [13]

On a similar note, in *Immaterial Architecture*, the researcher Jonathan Hill contends that architecture, as we understand it today, is inextricably entangled with the practice of representation. An evidence of this, he states, is that some very influential architectural works have only existed in the form of drawings and models. As Hill claims:

> "Sometimes a building is not the best means to explore architectural ideas. Consequently, architects, especially famous ones, tend to talk, write, and draw a lot as well as build. Serio and Andrea Palladio are notable early exponents of this tradition, and Le Corbusier and Rem Koolhaas are more recent ones ... As architects draw buildings and do not physically build them, the work of the architect is always at a remove from the actual process of building ... Independently or together, drawing, writing and building are all examples of architectural research and means to consider and develop architectural design and the architectural discipline ... If everyone reading this text listed all the architectural works that influence them, some would be drawings, some would be texts, and others would be buildings, either visited or described in drawings and texts." [14]

Whether referring to the built or to the unbuilt, the realm of architectural representation provides a fertile ground from which this practice might be interrogated and reinvigorated. Rather contentiously, we want to advocate that the doll's house might play an equivalent role in regards to the practice of interiors.

References

[1] As pointed out by Hill, J. *Immaterial Architecture*, p. 33. (Routledge, London, 2006)
[2] Rice, C. *The Emergence of the Interior* (Routledge, London, 2006).
[3] Bornet, C. *Dolls' Houses: a History of Domestic Life, Architecture and Design in Miniature.* (V&A, London, 2007).
[4] Berger, J. *And Our Faces, My Heart, Brief as Photos,* pp64 Writers and Readers (Bloomsbury Publishing plc, London, 2005)
[5] The problematic around authorship in spatial design and the role of the user is discussed in detail in Hill, J. (ed.). *Occupying Architecture: Between the Architect and the User* (Routledge, London, 1998).
[6] Stewart, S. *On Longing: Narratives of the Miniature, the Gigantic, the Souvenir, the Collection,* p. 61. (The John Hopkins University Press, Baltimore and London, 1984). See also Tabor, P. Striking Home: the Telematic Assault on Identity. In Hill, J. (ed.), *Occupying Architecture,* pp. 217—228.
[7] Stewart, S. *On Longing,* p. 61.
[8] Stewart, S. *On Longing,* p. 44.
[9] Stewart, S. *On Longing,* p. 58.
[10] Stewart, S. *On Longing,* p. 54.
[11] Warner, M. *Phantasmagoria: Spirit Visions, Metaphors, and Media into the Twenty-first Century,* pp. 160—162. (Oxford University Press, Oxford, 2006).
[12] Warner, M. *Phantasmagoria,* p. 161.

[13] Quoted in Forty, A. *Words and Buildings A Vocabulary of Modern Architecture*, p. 29. (Thames and Hudson, London, 2000).
[14] Hill, J. *Immaterial Architecture*, pp. 37—39.

Acknowledgements

The authors gratefully acknowledge the participation of Allan Sylvester, Abi Abdolwahabi, Mami Sayo and Helen Warren in the fabrication of the Secret House, and the participation of Pooja Asher, Erica Calogero, Ana Matic, Sagit Yakutiel and Jenny Wynness in the fabrication of the Knitted House.

Ana ARAUJO
University of the Arts
Department of Architecture
Chelsea College of Art and Design
16 John Islip Street
London SW1P 4JU
a.araujo@chelsea.arts.ac.uk
44 7876426894

Ro SPANKIE
University of Westminster
35 Marylebone Road
London NW1 5LS
r.spankie@westminster.ac.uk
44 7932621499

Suzie ATTIWILL
RMIT University

BETWEEN REPRESENTATION AND THE MIRROR – TACTICS FOR INTERIORISATION

Introduction

The title of the paper "Between representation and the mirror" refers to a tale – "The Legend of Painting" in the book *The Midnight Love Feast*, a story about a couple who are separating and decide to celebrate their last night together with a feast and friends – each of whom is invited to tell a tale. "The Legend of Painting" is one of the tales; it is about a Caliph of Baghdad who desired to have the most wonderful painting in the world. He commissioned a Chinese painter and a Greek Painter to do this in a room of his palace. Each was allocated a wall at either end of a room divided in two by a curtain. When the Caliph asked the painters how long it would take each of them, the Greek replied as long as it takes my Chinese friend, who then replied three months. When the time came, the court gathered for the unveiling

> " ... a magnificent cortege in which nothing could be seen but embroidered robes, plumes of waving feathers, jewels of gold, engraved weapons. Everyone first assembled on the side of the wall painted by the Chinese. A unanimous cry of admiration went up. The fresco represented the garden of everyone's dreams, with trees in blossom and little bean-shaped lakes spanned by graceful footbridges. A vision of Paradise that no one tired of looking at. So great was their delight that some wanted the Chinese to be declared the winner of the contest without so much as a glance at the work of the Greek. Soon however the Caliph ordered that the curtain dividing the room should be drawn aside, and the crowd turned round. And as they turned, an exclamation of amazement escaped them. What had the Greek done,

then? He had painted nothing at all. He had contented himself with covering the entire surface of the wall, from floor to ceiling with a vast mirror. And naturally this mirror reflected the Chinese painter's garden in the most minute detail. But then you will say, what made this image more beautiful and more stirring than its model? It was the fact that the Chinese painter's garden was deserted and uninhabited, whereas the Greek's garden was alive with a magnificent throng in embroidered robes, plumes of waving feathers, jewels of gold, and engraved weapons. And all these people were moving and gesticulating, and recognised themselves with great delight. The Greek was unanimously declared the winner of the contest" [1].

Here is an example of interior tactics in terms of producing relations between people and their environment where surface becomes a site of meaning and events. Different kinds of surfaces are useful to distinguish. There is the surface of representation, which places the viewer at the centre of the world, a rational and self-reflexive Cartesian subject ("I think therefore I am"). The other – a reflection, a mirror which locates the viewer as the site of embodied perception. Both of these surfaces are familiar to interior design as a way of thinking and working. As models of Cartesian and phenomenological philosophy respectively, this kind of thinking is implicit and implicated in the processes of interiorisation.

Yet something else is occurring in this tale – where there is an engagement with composing forces beyond the states of representation and reflection. In between the two surfaces bursts life in all its glittering materiality and movement – the surfaces of representation, mirror, velvet, gold effect a folding which interiorises and composes, albeit momentarily, the vitality of energies and forces.

> "Rather than human consciousness illuminating the world like a search light, it is the case that the world is "luminous" in itself" [2]

and this is what is celebrated in the tale.

Two tactics which re-position the concept of interior are evident above. One is a focus on surface as distinct from space. Interior design is often referred to as a spatial discipline. However this seems either to amplify the idea of containers or, if it moves to relational conditions, then it becomes a kind of point thinking between things where there is a relation *to* something. This questioning of the primacy of space finds resonance with ecologist/psychologist J.J.Gibson's provocative claim:

> "We live in an environment consisting of substances that are more or less substantial; of a medium, the gaseous atmosphere; and of the surfaces that separate the substances from the medium. We do not live in space" [3].

The shift to processes of interiorisation involves surfaces, materialities, light and movement; there is a sense of a relation *in* as distinct from *to*. There is not something to have a relation to – which needs things to exist before the relation; rather we are already *in* the world.

Exhibitions as arrangements of relations between things – subjects and objects – offer up many examples to think through these ideas and relations of "to" and "in", and to experiment. Donald Preziosi, an art historian, writes:

> "What the subject sees in museological space, in the "picture" or in the "frame" of the museum, is a series of possible ways in which it can construct its own life as some kind of centred unity or perspective that draws together in a patterned and telling order all those diverse and contradictory experiences and desires. It is in this sense that the new museum can be seen as working to put all things into a perspectival system of new and clearly related positions." [4]

Most exhibitions produce compositions which effect this kind of positioning – i.e. representation or reflection; relations of "to".

However in this paper, and in my research, I am interested in tactics where there is an attempt to experiment and question the self-given quality of The Interior of the subject – to question the privileging of identity and self through the emphasis of a stable interior which dominates interior design thinking and discourse. Shifting the concept of interior from "Being" to "becoming", from "is" to "and", from subject to process as a tactic, and how this then becomes a question of design not psychology. In contrast to Preziosi's diagram, which focuses on an idea of centred unity and a subject who makes sense, is posed a different diagram where

> "an element in experience … comes before the determinism of the subject and sense. Shown through a "diagram" that one constructs to move about more freely rather than a space defined by an a priori "scheme" into which one inserts oneself, it involves temporality that is always starting up again in the midst, and relations with others based not in identification or recognition, but encounter and new compositions" [5].

This paper selects some exhibitions which do this – in contrast to Preziosi's diagram where the self desires stability through centring and an identification of a fixed being, an emphasis on movement and transformation opens up the interior to exterior forces in a process of constant becoming.

Exhibition Tactics

In turning to consider exhibitions, it is telling to observe how the concept of the gallery space as white cube continues to be accepted as a space where there is minimal interference with the exhibition of art and the viewer's engagement with it, i.e. there is no intervening mediation of the meaning. This subscribes to the idea that both the art object and viewing subject can have a direct, unmediated relation where the interior of the art object is experienced by the subject, or the viewing subject is privileged in terms of their experience of the work, or there is collaboration between the two. The gallery space as white cube is positioned as a neutral spatial container which does not interfere with the communion between art and viewer. A space with no exteriors! While this has been critiqued extensively – Brian O'Doherty's *Inside the White Cube*

[6] and installation art since the 1960s have challenged and contested this concept – the desirability of the white cube as perceived neutral space for the viewer to engage with the artwork and the artist to present work continues to dominate the design of galleries and is evidence of how such ways of thinking continue to be both pervasive and persuasive.

The following are three exhibitions which attempted to shift the centrality of the viewer as a stable, centred "I" to a composition which produces encounters via surfaces with processes of becoming and transformation as distinct from surface as representation or a reflection of one's self-expression. These exhibitions took place in the early twentieth century, during the 1930s and 1940s – Alexander Dorner's atmosphere rooms at the Hannover Landesmuseum; El Lissitzky's abstract cabinet, one of these atmosphere rooms, and Frederick Kiesler's Surrealist Gallery, part of the *Art of This Century*.

During the twentieth century, there have been many exhibitions by artists which have also experimented with questions of what happens in the encounter between art and viewer. Claire Bishop's book *Installation Art* is a stimulating account of contemporary art from the 1950s to the present as one of experimentation with different kinds of viewer/art relations. Installation art, she writes, sought

> "to provide an alternative to the idea of the viewer that is implicit in Renaissance perspective: that is, instead of a rational, centred, coherent humanist subject" [7].

Bishop's four models of viewing subjects: psychological/psychoanalytical; phenomenological; Lacanian; and political; offer up much to consider in terms of relational models for interior design. It is also interesting and thought-provoking how this exposes much interior design discourse which implies, and relies in an unquestioned and implicit way upon a subject as centred and stable.

While the models presented by Bishop are useful to work through in a re-conceptualisation of the concept of interior, the focus of this paper is on a process of interiorisation as one of design and one of mediation involving design tactics with surfaces, materials, light and movement; a kind of in-between position, neither viewer nor artist, like the Tournier story; a process which constructs

> "a temporary and virtual arrangement according to casual, logical and temporal relations" [8].

Alexander Dorner

Contemporary curator Hans Ulrich Obrist, in an interview on contemporary curatorial practice, drew my attention to the practice of Alexander Dorner. For Obrist, Dorner is someone who contributed to the transformation of exhibition practices and museums through making dynamic

> "the often too static museum and to transform the neutral white cube in order to assume a more heterogeneous space".

According to Obrist, Dorner used "the museum as a laboratory", "as a locus of crossings for art and life" and "as an oscillation between object and process" [9].

Dorner, born in 1893, was the director of the Hannover Landesmuseum from 1922 to 1936. In 1937, along with many others, he escaped Gestapo persecution and went to New York. From 1938 to 1941 he was the director of the Rhode Island School of Design Museum, and died in 1957. This paper will concentrate on his atmosphere rooms and a publication he wrote while in America titled *the way beyond 'art'*, first published in 1947 and republished in 1958.

Dorner described art as

> "an aggressive energy seeking to transform the visitor" [10]

and developed a theory which challenged the dominant ideology of art as a container of inherent, immutable, unchanging meaning which could be engaged with at different times. He believed that the viewer was also contingent rather than a stable, centred entity. He desired an engagement with the current – literally, in terms of energies – and dismissed Surrealism and Romanticism for their inward concerns with self-expression and symbolism.

the way beyond 'art' is like a manifesto of his thinking and as he writes in the opening pages:

> "I have reached this conclusion not through theoretical speculation but through long practical experience" [11].

Dorner invited the pragmatist philosopher John Dewey to write the introduction. Dewey focused on the repositioning of the concept of "The Individual" as a vital contribution of Dorner's work and writings.

> "In the older view, a person as individual was thought to be a fixed element in a given larger whole: departure from this fixed place was heresy, in matters of belief; disloyalty in matters of overt action. Later what was called 'The Individual' was cut loose entirely, and was supposed to be fixed in himself – a synonym at the time for 'by' himself, or in isolation. The author [Dorner] effectively calls attention to something fundamentally important, but usually ignored: the assumption of immutability is common in both cases. In the first instance, the artist was 'servant of absolute form'; in the second he was taken to be himself absolute and hence 'spontaneous creator'. Against these fixations, Dr Dorner points to the personal individual as a partaker in the 'general process of life' and as a 'special contributor to it'. This union of partaker and contributor describes the enduring work of the artist." [12]

These comments take us back to the gesticulating courtiers in the world where it is neither the surface of representation nor self projection – where the individual is fixed in a larger whole or a self-contained knower – but of participation and contribution. It is not a huge leap to position Dewey's words within, and as a critique of, current interior design practice where a holistic approach to design and the human-centred approach continue to dominate contemporary practice.

Dorner was also critical of three-dimensional space: he referred to it as a "cage of certainty-giving space".

> "In the place of static or semistatic causation we now find the dynamic ground of SELF TRANSFORMATION. ... There is only one way to cooperate with this energetic substratum: through a constant and active transformation of the life process" [13].

Individuals and space were associated with the notion of Being; eternal, immutable and static conditions of identification and closure. In contrast Dorner advocated processes of becoming which engaged with life, growth, energies, time and hence were transforming rather than fixed and eternal.

Atmosphere Rooms

Dorner:

> "Only one point of view can be behind a museum's arrangement as well as behind its activities: namely 'How can it become, to all people, a source of understanding and a living force for active life?'" [14].

His tactic was to produce atmosphere rooms, which he distinguished from period rooms or representations of a specific style. There is a resonance here to *The Legend of Painting* and its atmosphere. These atmosphere rooms were produced through an attention to design aspects of each room, that is layout, sightlines, circulation, lighting, colour and arrangement i.e. tools of interior design. Often working against the interior architecture, Dorner attempted to actualise an encounter which was neither representational in terms of presenting the past as eternal and contained nor as an experience produced wholly by the viewer but as atmosphere, of life and energies which enfolded the present as part of an ongoing process of becoming. The interior of the room then is repositioned together with the viewer – where the encounter does not depend on either a fixed relation of representation or one of relativity i.e. from the viewer's subjective position. Rather than a relation *to* something, a relation *in* a world as dynamic and transforming is fostered. [This distinction is a tool taken from Deleuze].

Different rooms from different times followed in chronological order, each evoking an atmosphere as distinct from representing styles. Cauman, Dorner's biographer, takes one on a walk through the rooms in *The Living Museum*. Beginning with the Medieval rooms which were painted in dark colours since medieval churches did not have light interiors:

> "The rooms receded; permitting only the works of art to stand out and leaving the towering crucifixes and shining alters as the focal points of display. The gold ground and the mystical soft forms of late Gothic altarpieces swam in their particular 'reality'".

In contrast, the walls and ceilings of the Renaissance rooms beyond were a clear white or grey,

> "the new conception developed in this period was of clearly defined volumes of space – cubes and hemispheres – with structural elements forming the defining

frame. Perspective in Renaissance painting was used to make this geometrical picture of reality plain to the senses. The clear, light walls of the Renaissance galleries emphasised the cubic character of the rooms. The pictures were like views lit into the walls; their frames played the part of window frames."

In the Baroque galleries – backgrounds of red velvet, framed in gold, where

> "the picture of space lost its clear definition, becoming far deeper and assuming an active, levitational quality. The surrounding wall and ceiling structure, no longer defining the space so sharply, fused with it, creating a greater impression of unity than in the Renaissance galleries" [15].

The Abstract Cabinet

Dorner commissioned the Russian constructivist El Lissitzky (1890–1941) to actualise the atmosphere room which presented Abstract art. For Dorner, abstract art engaged with the energies of the current and did not retreat into individualism like Surrealism and Romanticism. Referred to by Alfred H. Barr Jnr., director of MoMA, as the most famous single room of twentieth century art in the world, Dorner claimed that its significance was due to the fact that it was

> "the first attempt to overcome the fixity of the gallery and the semi-stasis of the period room, and to introduce modern dynamism into the museum by representing a vision of the respective reality of the style" [16].

This was achieved by tactics which engaged with surfaces and movement as a process of composition and encounter. As Cauman noted

> "this room had the unprecedented ability of transforming itself, of changing its identity as the works changed theirs. There could hardly have been a more striking contrast than that between the dynamism of the new room on the one hand and, on the other, the balance and repose of the Renaissance galleries" [17].

In *the way beyond 'art'*, Dorner describes the room in all its vitality:

> "The walls of that room were sheathed with narrow tin strips set at right angle to the wall plane. Since these strips were painted black on one side, grey on the other, and white on the edge, the wall changed its character with every move of the spectator. The sequence of tones varied in different parts of the room. This construction thus established a supraspatial milieu for the frameless composition. This visual mobility was further increased by a placing of a sculpture by Archipenko in front of a mirror. The mirror reflected the reversed side of the metal strips, not the side seen by the spectator. Thus the mirror effect extended the elusive wall construction in such a way that that construction changed its identity in continuing. (This feature is indeed a true symbol of the new concept of CONTINUITY AS SELF-TRANSFORMATION. In contrast the mirror effect of the Baroque created a balancing replica of a static space arrangement.) All display cases and picture mounts were made movable to reveal new

compositions and diagrams. This room contained many more sensory images than could have been accommodated by a rigid room. Mobility exploded the room, as it were, and the result was a spiritual intensification, proportionate to the evolutionary content of the display cases which tried to demonstrate the growth of modern design in its urgent transforming power" [18].

Frederick Kiesler

Frederick Kiesler (1890–1965) was an architect who worked in areas of exhibition and retail design. Continuity and transformation as temporal dynamic were also vital to his thinking about design. Kiesler:

> "The traditional art object, be it a painting, a sculpture, or a piece of architecture, is no longer seen as an isolated entity but must be considered within the context of this expanding environment. The environment becomes equally as important as the object, if not more so, because the object breathes into the surroundings and also inhales the realities of the environment no matter in what space, close or wide apart, open air or indoor" [19].

Kiesler left Europe for New York in 1926. In 1942, Peggy Guggenheim invited him to devise "a new exhibition method for objects" for her *Art of This Century* gallery which involved four exhibition spaces: the *Surrealist Gallery*, the *Abstract Gallery*, the *Kinetic Gallery* and the *Daylight Gallery* [20]. Each of the exhibitions employed tactics to effect spatial continuity where the viewer was brought into contact with a dynamic. While Dorner arranged surfaces to produce atmosphere rooms and El Lissitzky made the surface dynamic, Kiesler removed the frame which produced boundaries, defined boxes and insides/outsides. Kiesler's main concept was the *Endless House*:

> "When the moment comes when we want to move a wall way out, to breathe more fully – yes, when we want the ceiling to be higher, or the whole area to change into another shape – that is where the Endless House comes in. Because it has twofold expression: first, it has the reality of the walls and the ceiling and the floor as they are ... but also a lighting system ... so that by changing the lights ... one can expand or contract the interior in an illusionary way. You can't do that with boxes." [21]

With the design of the *Surrealist Gallery*, Kiesler painted the surfaces of the interior architecture black and installed curved wooden walls. Unframed artworks were attached to these walls by adjustable arms made from baseball bats. Frames removed, the artworks became part of the environment and interior/exterior divisions were removed. He used the term "spatial-exhibition". Seats within the gallery enabled different relations between the works and viewers. Part of the design, these seats were used in a multitude of configurations from sitting to display. The lighting was also critical to the encounter – with different lights switching on and off at different intervals, acting as attractors drawing viewers to different works at different times. There were also special sound effects.

In a review of the exhibition titled *The Violent Art of Hanging Paintings* – Edgar Kaufmann, critic and design curator, criticised the exhibition for preventing an engagement with what he positioned as the inherent qualities of the paintings:

> "A primary fact about every painting, whatever its quality or function, is that it is a focal point. In it, for whatever he's worth, the artist has concentrated his vision, his emotions, his understanding, his craft. Whether pictures are assembled in a decorative scheme, in an intimate presentation, or an expository survey, this factor remains unchanged."

While Kauffman wrote of "the atmosphere of dynamics which he [Kiesler] creates forcibly recalls the investigations of modern science, where gravity has no hold and matter and energy are interchangeable ...[Kauffman lamented the fact that] works based on a human scale of vision and empathy must be lost" [22]. For Kauffman, stability is what is at stake here, and without it, one is left with disorientation and violence.

Interiorisation / the Interior / Interiority – a Conclusion

These tactics and exhibitions offer up a way of thinking not just about exhibitions but questions of interiorisation, interiority and interior. The experiments of Dorner, El Lissitzky and Kiesler challenged the concepts of an inherent, immutable, stable object or subject which could be engaged with via representation or as self-reflection/projection. For them, it was a question of design, of working with surfaces to engage a dynamic and transforming environment. Their practices and ideas offer up lines of thinking which one can pick up and use as a way of working through some current problems.

The other tool which has been used through out, albeit with little direct reference, is the thinking of French philosopher, Gilles Deleuze. Deleuze dismisses the concept of interiority as it

> "refers to the thought, dominant in Western philosophy since Plato, that things exist independently, and that their actions derive from the unfolding or embodying of this essential unity".

For Deleuze, one must not

> "look to the internal or intrinsic "meaning", "structure" or "life" of the terms involved (whether they be people, a person and an animal, elements in a biological system, and so on). ... organised beings are not the embodiment of an essence or idea, but are the result of enormous numbers of relations between parts which have no significance on their own. In other words, specific beings are produced from within a generalised milieu of exteriority without reference to any guiding interiority". [23]

For Deleuze,

> "an interior is only a selected exterior; an exterior, a projected interior". [24]

These ideas challenge interior design and invite one to re-think "interior" and in the process re-conceptualise the practice of interior design.

The practices of Dorner, El Lissitzky, Kiesler and Deleuze challenge dominant and dominating concepts of interior which come from Cartesian, phenomenological and humanist underpinnings. Their ideas cannot easily be dismissed as abstract philosophical concepts because as ways of thinking they shaped tactics and tools which can be used in practice. The re-conceptualisation of the concept of interior evident in their practices involves a shift from an essentialist, self given, *a priori* position as either inside of a box (architecture) or the inside of a person (subjectivity).

It is apparent that in the twenty-first century, the concept of interior is in crisis, i.e. stability is no longer assured or even desired; enclosures and dialectical divisions between inside/outside, interior/exterior disputed. The concept of "interior" is critical at the beginning of the 21st century and therefore we are poised at a moment of potential for interior design. This tends to effect a reactive reinforcement of existing ideas of enclosure, certainty, identity and stability. The search for identity within the discipline of interior design pursues this direction. It also invites the possibility of thinking differently – finding tactics and tools which open up the concept of interior beyond representation and reflection, engaging interior as a dynamic process of making, of interiorisation, of interior design.

References

[1] Tournier, M. *The Midnight Love Feast*. trans. B. Wright. (Collins, London, 1991) p. 189.
[2] Marks, J. Representation. In Parr, A., ed. *The Deleuze Dictionary*, (Edinburgh University Press, Edinburgh, 2005) p. 228.
[3] Gibson, J, J. *The Ecological Approach to Visual Perception*, (Houghton Mifflin Co., Boston, 1979) p. 32.
[4] Preziosi, D. Brian of the Earth's Body: Museums and the Framing of Modernity. In Duro, P., ed. *The Rhetoric of the Frame. Essays on the Boundaries of the Artwork*, (Cambridge University Press, USA, 1996) p. 106.
[5] Rajchman, J., Introduction in Deleuze, G. *Pure Immanence. Essays on A Life*, trans. A, Boyman, (Zone Books, New York, 2005). p. 15
[6] O'Doherty, B. *Inside the White Cube: The Ideology of the Gallery Space* (Lapis, San Francisco, 1986).
[7] Bishop, C. *Installation Art. A Critical History*, (Tate Publishing, London, 2005) p. 13.
[8] Stagoll, C. Plane. In Parr, A., ed. *The Deleuze Dictionary*, p. 205.
[9] Obrist, H, U. http://www.thing.net/eyebeam/msg00373.html [Accessed on 26 April, 2008] (1998).
[10] Cauman, S. *The Living Museum. Experiences of an Art Historian and Museum Director*, (New York University Press, USA, 1958) p. 170.
[11] Dorner, A. *the way beyond « art »*, (New York University Press, New York, 1958) p. 15.
[12] Dewey, J., Introduction. Nov, 1946. In Dorner, A. *the way beyond « art »*, p. 10.
[13] Dorner, A. *the way beyond « art »*, p. 32-33.

[14] Cauman, S. *The Living Museum,* p. 111.
[15] Cauman, S. *The Living Museum.* p. 89-90.
[16] Cauman, S. *The Living Museum.* p. 108.
[17] Cauman, S. *The Living Museum.* p. 100.
[18] Dorner, A. *the way beyond « art »,* p. 114-115.
[19] Kiesler, F. Second Manifesto of Correalism, published in Art International 9 March 1965. In Phillips, L. *Frederick Kiesler,* (Whitney Museum of Modern Art, New York, 1989) p. 83.
[20] Peggy Guggenheim quoted in Phillips, L. *Frederick Kiesler,* p. 150.
[21] Philips, S. Introjection and Projection. Frederick Kiesler and His Dream Machine. In Mical, T. ed. *Surrealism and Architecture* (Routledge, London, New York, 2005) p. 149.
[22] Kaufmann, E. The Violent Art of Hanging Pictures *Magazine of Art*, 1946, p. 108.
[23] Roffe, J. Exteriority/Interiority. In Parr, A., ed. *The Deleuze Dictionary,* p. 95.
[24] Deleuze, G. *Spinoza: Practical Philosophy*, trans. R. Hurley, (San Francisco: City Lights Books, 1988) p. 125.

Associate Professor Suzie ATTIWILL
Interior Design, RMIT University
GPO Box 2476
Melbourne
Australia 3001
suzie.attiwill@rmit.edu.au
+61 3 9925 3498

Brigid COLLINS

DJCAD Duncan of Jordanstone College of Art and Design / University of Dundee

Valerie ROBILLARD

University of Groenigen

WORD, IMAGE, AND THE SPACE BETWEEN: A PRAGMATIC APPROACH TO LITERARY THEORY AND ARTISTIC PRACTICE

Introduction

"The real developments, the innovations, in art and life, whether in literature or painting, depend on the manner in which the elements of one medium are translated to the conditions of another."

Bram Dijkstra[*]

The interaction between the visual and verbal arts has received much attention since the latter half of the 20th century and the extent to which any medium can be "translated to the conditions of another", to quote Bram Dijkstra, has stood at the center of the debate surrounding the "sister arts" tradition.[†] In spite of such academic debates, however, artists and writers themselves have continued collaborating in a variety of interesting ways that far outrun any theories developed to articulate the complex interactions that arise from such interdisciplinary "crossovers".

---

[*] *Cubism, Stieglitz, and the Early Poetry of William Carlos Williams*, p. ix.
[†] See, for example, G.E. Lessing's *Laocoon: An Essay on the Limits of Painting and Poetry* (1776), in which Lessing argues that art and poetry cannot present images in the same way, as the first is spatial, fixed, and the second is temporal.

One of the central concerns of interarts discourse has centred on the forms and functions of "ekphrasis", * a medium of expression that is one of many representational techniques available to writers and, which has become increasingly popular with poets, particularly since the latter half of the 20th century.† In practice, ekphrasis is an act of mediation: the artist's perception of "reality" is re-imaged by the poet/writer, which, in turn, is re-imaged in the mind of the reader. It is this sequence of interpretive "events" that contributes to the complex nature of ekphrastic texts, because these are inextricably bound up with, among many other factors, cognition and cultural codes. Furthermore, as James Heffernan points out, ekphrasis

> "never aims simply to reproduce a work of visual art in words, so there is no point in judging ekphrastic poetry by a criterion of fidelity to the work it represents. We can much better judge it by asking what it enables us to see in the work of art or even just to see, period."‡

The manner in which "seeing" is facilitated in such texts continues to be the subject of critical discourse; indeed, much has been written on the topic and a variety of approaches offered. To date, these approaches have been largely logocentric, in other words, have centred on the original sense of the term "ekphrasis", which privileges the translation from the visual to the verbal. It has become increasingly clear, however, that similar operations come into play when verbal texts are translated to visual works of art. The goal of our research collaboration has been to explore the variety of ways in which visual artists might create works that establish complex and varied ekphrastic relationships with verbal texts that go beyond illustration (or exemplification) of their source texts. The first part of this essay (Robillard) will demonstrate the usefulness of revising the notion of ekphrasis to accommodate the responses of the visual arts to the verbal arts (a topic often falling under the heading of "illustration"); the second part of this essay (Collins) will demonstrate the pragmatics of this revision through practical application in undergraduate projects.

Revising the Term "Ekphrasis"

Because similar operations can be discerned between translating from visual to verbal texts and vice versa, my earlier "Differential Model" (Robillard, 1998)§, which was

---

* This term originates in early Greek rhetorical practice, where young scholars were trained to describe objects or artworks as clearly as possible in order to bring them vividly before the 'mental eye' of the listener (in other words, to create 'energeia').

† The number of poems written in English in the latter half of the 20th century on Brueghel and Vermeer alone is remarkable. For example, Gisbert Kranz, in *Das Bildgedicht (1987)*, mentions over 75 poems written on Brueghel's *Fall of Icarus* – and there have been even more since the publication of Kranz's monumental reference work.

‡ *Museum of Words: The Poetics of Ekphrasis from Homer to Ashbery*, p.157

§ First published in *Pictures Into Words: Theoretical and Descriptive Approaches to Ekphrasis*, 1998.

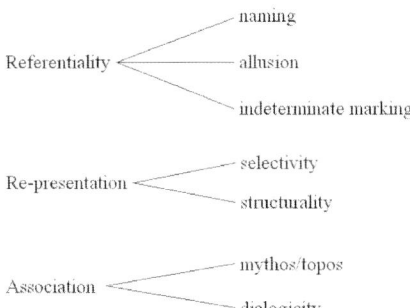

Figure 1

originally aimed at classifying varieties of ekphrastic references in verbal texts, was revised to include both "verbal" and (what I will call) "visual" ekphrasis.* The resulting typology categorises the manner and degree to which verbal and visual arts interact and is based on my classification of ekphrasis as a variant of "intertextuality" (the idea that texts are shaped by earlier texts).† The revised model (Figure 1) is described below:

This typology has been designed to differentiate explicitly-marked ekphrastic texts from those which signal more subtle relationships with their verbal/visual pre-text(s). Each heading is divided into three subheadings. The first category in the typology, "Communicativity", proceeds from the assumption that ekphrastic texts, because they are specific to particular (art)works, will in some way mark their source. This marking can be explicit, as in "naming", where the source is stated clearly in the title or elsewhere in the (art)work. Allusion, a more subtle type of communication, might take the form of a reference in the title (or elsewhere) to some important aspect of the source text and would rely on some (literary/art historical) knowledge on the part of the viewer. "Indeterminate markings", the most complex types of references, are subtle "clues" placed within a text or artwork which only a handful of viewers/readers (in Stanley Fish's words, an "interpretive community"‡) might recognise as referring to a particular verbal/visual source. The following category, Re-presentation, is designed to account for the degree to which the original work is depicted in the new.§ The sub-category

---

* Published in 'Beyond Definition: A Pragmatic Approach to Intermediality', in *Media Borders, Multimodality, and Intermediality*, Lars Elleström, ed. (London: Palgrave MacMillan, 2010), 150-162.
† I use the term 'text' to refer to both visual and verbal communication.
‡ *Is There a Text In This Class?*,1980.
§ I have written the term with a hyphen in order to avoid the synecdochal problem (part-whole relationships) presented by the term 'representation' and mimesis in general. Here, it means simply to 'present anew'.

"selectivity" refers to the number of details from the original text which are incorporated in the new text. "Structurality" refers to the re-presentation of the shape or construction of the earlier work. A poem structured around the organisational properties of a cubist painting, for example, would be highly "structural" in this typology; an illustrated text that in some way attempts to follow the narrative sequence of its verbal per-text would establish a structural relationship with it. (In both cases we can speak to some degree of "structural analogue"). Finally, the category "Association" accounts for texts which refer to conventions or ideas associated with the source text or are autoreflexive additions of the artist/writer. The sub-category "dialogicity" refers to the semantic or ideological tension created between the original text and the new.[*] The sub-category "mythos/topos" is designed to account for the manner in which texts refer, for example, to various conventions or cultural codes that play an important role in the generation of source-texts during a particular period.

To illustrate this more complex type of relationship, I would like to briefly turn to the variety of choices that might be made in a visual re-presentation of Tennyson's "Lady of Shallot". One response might emphasise the feminine task of weaving and the details of the domestic interior, as these were important to the 19th century's view of the woman as the "angel in the house"[†], or the artist might consider the notion of the "femme fatale" convention of the time and suggest in his/her work that the lady's plight is the result of a break in society's (or her own) moral fabric. In both cases, the artist focuses on contemporary cultural codes and norms of the period in which the poem was written. On the other hand, the artist could address the original text in the context of contemporary thought of his or her own times. For example, a visual response to "The Lady of Shallot" might forgo all original details of the poem in favour of contemporary feminist attention to the plight of the single woman in a male society. In this case, the only ekphrastic reference would (necessarily) be contained in the title of the artwork or in some other verbal naming within the painting itself, and the remainder of the work will be largely associative or even autoreflexive (reflecting personal concerns). These are largely dialogical responses, as they place the original text in a new context.

Ekphrasis and the "Poem House"

To demonstrate the usefulness of this typology in accounting for the ways in which artists address verbal texts, I would like to turn to the work of my co-author, Brigid Collins, an artist, illustrator, and lecturer whose "poem houses" not only inspired the inversion of the Differential Model to account for "visual ekphrasis", but have also

---

[*]   The terms 'selectivity','dialogicity', and autoreflexivity used here have been adapted from Manfred Pfister's Intertextual Scales set out in his article 'Konzepte der Intertextualitität, in Broich, U. and Pfister,M, eds, *Intertextualität: Formen, Funktionen, anglistische Fallstudien*, 1985.

[†]   A term derived from Coventry Patmore's 19th century poem of the same title, which defined the virtues of the ideal Victorian woman: a selfless and devoted wife and mother, who was, above all, modest and submissive to her husband.

Figure 2

proven an invaluable source of inspiration for designing and collaborating on interart projects at the university level. The question of "ekphrasis" opposed to "illustration" is raised most poignantly by Collins herself when she asserts that she has

> "certain reservations about using the word 'illustrate' in connection with her 'poem houses' based on the poems of Seamus Heaney, as 'it is a different process from what is normally understood by book illustration'".*

What her work does is to

> "reconcile the sense of apparent conflict between the cerebral and sophisticated qualities inherent in the world of ideas and the tactile, earthy qualities"

of poetry's images and subject matter.† In Collins' artistic response to Heaney's poem "Digging", for example, we find a number of ekphrastic operations at work. Considered in the context of the Differential Model, this poem house (Figure 2),

---

* In conversation with Brigid Collins. (Collins' Poem Houses were also used to illustrate Heaney's speech 'Room to Rhyme', given at the University of Dundee, and published by the University in 2004)

† *Room to Rhyme*

addresses the verbal text in a variety of ways. In the first place, communicativity is high. In both book, *Room to Rhyme*, and in exhibition, the title "Digging" and the name of the poet have been clearly communicated – or "named". In the category of "Re-presentation", Collins' artwork is high in selectivity, as the poem's central images (the act of digging and the act of writing) are represented throughout by spade and pen-like forms. Furthermore, words from the text itself are typed on strands of parchment and strung throughout the artwork, although not in a structural imitation. What is most intriguing about Collins' work is that this is where direct re-presentation (or "illustration") stops. From this point on, Collins lays aside the organisation of Heaney's poem and arranges details and images according to her own "personal journey through the text".[*] We can, by means of the Differential Model, suggest that, although Collins clearly re-presents Heaney's poem in a number of concrete ways, the autoreflexive nature of the work largely informs its final structure and reconfigures it to place it in a new context. It is, therefore, equally Re-presentative and Associative as it re-presents the objects in the text, but is not based solely on what the poet puts on paper but on Collins' experience of it.

Exploring Collins' work through the vehicle of a differential typology helps illuminate the ekphrastic capability of visual texts. Nevertheless, this kind of exploration also makes clear that typologies and models are imperfect, as they can prove exclusive and/or reductive. For example, what is *not* accounted for here is Collins' use of materials in place of words – or materials placed alongside words. It is important to note here that current research within a new and developing field of interarts studies – Intermediality – has provided new ways of exploring the interaction between the arts and other media. In this field of study, Collins' work would be considered a composite or hybrid artwork, one made of the confluence of more than one medium: in this case, of verbal text and solid materials. There is, indeed, much to learn about the ways in which the visual and verbal arts interact, and it is becoming clear that collaboration between practitioners in both fields is essential to the development of the means by which to articulate these interactions. Research directed at defining and categorising the operations between words and images is inextricable from the discoveries in the field of Art and Design itself.[†] If we are to expand these research areas, a good place to begin is with the development of interart projects at the undergraduate level. The following is an account of just one of a series of "word and image" projects that we have developed for Duncan of Jordanstone College of Art and Design at the University of Dundee, using pragmatic means to demonstrate and extend our individual research findings.

Valerie Robillard

---

[*] In conversation with Brigid Collins.

[†] Indeed, leading professional organizations in word and image, such as the International Association of Word and Image (IAWIS) are increasingly in close cooperation with comparable Art associations, particularly through the sharing knowledge in international conferences. (An example of this is the place allotted to IAWIS at the College Art Association's conference in February, 2009)

A Poetic Revolt: The Poetics of Installation

Brigid Collins

In response to the research into "visual ekphrasis" outlined above, a series of projects was devised by myself and developed in collaboration with Dr. Robillard. These projects have been undertaken by a group from the second year of the undergraduate programme in Interior and Environmental Design, at Dundee, initially by means of a one-day workshop. The project was designed as follows:

1. A Poetic Revolt

which introduces the students to the possibility of engaging poetry and 3D space, followed by a project in two distinct phases:

2(a) The Poetics of Installation

The design and making of full-scale 3D installations, exploring ideas derived from selected poems, which were to go on to provide a springboard for the design of:

2(b) A House For A Poet

This phase of the project challenges accepted methods of approaching the design of interior architecture, shunning the accepted route of studying precedents (initially, at least) in favour of following a more personal "interior" journey, triggered by the study of a poem, thereby demonstrating a means by which a poetic route towards the design of more human-centred living and working space(s) becomes tangible.

1. Introductory Workshop: A Poetic Revolt

This project was initially inspired by the claim made by Catalan artist and poet, Joan Brossa (1919–98) that his paintings, constructions and installations were actually "poems" in their own right. Through an analysis of some of these works, Valerie Robillard, in an introductory lecture to students and staff, examined the ways in which these might – or might not – follow established rules of poetics which inform our conception of form. In the same lecture, Robillard also introduced her research into the subject of "ekphrasis". Inspiration for this part of the project comes directly from Brossa's experiments with form, in that an important reinterpretation took place in his work – not just in terms of poetic form, but even in terms of what represents a poem. Brossa's assertion that poetry and art can achieve a similar effect in terms of image (in direct opposition to Lessing) can be seen as a kind of personal, internal revolution, or a "poetic revolt" against a perceived hierarchy between words and images.

Continuing the revolutionary reinterpretation of poetic form and convention which had occurred during the early twentieth century, Brossa, according to Manuel Guerrero:

Figures 3 and 4

"carried through to its ultimate consequences his experimentation with language... testing out different poetic forms, and subsequently liberating himself from the traditional forms...in order to arrive at new, synthetic poetic forms such as the visual poem or the object poem, or to carry on experimenting at the limits of the literary tradition."*

In response to visual information such as Brossa's installations and "poem-objects" (Figure 3) and on recent "Poem-House" forms, developed by myself (Figure 4), in response to my own sense of the 3D space suggested by certain poems, students were asked to work in small groups to develop ideas for their own "poem-object", inspired by the images in and form of, a given poem.

The choice of poems offered encompassed either structurally "closed", or traditional, e.g. the sonnet, sestina, or villanelle, with their strong structure, metre and rhythm and "open", or modern in form and avoiding traditional poetic conventions. In both cases, the students were encouraged to focus closely on the images and figures of speech (e.g. metaphors) that informed the poems. Groups were guided through this experimental process by Robillard and myself over two studio sessions, after which each group gave a short presentation, outlining their idea(s), demonstrated in three-dimensions, as "Poem-Objects". Lively discussion ensued on ways in which these ideas might be developed into full-scale installations and a list of poems – examples of both "closed" and "open" poetic forms – was introduced from which each group was asked to make a selection as the basis from which to proceed.

---

*   Guerrero, p. 27-28

2(a) Project: The Poetics of Installation

The second task centred on the creation of a *"poetic"* installation, by means of first designing and then making (also in groups) over a period of three weeks. This was to be a full-scale 3D space, reflecting the images, form and mood of a *chosen* poem. Using Robillard's "ekphrastic" model, students were asked to consider the incorporation of the formal structural elements of, as well as words and/or lines from the poem(s) selected, into their installations. What each group was constructing could be seen as a "poem-house" – a space which each poem could physically occupy.

Robillard's lecture on "visual ekphrasis" had been designed to encourage students to consider how poetic form could begin to suggest ways in which their "poem-object(s)" and ensuing installation(s) could be spatially organised. Images from the poem would, inevitably, suggest many kinds of ideas, some of which could be used to influence the mood of the space within the installation inspired by it. While each of the resulting "poem-objects" could be viewed as a maquette for "real" space, they could equally be seen as a "mood" space(s), setting a tone from which to progress to the design of a full-scale 3D installation. The making of the installations proved to be an huge learning curve for all involved and this paper can only begin to reflect the excitement of seeing a poem transform, breathing life into a three-dimensional space. As the architect, Tom Morton, observes:

> "architectural space and poetry are closest during the process of struggle to articulate a feeling, an idea, a relationship, be it through physical form, or words, alongside their shared need for an underlying structure, or form".[*]

It is in this place that the "poetic revolt" already referred to could be said to begin. As the selected examples (below) from the range of outcomes will illustrate, the results of this project clearly demonstrate that the process of designing, building and recording the installations produced during this phase went on to provide a highly effective springboard into the second part of the project. Any tensions that may have arisen between form and feeling – as a result of the restriction implied by poetic structure (form) – subsequently served to suggest routes toward the designing of interior architectural space that are at once unprecedented, innovative and inspiring.

2(b) Project: A House for a Poet

Forming the second phase of the project, and closely inter-connected to Robillard's introductory lecture, *A House for a Poet* was led by myself, with Andy Milligan (I&ED Course Director). Each student was instructed to begin to connect explicit or implicit aspects of the poetic installation which they had collectively created, and to go on to

---

[*] Tom Morton, of Arc Architects, Fife, Scotland, from his unpublished essay, *Architecture, Poetry and Ecology: Process and Product,* written as a reflection on a collaborative project in which we were then engaged, along with a Poet, Larry Butler and a Jewellery and Metalwork Designer, Teena Ramsay, *A Place Where Thought Happens…*

Figures 5 and 6

"translate" these into a formal interior scheme– to design a living/working space for a poet within a traditional Victorian house, currently used as office space. The site, a small terraced house at 22 Springfield, Dundee (Figures 5–6) retained a number of period features, as well as having a small garden area, to the rear.

The paradox between the directness and authenticity of a poem, and its "other", visual, translation was to be a central theme in the students' work, inspiring ideas for the building and its interior space(s). Indeed, the poetic installations, which they had been constructing, were themselves most likely to have provided direct inspiration for their creative ideas for the spatial reorganisation of the building.

3 Case Study: Project by Cochrane et al

A group of five students* worked as a team during both the workshop and the installation phases of the project. The "poem-object" constructed by these students during the workshop was took its inspiration from a poem by Dylan Thomas (1914–53), "Do Not Go Gentle Into That Good Night". An example of the poetic form, the *vilanelle*, this poem is made up of 19 lines, 8 of which take the form of a refrain, being one or two lines, repeated at the end of each stanza, almost like a chorus. That this form (villanelle), which is a form of French "light" verse, is here used to address a dying man lends an ironic tone to the poem, adding to its poignancy. The poet breaks with tradition by alternating the lines of the refrain, reflecting the rebellion that the poem calls for. The effect of this is to cause the reader to be flung outwards, "Rage, rage against the dying of the light" whilst being pulled back in, at the end of the following, and each

*   Lindsay Abercrombie, Alanna Cochrane, Laura Inghram, Joanne Stewart and Lang Yang.

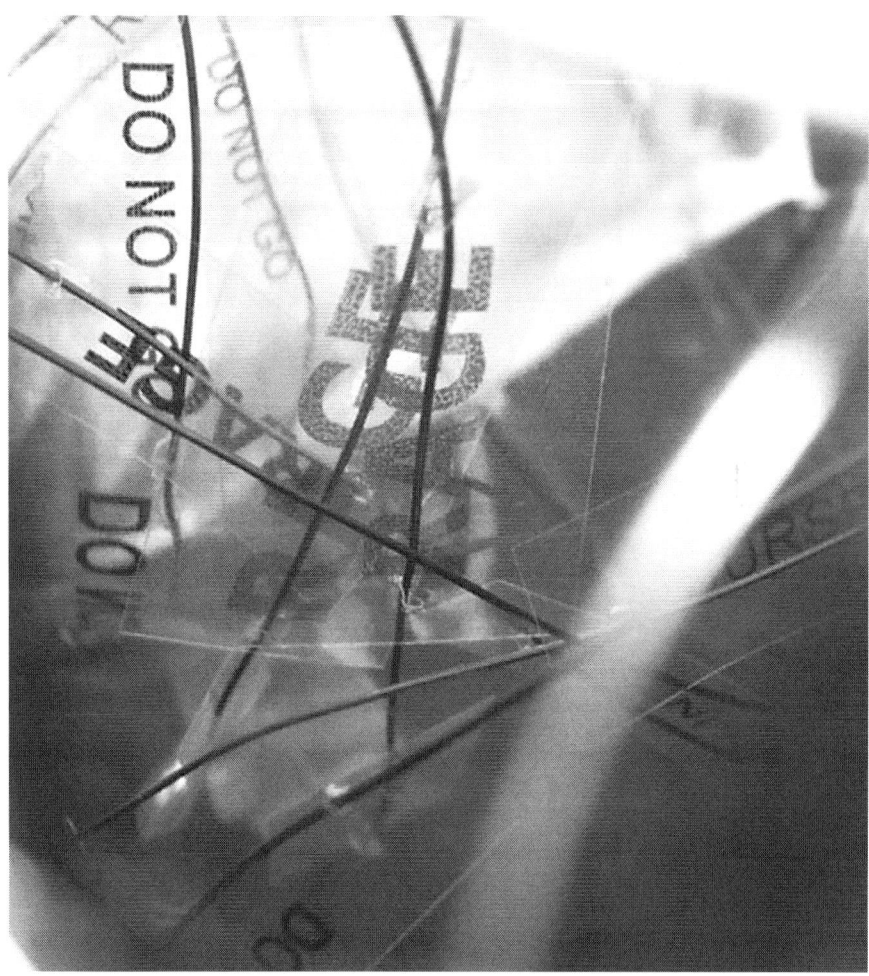

Figure 7

subsequent alternate stanza, by the second refrain, "Do not go gentle into that good night", as if in answer to, or seeking a resolution with, the first.

The *poem-object* created by the group (Figure 7) had reflected aspects of both the form and the feeling of the poem, being an almost fully closed cubic structure, but incorporating flashes of red wire, escaping from the basic form of the cube, representing the anger and rage of the initial refrain. The monochromatic colour scheme of its structure, alternating between back and white, is symbolic of the extended dualistic metaphors within the poem – of life/death, day/night, rage/acceptance – as well as the forward/backward motion created by the alternating refrains. Closer inspection of the

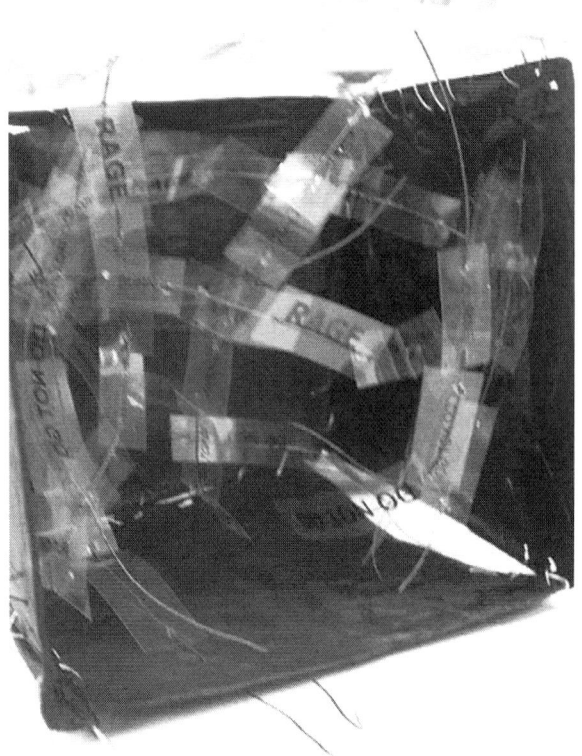

Figure 8

"poem-object" reveals an interior brimming with activity, reflecting a life-force at work, attempting to break free whilst, paradoxically, being restrained by its own structure (Figure 8), tensions which are successfully illustrated by this energetic *poem-object*, so full of life and rage contained.

The group, energised by the experience of conceiving and then producing work so quickly – over approximately six hours – went on to select a poem from the shortlist provided. The poem they chose was "Metaphors", by Sylvia Plath (1923–63). One of the group, Alanna Cochrane, understood the poem to be a riddle about pregnancy (Figure 9), stating that:

> "The various metaphors the poet uses suggest the idea of something being inside, or enclosed by something else. The exaggerated imagery that Plath uses seems to be expressing her view of the female body as being unstable. Feeling the images that she creates about pregnancy to not be entirely positive ones inspired me to begin to imagine how someone might experience our installation."[*]

---

*   In conversation with Alanna Cochrane (April, 2005)

Figure 9

In approaching the design of *A House for a Poet*, the student uses this idea of enveloped, or enclosed, growth to inspire the spaces she has designed within the building. Regarding this process, she reveals (Figure 10) that:

> "when looking at the poem again, I decided to analyse its structure more fully, focusing mainly on the enjambment that is evident within it. I began to view the punctuation as a kind of plan of the poem and then compared this with the plans of the existing building."*

What drew her attention most was the exclamation mark, at the end of the fourth line of the poem (Figure 10): "O red fruit, ivory, fine timbers!" (line 4) – the effect of which is exaggeratedly dramatic as a result of the poet's decision to use this particular punctuation.

Also, when overlaying plans of the building with a plan she made of the poem's punctuation (Figure 11), Cochrane noticed that the position of the exclamation mark fell in exactly the same position as the stairwell, cutting through each of the floors. Deciding to follow through with this experience of the poem, in relation to the building, this would go on to become a feature, around which her design for the space would develop. The very words chosen by Plath to emphasise, through her use of punctuation, were to become important to the resulting design, the "fine timbers" recurring as a physical motif throughout the house, for example.†

The paradoxical facets of the functional – structural/architectural – contrasting with the

---

* Ibid.
† Coincidentally, Brossa had devised one of his visual poems, based on the notion of making punctuation three-dimensional, for a small park included in the layout for the Velodrome d'Horta, in Barcelona. Designed by architects Esteve Bonell and Francesc Rius and inaugurated on the opening day of the World Cycle Racing Championships (1984), this was the first of Brossa's visual poems that could be three-dimensionally experienced by the public.

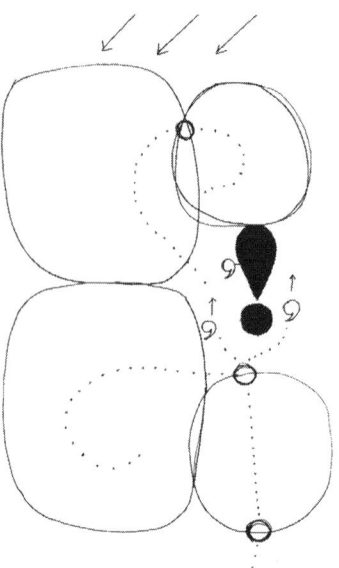

Figures 10 and 11

emotional – soft/organic – in pregnancy, that had created a particular sense of tension in the installation, inspired by this poem now came into play in the design for the house. Cochrane selected a highly functional motif with which to attempt to express the notion of growth throughout her design for the house (Figure 12). Further inspiration for this approach then came into play from the work of Frank Gehry (Figure 13), Richard Rodgers (Figure 14) and Greg Lynn*. The newel, or central pillar of the staircase structure that Cochrane designed opens out, in what she refers to as a "flowering of growth"†, at the top of the staircase, just as the central supporting structure for the installation had done (Figure 15). This "flowering", expressed structurally as a series of dramatic arched forms (Figure 16), radiating from the top of the staircase and spanning the upper level of the house.

It is here that Cochrane has chosen to locate the study, or work area for the poet since, as she puts it:

---

*
    (i)   Frank O. Gehry's designs (from 1989), in bent plywood, for the Knoll Furniture Company (Figs.34-35);
    (ii)   The cedar-clad funnelled roof structure employed by Richard Rodgers in his design for *The National Assembly for Wales* (2005), in Cardiff (Figure36);
    (iii) The forms and philosophy of Product/Interior/Architectural Designer, Greg Lynn, for his company FORM, whose designs include an *'Embryological House'* which uses a *"vital, evolving, biological model of embryological design and construction."* (Available: http://www.glform.com.html)

†   In conversation with Alanna Cochrane (April, 2005)

Figure 12

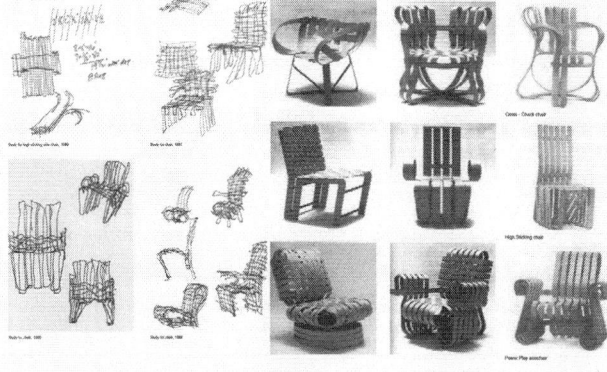

Figure 13

Figure 14

Figure 15

Figure 16

"I considered that, if the structure of the space expresses a kind of flowering of growth, then it will also inspire a flowering of ideas in the mind of the poet who spends time there..."*

This is central to the meaning embedded in Cochrane's concept for the design of the house.

* Ibid.

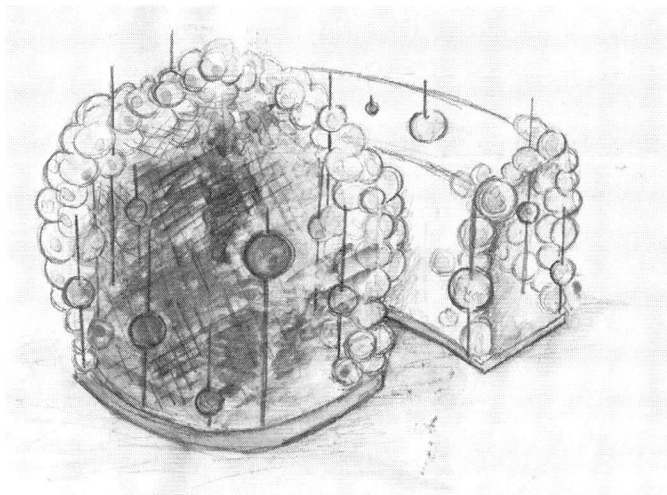

Figure 17

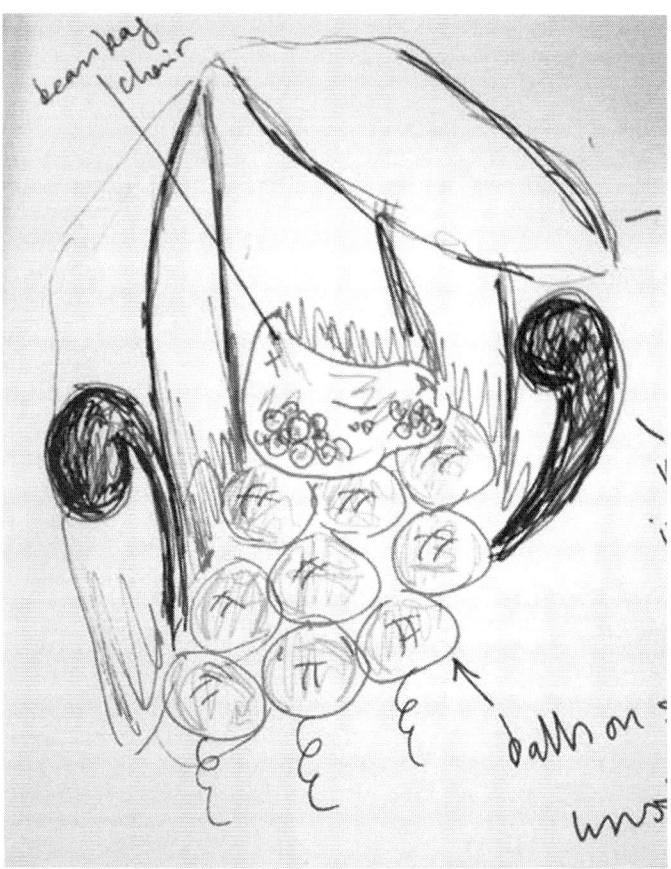

Figure 18

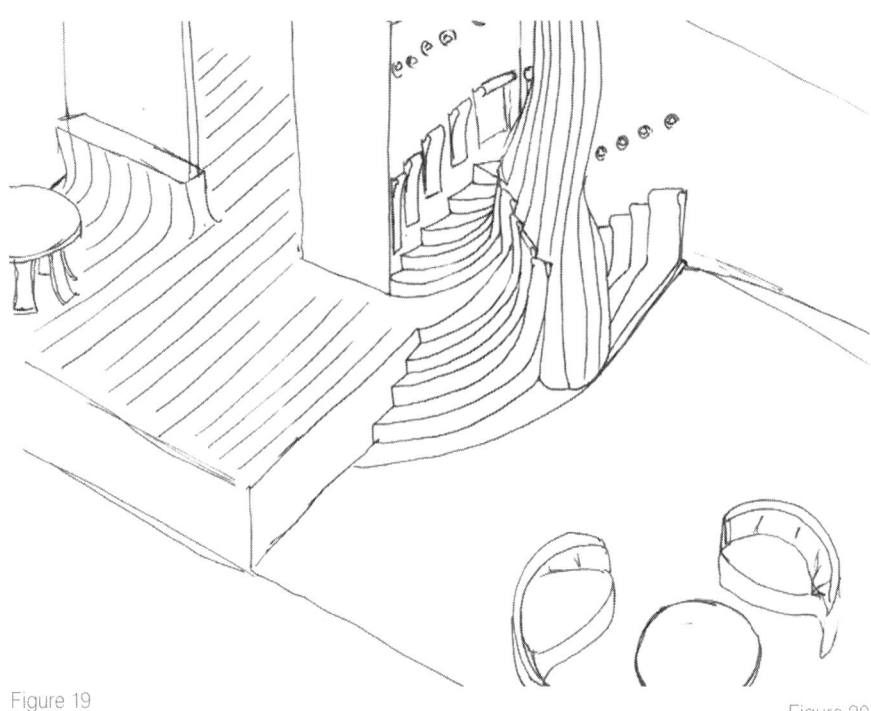

Figure 19

Figure 20

The number nine also transpired to be significant in her design, as it had been in the installation (Figure 17) and is in the poem itself: "I'm a riddle in nine syllables" (line 1). In addition to the fact that there are nine lines in the poem, the form of the number 9 itself also interested Cochrane, who compares it to both the form of a comma, in punctuation (Figure 18), as well as to the form of a human embryo (Figure 18) and to the female reproductive organs. Taking this motif and transposing it, in various ways, around the house (Figure 19), she successfully articulates the movement of the human form through space, by using it to form the shape of the handles of the doors in the house (Figure 20) – an inevitable place of pause, or punctuation – in our progress both through interior space and in our transition from interior to exterior space, and vice versa.

That Cochrane decided to emphasise the opening and closing of doors between each of the spaces in this way adds to the sense that punctuation has not only been crucial to the development of her concept but that it is also being singled out as being of significance in the journey through the spaces of the house: "A door opens. A door shuts. A glimpse has been had…"[*]

Conclusion:

The discoveries made by this group during the course of what transpired to be a genuinely groundbreaking project, clearly demonstrate that the structure, tone and images – the form and feeling – within a poem have directly and profoundly influenced the design of interior architectural space in ways that could not have previously been envisaged.

The research being carried out by Valerie Robillard and myself aims to contribute to an exploration and promotion of alternative interpretations of designing and seeks to draw on an alternative, poetical view of knowledge:

> "Poetry is [thus] an authentic instrument of knowledge and investigation of the complexity of the human being, of the reality of the world we inhabit"[†]

That the principles central to the experimental approach illustrated in this paper are potentially transferable across other disciplines remains largely unexplored, but I suggest that in the struggle to find new routes towards the uncovering of knowledge that may be closer to our realities in disciplines such as design, explanation and control undoubtedly have their place but perhaps can also accommodate other forms of experience. That poetry is capable of providing routes towards this possibility, being, as Guerrero argues,

> "the free expression of the human presence in the universe… It is the alteration of meanings, the switching of meanings, the disorder of meanings, the liberation from the one exclusively "correct" sense that is affirmed by the language of the poetic revolt"[‡]

---

[*]   Plath, quoted in Herbert and Hollis, 1992
[†]   Guerrero, 2001, p.30
[‡]   Guerrero, 2001, p.32

continues to propel both joint and independent research activity undertaken by myself and Valerie Robillard.

Works Cited

Dijkstra, Bram, *Cubism, Stieglitz, and the Early Poetry of William Carlos Williams: Hieroglyphics of a New Speech*. Princeton: Princeton University Press, 1969.

Fish, Stanley. *Is There a Text In This Class?* Cambridge and London: Harvard University Press, 1980.

Heffernan, James A. W. *The Museum of Words: The Poetics of Ekphrasis from Homer to Ashbery.* Chicago and London: University of Chicago Press, 1993.

Kranz, Gisbert. *Das Bildgedicht: Theorie, Lexikon, Bibligrapie. Vols 1, 2.* Koln: Bohlau, 1981. Vol. 3. Koln: Bohlau, 1987.

Lessing, G.E: *An Essay on the Limits of Painting and Poetry, (1776)*. Baltimore: Johns Hopkins University Press, 1984, trans. E. McCormack.

Pfister, Manfred, Scaliering Intertextualität, in *Intertextualität: Formen, Funktionen, anglistische Fallstudien*, U. Broich and M. Pfister, eds. Tübingen: Max Niemeyer, 1985.

Robillard, Valerie, 'In Pursuit of Ekphrasis: An Intertextual Approach', *Pictures into Words. Theoretical and Descriptive Approaches to Ekphrasis*, Robillard and Jongeneel, eds. Amsterdam: VU University Press, 1998, 53-72.

'Beyond Definition: A Pragmatic Approach to Intermediality', in *Media Borders, Multimodality, and Intermediality*, Lars Ellestrom, ed. (London: Palgrave MacMillan, 2010), 150-162.

Boland, E. and Strand, M. *The Making of A Poem: A Norton Anthology of Poetic Forms,* London: Norton, 2000.

Herbert, W.N. and Hollis, M. (Eds.) *Strong Words: Modern Poets on Poetry*, UK: Bloodaxe Books, 2000.

Guerrero, M. (Ed.) *Joan Brossa or The Poetic Revolt,* Barcelona: Fundacio Joan Brossa/ Fundacio Joan Miro/ Generalitat de Catalunya, 2001.

Hughes, T. (Ed.) *Sylvia Plath: Collected Poems,* London: Faber and Faber, 1981.

Robillard, V. and Jongeneel, E. *Pictures Into Words*, Amsterdam: V. U. University Press, 1988.

Thomas, D. Collected Poems of Dylan Thomas 1934-1952, USA: New Directions Corp., 1971.

List of Figures

[1] Robillard, V. (1998) Visual Ekphrasis (Ekphrastic Model), Robillard, V. and Jongeneel, E. (1998) *Pictures Into Words*, Amsterdam: V. U. University Press.
[2] Collins, B. (2004) Digging, in Heaney, S. (2004) *Room to Rhyme*, UK: University of Dundee.
[3] Brossa, J. (1984) Visual Poem in the Velodrome d'Horta, Barcelona (unknown photographer).
[4] Collins, B. (2002) Poem-House: *One thing we knew...*(Burnside, J.) Private Collection.
[5] Cochrane, A. (2006) 22, Springfield, Dundee.
[6] Cochrane, A. (2006) 22, Springfield, Dundee.
[7] Yang, L., et al, (2006) Poem-Object: *Do Not Go Gentle Into That Good Night (Thomas, D.)*
[8] Yang, L., et al, (2006) Poem-Object: *Do Not Go Gentle Into That Good Night (ditto)*
[9] Yang, L. (2006) Installation: *Metaphors (Plath, S.)*
[10] Yang, L. (2006) Installation: *Metaphors (ditto)*
[11] Cochrane, A. (2006) Plan of Punctuation in the poem *Metaphors*.
[12] Cochrane, A. (2006) Sketch of staircase (concept of growth).
[13] Gehry, F. (1989) Sketches of Chair Designs for the Knoll Furniture Company and Gehry, F. (1989) Chair Prototypes for The Knoll Furniture Company.
[14] Rodgers, R. (2005) The National Assembly for Wales (photographer unknown).
[15] Yang, L. (2006) Installation: *Metaphors* (plan view, under construction).
[16] Cochrane, A. (2006) *A Flowering of Growth* (CAD image).
[17] Cochrane, A. (2006) Sketch for Installation: *Metaphors*.
[18] Cochrane, A. (2006) Sketch for Installation: *Metaphors*.
[19] Cochrane, A. (2006) Sketch of Ground Floor.
[20] Cochrane, A. (2006) Door in Basement (CAD image).

Andrea MINA
RMIT University

Peter DOWNTON
RMIT University

MANUAL MODELLING: A PEDAGOGICAL TOOL

Introduction

Models in architecture, and most other design areas, serve as representations of design intentions. Frequently, such models are made after designing has been done by other means; sometimes designing is done while making models. In either case they serve a function in the overall process of designing something such as a space and bringing it to completion. In most cases the model serves as a communication device which enables the transfer of intent and information from one body to the next, be it from the designer to the detailer or from designer to the client. The emphasis in these models is on the thing that will be constructed. Clearly, there are a number of ideas or concepts informing the design which are to be expressed in the design. These are often discussed in a design process, but they are not singled out for examination in their own right.

The discussion here grows from an effort examine the modelling of ideas in a fairly pure form by running a design studio where this somewhat artificial task could be conducted as part of the overarching Homo Faber research project[*]. The studio was named "Manual Ideas" to express the connection of the hands and processes of thought, and centred on investigating the physical modelling of ideas. Strictly, ideas can be modelled by other ideas – this is part of metaphor. In the studio ideas were to be modelled by small physical objects. The process still entails metaphor, but a shift of medium is also required, and this was the process of greatest interest, focus and difficulty.

---

[*] Three year long Australian Research Council funded grant. Principal Investigators: Professor Mark Burry, Professor Peter Downton, Professor Michael Ostwald, Associate Professor Andrea Mina.

The Interior Design students engaged in this design studio were predominantly from second year with a couple from third year. The projects set in the studio asked students to make physical models to say something about some rather unphysical ideas. As an initial project they were each asked to model an idea they selected from a provided list that included terms such as "comfort", "responsibility" and "isolation"; next they had to select and address in modelled form, two of these ideas juxtaposed in some way. For their third project students were asked to think of three spaces each with a different function and concentrate on modelling the relationships between the spaces and also develop the narratives surrounding the spaces and the ways in which they related. From this they progressed to dealing with issues of varying scales by identifying three activities – one for a single person, one for five and a third for twenty people. For their final project, students reflected on the idea of "home" and sought to model this for themselves. While there was some universality in this, people quickly realised this could only be dealt with by developing highly subjective definitions of home based on their personal experiences. From this base, they were more able to explore the degree to which these were more widely shared and, by this means, at least offer echoes of familiarity and trigger feelings of recognition to a broader audience.

It was evident throughout that the models produced were often the result of rich thought and complex ideas, but that there are great difficulties involved in giving physical form to a set of ideas not typically thought to have physical components. Frequently the pieces produced were soaked in metaphoric layers, but the intended readings could not be accessed without the author's guidance. Once some small insight into the approach was provided by the author, reading of the model and an understanding of the author's modes of expression and exploration unfurled.

The fifteen sessions of the studio took the form of group conversations led by Andrea Mina and Peter Downton. These conversations covered the ideas themselves, their exploration and subsequent representation through a three-dimensional model, critiques of the ideas and of the modelling, discussions of possible further directions of discovery and the materials and techniques for making. Actual making was done elsewhere. Karen Hamilton (both an interior designer and jeweller) conducted a workshop-based weekly session covering making, materials and techniques and requiring students to undertake some set making assignments. Andrea and Peter could also address such issues, but the principle focus of the studio sessions was about the ideas in each project and their development and expression in the models.

Models as Foci of Conversation

Students' models served as foci of the weekly conversations; without the objects on the table the discussions would neither have been as rich or as interesting to the participants. Those sitting around the table showed their own work and appreciated, supported and critiqued the work of their peers. The fact of having invested personal concerns and effort in a model makes the producer's interest in it considerable. If it has been undertaken with care and commitment, the author has intellectual and emotional attachment to the work, and an interest in promoting and defending it. In nearly every case, students had an interest in hearing thoughts from others about what might have been different and what might be done in a future model. Almost regardless of the topic and quality of a model, it served to facilitate conversation and hence learning. This can be also said of designs that are described through images and pinned on the wall. However, in this instance, because the work is small and positioned on a table, a normal conversational situation is established. With drawings on the wall, the typical crit group is arrayed in a shallow semi-circle with the studio leaders and/or other critics nearest to the images while the remainder of the studio group is at various distances. It also means that the conversation is at the front and tends to be a performance watched by an audience. Circling models on a table, the studio members and leaders are in a more equal arrangement. People in this case often moved so as to get closer views – even if this meant they crouched or stood rather than sat. There is much to be said regarding the actual handling of an object in contrast to the detached viewing of an image located on the wall. This setting encouraged everyone to offer opinions and share concepts, techniques and experiences.

Whilst the conventions of architectural drawings demand the author convert ideas and desires into a formal language, which is in effect an abstraction of reality, the physical model provides a more direct representation of intent which is more easily understood by others. In this way the students' intent and subsequent outcomes as communicated by the models became readily available to all which in turn induced an atmosphere conducive to the free flow of conversation.

This role of models as facilitators of a conversation is easy to overlook, but was shown to have considerable significance in this studio. That they were mostly small models – often around palm size – and therefore required fairly close examination is important. It led to reasonable physical closeness, concentration on the object and therefore the ideas under discussion, and these behaviours helped produce the observed richness of the conversations. Clearly the participants have to be motivated, thoughtful, appropriately verbally adept, and not overcome by nerves. The contention here is that the models helped the students to prepare and contributed in the ways discussed above. They thus aid learning. They focused the thinking about the ideas; they were an integral part of the translation of those ideas into physical forms; they were central to learning about making; and, in addition, they were part of the process of learning from others. Of principle concern here is that through facilitation of conversations they encouraged sharing of knowledge and triggered ideas in different members of the group.

Conversation's Role in Evaluation

The role of the models as facilitators of conversation and hence learning extends to their contribution to evaluation. In design, and more widely in practice, models are constantly assessed and evaluated against a wide array of criteria – some clearly specified and well articulated others that are intrinsic, unexamined and possibly unshared. Some evaluation is almost instantaneously carried out by designers and results basically in a yes or a no, a decision to continue with the directions represented by the model or to veer in another direction in the search space of design ideas. A similar and more protracted process is conducted by groups of designers, or groups involving others, maybe consultants or clients. In these cases conversation is necessary to share values, debate degrees of success and discuss alternative future paths. Individual designers parallel these conversations by conducting their own internally or even vocalise them and debate with themselves as a means of evaluating their progress. Again models have a role in conversations.

In the studio circumstance there was also a frequent evaluative component to the conversations. This had at least two forms. Mostly evaluation played a role in discussions about what could be better. Obviously this entails values and positions about what should be the case. The studio leaders attempted to provide a democratic space of engagement and conversation by trying to argue these positions rather than asserting them as unchallengeable certainties. We also encouraged students to reflect on, and openly report, the values they brought to their evaluations of the work of themselves and others. In this way conversations quickly spread to encompass ideas that were not about a model although brought into being by a model.

Each model, and the process around it, had to be assessed for the purpose of awarding a grade to each student. In one session each student was required to submit a grade for every model presented including their own; these results were averaged and formed part of the overall grade of that project. The final project assessment was a special event with guest critics and reduced input from studio members. In physical layout and relations of people to work, it mirrored the crit panel outlined above. Utilising these processes, the models again served as facilitators of conversations – between students, students and staff, and between staff (including guest critics) – they were conversations debating values and degrees of success.

In what sense are these outcomes "Models"?

It is simple to call the objects produced by the students in the studio models because they are small, carefully made, and can be understood as representing something. They look like models. This is somewhat simplistic and it is revealing to consider why.

What are these things made in the studio models of? Nothing at all – they do not represent something that is extant. They are not models of works from the canon of architecture or interiors for instance. Compare them with the types of models seen in design practices and which take their place as part of a design process intended to result in perhaps a building or a product. These models may be made during the designing process as thinking and designing tools, or they may be made after at least initial designing, as representational and communication tools – usually for showing others (probably clients) the present state of the design. This class of models is projective. Such models are intended to describe what will come into existence in the final product or building; they serve a function in making the final building exist. Effort is spent to make the final outcome like the model. The model represents an intention; the outcome can be understood as representing the model.

None of this is true for the models made in this studio. Some of the pieces could, with various degrees of structural and detail effort, be scaled up one, two or even five hundred times and made into a (small) habitable building. This was never specified in the studio. In two of the projects there was a specification that spaces for an activity or for a number of people be designed, but the focus was on these and their relations to other spaces. So, the pieces were not models of extant buildings, nor were they models for intended buildings – even if some could potentially become so. One useful descriptor of a model is that it can be used to answer questions of interest to an interrogator that could be asked of the thing or system modelled. It can be seen that a model of an existing building, or a model representing an intended building, can both be used in this manner. It is difficult to say whether-or-not this is true in the case of the models of ideas in this studio. The answer hinges on the degree to which the relations between the ideas and the model can be understood as well as the qualities of relations.

One last examination of the characteristics of these models is necessary. That they are models of something existing or something intended was ruled out above. As physical things they do not represent other physical things; they are themselves. These models are ends in themselves and in this sense are not models at all, but final outcomes. Such objects are common in design schools. They are easier to produce in terms of time and resources than buildings or products. They do not have to satisfy the dictates of construction, costs, clients or regulatory requirements that intended future objects are subject to; rather their ends are educational. Full size objects occasionally get constructed in architecture and interior courses, but they are typically portions of a possible whole or something such as a small shelter. There is sense in which the models made for this studio are full-size; they are the size they were asked to be. They are in their intended materials, not in a material chosen to simply represent a future building material. If they are regarded as being at a scale smaller than one to one and at least tentatively considered as potential full-scale structures then a range of adjustments in the way they are viewed is necessary, as sizes, thicknesses and fixings all become items requiring detailed consideration.

Armed with this cloud of ideas about the term "model" and even accepting doubts about whether it is the right term to describe what the students made, we will continue to use the term as it is the word most likely to be applied to them by others.

Materialisation

The students had to establish a way of understanding the idea or ideas that were the givens of any one of the projects. They also needed to find a way of dealing with their particular views in a physical form, what materials to use and how to make their model. Such things often do not evolve sequentially, and if they do, the order in which they unfold may vary from instance to instance. It seems that most often these matters at least partially co-evolve and mutually inform and shape one another. Confronted with a mute object the viewer can conjure concepts concerning the ideas embodied in the object. but these may easily be at odds with the intentions of the maker. Minimally, the maker needs to provide a small key to unlock their intended ideas; and once this understanding, the relation between the ideas being dealt with and the model presented can be unravelled, enriched and explored by the viewer. Once this narrative is shared, the viewer's ability to understand the piece entirely in their own terms is reduced, while the maker's intentions become available in varying degrees. The reading is then potentially played out as a resolution of the tensions between the two understandings.

The processes of moving from idea to physical form entails many possible choices, decisions and evaluations. How arbitrary are choices of forms and shape to express ideas? On what grounds, for example, does a designer decide that something round (maybe a circle or a sphere) symbolises or represents the universal, or completeness, or calmness? Sometimes the choice involves selecting an historic cultural archetype that has been valued in one or more cultures for centuries; sometimes the choice rests on an original argument. There are variations in the degree to which the representational form can be shared. In the case of the argued representation, new insight or understanding may be offered as an alternative to the comfort and "rightness" of the culturally entrenched form. The choice process can be predominantly emotionally driven or it might be essentially intellectual.

Designers derive forms for their current task from their personal catalogues of forms, re-using, re-interpreting and evolving prior forms. Part of the success of the mapping of form onto idea results from the degree of literality employed. Too much abstraction leads to unintelligibility; too little results in cringe-worthy banality. The tasks for the students in this studio entailed pitching their ideas and physical mappings at an appropriate level of literalness.

Outcomes

The richness of thought and content in the work produced is best discussed by contrasting the different approaches adopted by Vaughan Burns and Katie Collins. Vaughan's response to modelling the idea of complexity (Figure 1) was to engage with the idea of a complex ecological system composed of a number of disparate elements which through their inter-dependent relationships form a coherent and harmonious whole. This was achieved through the making of a sphere composed of many parts made from contrasting materials. The junctions between these materials were in themselves formed along highly complex edges further adding to the articulation of complexity. Katie, set the task of modelling the idea of isolation, (Figure 2) used her model as a form of machine which demanded the active participation of the viewer to articulate her intentions. Through the use of pulleys and thread fourteen small components, initially located as a unitied and interlocking whole at the centre of a sphere made from five circles of wire, were able to be individually moved apart to the edge of the sphere. Her machine enabled the generation of space through distance with isolation manifest as the gap in-between.

Figure 1

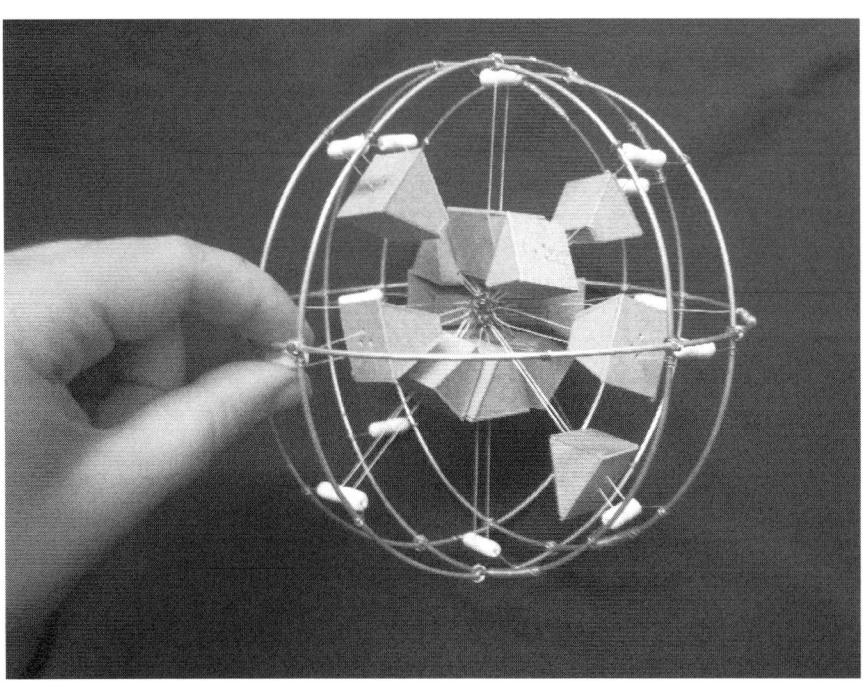

Figure 2

Manual Modelling 199

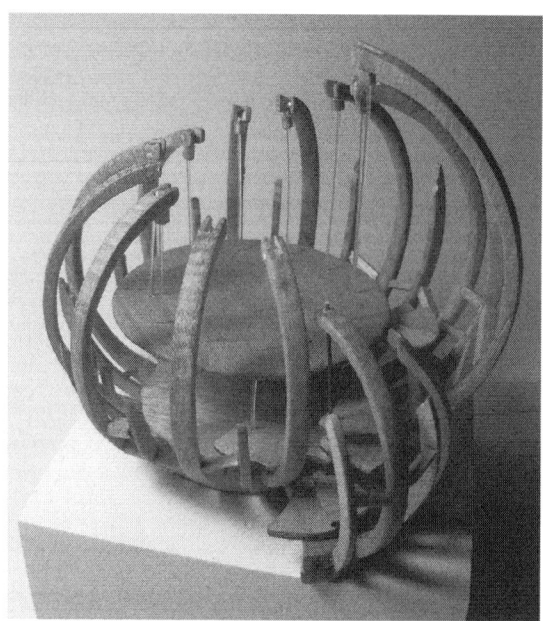

Figure 3

In response to brief #3 Vaughan modelled the activities of reading, story-telling and watching (Figure 3). His composition of spaces is held together by a series of curved ribs from which varying sized circular platforms are suspended. The watching space dominates the composition being accessed via a spiral staircase. The story-telling space is located below in a space illuminated by light filtering through the open lattice structure. This space is privileged by its central location and large scale as it serves as the forum for social construction through the dissemination of the stories and knowledge gained from the reading space located at the foot of the composition. The reading space is conceived of as a quiet and introspective space.

Katie addressed the idea of a dinner party narrative through her machine (Figures 4a, 4b). This involved the narration of a linear timeline experienced by the host involving the spaces of preparation, dining and cleaning. The artefact described a linear movement from one space to the next, working with the ideas of one space coming into being on the pretext of that which immediately preceded it, neither being able to be simultaneously occupied. These spaces were described by the space contained between two timber rings joined together by flexible brass plates allowing for the expansion and contraction of the central space. The preparation space is described through this space in its enlarged configuration followed by its contraction during the time of dining and by its ultimate collapse at the conclusion of the event.

The inspiration for Vaughn's response to brief #4 is from a quote by Thoreau who had three chairs at his cabin in Walden, "one for solitude, two for company, and three for society". He has modelled some of the elements which make up a community. The large communal singing space for twenty is made from aluminium shingles positioned to face upwards in the evocation of the uplifting power of music with the suggestion of an aspiration towards a higher level of being. His place for five is a dining space intended as a space of interaction, ritual and enjoyment, made with the shingles facing downwards in an effort to communicate a sense of grounding. The space for one is manifest as spherical; unique and individual yet made from the same shingle-like building blocks used to make up the other spaces. The composition is held together within a metal cuboid shaped frame (Figures 5a and 5b) which may be read as representing the universal nature of that required to make up community. Of interest is the linear nature of this outcome in contrast to his previous artefacts which are mostly curvaceous. This can be attributed to the fact of his being encouraged to engage with materials that are not as conducive to carving from a solid as had been his previous practice; a demonstration in the powerful influence materials have over outcomes.

However in Vaughan's response to modelling "home" (Figure 6) he reverted back to the familiar by carving timber to paper thinness. The genesis of his object is in the idea that the home is created around a fire. The etymology of "hearth" reaches back to the Greek goddess of the home Hestia, always the first to be honoured in rituals. Guided by the belief that if rituals are a chief ingredient in the creation of the home, then it is around the fire that these rituals revolve. Another reading has the model as a metaphor for homes with the structure inside the three "leaves" representing the physicality of houses and the abstract philosophical concept of the home the "leaves" themselves tightly wrapped about the central hearth.

Figures 4a and 4b

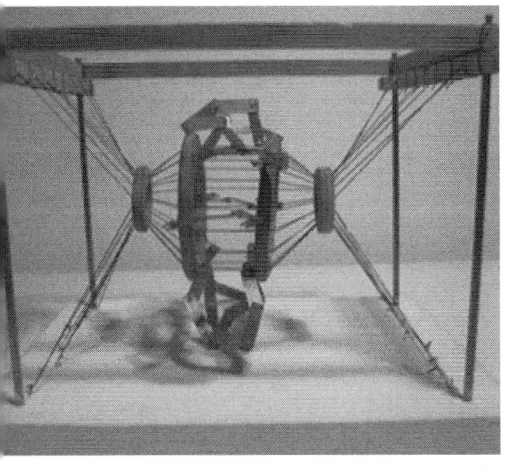

Figure 5a

Figure 5b

Most of the projects were done over three or four weeks each. In the first studio sessions for each project we discussed the ideas to be focussed upon with the conversations covering each person's initial views. Hearing the initial intentions of others and discussing the array of concepts circling the ideas led to an enriched conversational field which gathered momentum as the sessions continued. As inter-personal trust increased, the character of this conversation could become more open and personal. We made clear the notion that no one student held a patent over an idea but that ideas were accessible to all and it is in the physical manifestation of the idea through the use of particular materials and their relationships that the authors could lay claim to the ideas.

Usually in the second session of a project there were sketchy design ideas appearing – mostly on paper. By the third session these were more detailed, sometimes ideas were presented in the form of a modelled mock-up and sometimes there were the beginnings of a partially-built final model. For the last project a rough model in an easy-to-use material was specified as a required step. The final session for each project involved presenting each model to the group. Throughout, visual and written documentation of the projects were also required. These emphasised designing and making processes and later ones also sought reflection upon, and curation of, prior work. There was also a group conversational memory able to be drawn upon for commentary and comprehension.

Another albeit abstract form of materialisation was achieved through the photographs taken by the students of the spaces contained within the models as distinct from imaging the models as objects located on a surface within space. These photographs provided beguiling effects through their dissolution of scale and their abstraction of

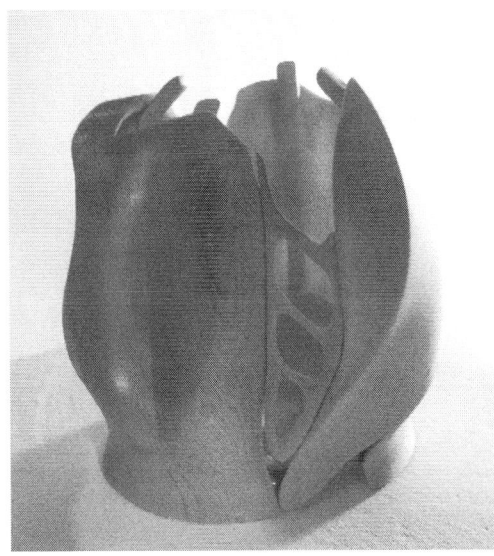
Figure 6

the materiality of the surfaces describing the spaces. Considering this was a studio for interior design students we felt it important to direct the conversations towards the making of spaces as distinct from the making of objects.

Materials

Except for a mock-up or when used in an exciting or entertaining manner, the common materials seen in studio modelling were banned. Card, balsawood and paper, typically asked to represent sheet and mass construction materials, were forbidden; foam-core was frowned upon. Students were challenged to investigate the expressive potentials of any other material. Timbers, metals, fabrics, plaster, and clay were used in a range of ways. However as the studio progressed the use of plaster became something to avoid. Far more unusual materials were explored – fish scales and bones, leather, Vaseline, oven-baked modelling putty, toilet paper and wax. Materials were mostly glued, but precise friction-fitting, and riveting were employed. Materials were cut, bent, carved, sanded, vacuum-formed, woven, knitted, crocheted, moulded and machine routed.

The large materials palette aided expressive possibilities when compared to those materials that were banned. A fabric might be much more useful to convey the idea of "comfort" for instance than is card. In the main, however, the relation between the materials chosen and the idea dealt with was not this direct. It is frequently the case that the kinds of materials used result in a more seductive outcome than can be produced by card or balsa. There is some danger in this – perhaps the making and materials are seducing the viewer, but the ideas embodied are ordinary. When, however, the ideas and the object are working in unison, the deployment of a fascinating and carefully chosen collection of materials supports and enhances the modelling of ideas.

Asking students to engage with material palettes that were in the main unfamiliar to them encouraged the production of forms and spaces that managed to negate preconceived outcomes. Of more interest was the manner in which these different materials were joined. The common use of glue was in many instances unsuitable which in turn led to the development of jointing techniques which in themselves began to influence the nature of the forms produced and their contained spaces. For example a circular form made from pieces of mirrored acrylic joined by metal rings produced space defined by the irregular angles of the planes of acrylic relative to each other. This in turn produced an interior space composed of multiple reflected images.

Conclusion

As the production of work progressed through the studio a sense of frustration was experienced by the studio leaders due to the enormous potential for design development contained within the models. In so far as the models were effective tools for the exploration and communication of ideas and consequently the production of meaningful conversations and the facilitation of learning, they also provided glimpses of future possibilities which were intentionally not further developed. We began to understand that it was through the objects' materiality and hence making of spaces that one could discover qualities of space which could not be preconceived. It became obvious the next step should be the exploitation of these discovered qualities through the design of specific spaces.

Associate Professor Andrea MINA
RMIT University
School of Architecture & Design
GPO Box 2476V
Melbourne
Victoria 3001
Australia
andrea.mina@rmit.edu.au
+ 61 3 9925 2648

Professor Peter DOWNTON
RMIT University
School of Architecture & Design
GPO Box 2476V
Melbourne
Victoria 3001
Australia
peter.downton@rmit.edu.au
+61 3 9925 2550

Cristina FIORDIMELA
Politecnico di Milano

THE MODEL AS TEACHING TOOL, EXHIBIT OBJECT AND MUSEUM INSTALLATION – DOMESTIC INTERIORS DESIGNED BY LE CORBUSIER MADE REAL

Introduction

This forms part of a research project on the theme of "Conservation, interpretation and museum conversion of residential interiors designed by the masters of the Modern Movement". The scope of this research is to compose a critical review of the processes of transforming architectural interior design projects into museum pieces which aim to preserve them and demonstrate their cultural value [1].

The museological conversion of interiors designed by architects involves a metamorphosis from private living space to architecture museum exhibit, with the aim of conserving, studying and communicating the meaning of that architectural project and the way it has changed over time. There are various ways in which this can be achieved and this depends on many factors: the specific local situation; the state of conservation; the history of the project; the availability of archive documents showing the original plans and modifications; even curatorial choices based on the approach to restoration involved in the design of the museum installation, and the way original fixtures and fittings are to be organised, and whether these are recreated or later reproductions of them are used.

However by examining some recent case studies it has been possible to identify some techniques which can be used to classify the different approaches to these projects in museographical terms, and they can be divided into two categories: museum conversions *in situ* [2] and the recreation of interiors within a museum.

The latter can be further divided into "the exhibition of period room motivated by a didactic purpose" [3] and the presentation of interiors designed by the Modern movement and then developed in the *Triennali* of the 1950s [4], which also make reference to the culture of the architectural project and the forms of three dimensional representation used for teaching purposes in schools of architecture.

The fact that the model can be walked through is a characteristic aspect of the representation of modern architecture where

> "whereas the participation of man in classical representative architecture could be observed from the presence of formal symbols and visual perceptions of the work, in the new bourgeois architecture and interior design there is a considerably closer and more direct relationship to this participation which does not simply imply a visual problem but rather requires the complete use of the architectural space" [5].

From the convergence of these different approaches to projects arise the recreations of domestic environments, in museums or travelling exhibitions and their configuration is determined by a synthesis of the reconstruction of the interior space and the museographical staging. The reconstructed interior is the result of many factors: critical reading of the architectural plans; whether it is possible to survey the original existing structure; the introduction of original furnishings or using later reproductions of them, the methodological approach to the project and what has been learned from this in the preparatory stages.

Therefore, in the context of a museum, a real scale model may carry a range of different meanings. Due to the diverse interpretative approaches employed, the recent museum reconstructions of Le Corbusier's interiors represent a brief review of case studies compiling the work of one architect, where the real scale model is presented as an architectural artifact which helps to inform the way in which the different parts and contents of the display are organised to fulfill their educational function. In the case of Le Corbusier, another level of reading of the model relates to how it relates to other models used by the exhibition designer to show, present and exhibit their own architectural designs [6].

The Real Scale Model as the Guiding Principle/Defining Feature of a Permanent Collection and Pedagogical Museum Experience

The model is at the origin of the idea behind architecture museums [7]. It can be created and interpreted in many ways, but above all it is its pedagogic value which is the most important quality in the context of a museum. This is true whether it is a preparatory study of a project or a whole or partial reproduction of a piece of architecture. The life-size copy of a habitation cell of the Unité of Marseilles, installed at the *Cité d'Architecture* in Paris, was designed at the same time as the outfitting of the gallery dedicated to modern and contemporary architecture. The museum already featured many architectural models and casts [8].

If it is true that each exhibition design corresponds to an interpretation of the content being exhibited, the same principle applies to the model. It can be seen as a critical reading of the architectural item and at the same time a device for conveying the content of the project and an educational experience [9]. So in this sense it is important, if the project is to be a success, to consider how a display using various media – drawings, virtual models, photographs, texts – can be integrated with the display of the life-size model. The latter takes on a multifaceted identity in museums: it is an exhibited object, a cognitive tool in which, according to Bruno Zevi,

> "architectural criticism is stated not in words but in the very language of architects, in 3-D reality" [10],

and in this case, as it can be walked through, a museum itinerary. A real scale model made by Le Corbusier himself provided inspiration for the Barcelona team of the GAO studio (Fernando Marzà, Josep Subirós, Eulalia Bosch) when they had to insert a full scale maquette of an apartment in the Unité d'Habitation in Marseilles.

They used the model to communicate the innovative aspects of the design. It is a very well-known image which has become the icon of the design itself, thanks to its communicative force. In this model Le Corbusier wanted to express the principle of distribution of space, expressed through the relationship between the habitation cell and the architectural structure. The same image was interpreted by GAO to convey, with the same media impact, the intersection of the reproduction of the apartment in the museum (Figure 1).

Figure 1: The intersection of the reproduction of the Unité d'Habitation Marseille apartment in Cité de l'Architecture, Paris. Image @ GAO

Marzà explains

> "The first image that came to mind was the very famous one showing a hand, perhaps Le Corbusier's, while it is inserting an apartment into the structure of the building. Le Corbusier used the metaphor of the relationship between a bottle (cell) and bottle rack (structure) several times, always in order to explain the Unité, and it was also reproduced in his written texts. Therefore, the representation of the Unité in the museum had to use that image again. The intersection between the structure of the Unité building and the gallery, both shown on the same scale, gave an exact image of that which had to be reproduced and how it had to be done. We decided to set up the full scale model at the far end of the gallery. This position offered a splendid view of the building" [11] (Figures 2, 3)

Figure 2: The reproduction of the Unité d'Habitation Marseille apartment in the gallery of the Contemporary and Modern Architecture Cité de l'Architecture 2007 Paris. Photo CF

Figure 3: The reproduction of the Unité d'Habitation apartment in the gallery of the Contemporary and Modern Architecture Cité de l'Architecture Paris 2007. Photo CF

From the start of the museographical and museological project, the model must be able to perform the double function of a comprehensive representation of Le Corbusier's contribution at the time of postwar architecture and also form part of the museum display, sited within the space represented and at the same time in the space where it is displayed in the museum. In other words the space actually defined by the real-life model must serve both as an immersion into Le Corbusier's interior space as well as providing an observatory over the museum space and the architectural structure of the building, which thus becomes part of the museum itself.

He tells us that the decision to entrust this job to a group of high-school students from 17 technical and professional colleges made it possible to salvage the mastery of technical skill and craftsmanship, applied to 1950s architecture, which was at risk of disappearing [12]. Just as Le Corbusier believed

> "one designs while making a model",

the executive phase of the museum model is similarly a time for verifying, but also for experimenting with new materials and for prototyping furnishings [13]. So the model is also the result of a process of background work and research, and offers inspiration for a critical reading of the mediums of representation. In this way the model can be understood as having a teaching and research function, where also the methodology of the planning and management phases of the project become part of the exhibit.

This aspect of the reconstruction, which constitutes the most original part of the project, is however not expressed in the final version of the model, which appears simply as a representative synthesis of an interior, but does not try to recreate the analogical, philological and didactic methods, which are simply implied. Werner Szambien, who in his *Le musée d'architecture* explores the theme of the reorganisation and installation of the Musée des Monuments Historiques –today the Cité de l'architecture- suggests that the meaning of an architecture museum based, in this way, around a collection of models and casts, can be innovative if it is designed to offer to the public a" double meaning: of the monuments and the way they are represented." In spatial terms such a vision can take shape, Szambien writes,

> "following three different lines: the architectural shell as an allegory of the content, conceptualizing the layering and interspersing the progress from one door to the next with areas for reflection [...] according to a pedagogy of discovery, which implies a vast range of ways to access knowledge." [14].

Instead the new arrangement adopts the logic of organised nineteenth century viewing galleries as a way of taking in everything in one gaze, giving rise here to a scenario in which the form of the real scale model is not related either to the perspective possibilities of the dimensions of the space in the architecture museum or to the communication techniques and display media used in contemporary museums.

The Real Scale Model as a Fragment of a Narrative Pathway

> "The moment you start to decide how to display and arrange a piece of architecture, the question of how it is to be organized is raised." [15].

The reconstruction of the Unité displayed at the Cité de l'architecture and Cabanon's real scale model in the exhibition entitled *Le Corbusier, un homme à sa fenêtre* [16], and set up by the students working under Michel Dudon, offer a comprehensive overview of Le Corbusier's interiors and are displayed in a way which follows both didactic and cognitive processes.

Figure 4: The reproduction of the Cabanon in the Musée de Beaux-Arts 2006-2007, Nantes. Photo @ Musée de Beaux-Arts de Nantes – Cécile Clos

The full scale model takes on a different meaning if its relationship to the flow of the museum display is considered as a primary aspect of its reconstruction on a par with its representative quality. In this way the model contributes together with the multiplicity of voices to compose a multimedia retelling of the architectural project, which is developed in the way the exhibit is displayed. This often happens in the case of temporary exhibitions for instance, which do not aim to provide a unitary vision of the domestic interior, but rather represent a critical interpretation which only deals with certain aspects of the architectural project. The model itself constitutes in its own way an installation inserted into that of the exhibition as a whole, with spatial connections linking them.

This is particularly evident in the recreation of the duplex, dual aspect apartment of the Unité of Marseilles at Tokyo's Mori Art Center, which was created for the exhibition entitled *Le Corbusier, sa vie et son œuvre, une vie de créativité* (2007) [16] and some years before in *Synthèse des Arts*(1986), where the partial reconstruction of an interior of the Unité d'habitation di Marsiglia by Ruggero Tropeano, defines one of the rooms through which the exhibition flows. The structure of the maquette also contained extensions of the main display in which it was possible to enter more deeply at the same time as viewing the main exhibition. The principle of the real scale model as a multimedia display is reinforced by graphical content on the surfaces of the exterior walls of the model, where a section of the ergonomic relationships which concern the design of the interiors and their furnishings is displayed. The organization of the layout of the exhibit in Tokyo is characterised by two other real scale reconstructions, that of Le Corbusier's *atelier* in the apartment in Rue Nungesser et Coli in Paris and the interior of the Cabanon, reproduced by the Cassina Study Center. In the reconstructed *atelier* works of art and original contents are shown. In this way the model takes on the function of a display cabinet of the interior which shows the contextual references to the objects exhibited in it.

The main question from a museographical point of view is how to differentiate between the original features from those which have been recreated and how to present clearly the model as a reproduction and also as part of a narrative in which it tells a tale [17]. The different layers of these spatial experiences which are concentrated in the real scale model evoke analogous situations to those which can be found in the museum conversion processes involved in *in situ* house-museums, where one of the crucial aspects of the project is to activate multiple layers of possible readings of the architectural composition of the interiors, by crossing the thresholds which mark the passage from private domestic space to public space.

The Recreation of an Interior Becomes an Exhibition Space for Contemporary Art

In 1987 Claudio Parmiggiani arranged a selection of his works inside the 1:1 scale maquette of the gallery at Villa La Roche. The model was built the same year, by the architect Jerome Habersetzer for the exhibition *L'Esprit Nouveau* [18] in the spaces of the Ancienne Douane des Musées in Strasbourg. Parmiggiani's works dialogue simultaneously with the old architecture of the customs house, and with Habersetzer's interpretation of the Villa La Roche gallery. The artist's attention is focused on the space as the object/container within a different architectural language, as well as the theme of the art collection, and on reconsidering the idea of architecture as a pure work of art. Arranged on the external walls of the maquette, the works highlight the loss of meaning between the external and internal environment in the reconstruction.

This experience brings to the museum the possibility of acting in an experimental way, working freely with the typological elements of the architecture of Le Corbusier's interiors, redefining their meaning in a topical context. The way the works are presented brings the intrinsic qualities of the gallery space up to date, creating an inversion in the rules of how to read the interior space being represented, from which its essence as an exhibition pathway can emerge as separate from the domestic environment of the villa.

The Lifesize Model of an Interior as an Autonomous and Itinerant Device Used in Exhibition Design

The Cabanon presented by Cassina, curated by Filippo Alison [20] reproduction takes the form of a travelling pavilion which fulfils the dual purpose of exhibiting the space of the Cabanon itself, while investigating the ergonomic and technological features of various furnishings. What makes this experience different from other reconstructions of the Cabanon is its strong museum-like character. This derives from the inclusion of an introductory space before visitors enter the reconstructed interiors. It is therefore an environment dedicated to conveying the design content, in this case by means of the projection of a story told through images. The purpose of the model as the representation of an interior is explicitly declared by the very structure of the pavilion. From the outside it has an anonymous appearance and is identifiable only through the graphics (Figure 5).

Figure 5: The reproduction of the Cabanon presented by Cassina in the park of Triennale di Milano, curated by Filippo Alison, Milano 2006. Photo CF

Figure 6: Pattern executed in research and development centre Cassina curated by Filippo Alison (2006) for the reproduction of the Cabanon

The re-transcription of the exterior space is thus negated. Instead, it is suggested inside, by using small dioramas placed near the windows. This has the purpose of showing the movement of the window leaves designed by Le Corbusier with the Mediterranean location in mind (Figure 6).

The lifesize reproductions of Le Corbusier interiors, a few recent examples of which have been cited above, show a sample of variations in the practice of creating lifesize models for museums, which raise questions about how to represent other interiors from modern architecture.

In such a transformation of a cognitive, analytical process, based on plans from the archive and on the history of criticism of modern architecture, the lifesize exhibition model is basically a way of representing a project for an interior in a museum context in which, as Alison explains,

"It's a case of reconstructing the phenomena around the thing, and not of the thing" [21].

References

[1] The definition of the Museum ICOM-UNESCO . Seul 2004. "A museum is a non-profit making, permanent institution in the service of society and of its development, and open to the public, which acquires, conserves, researches, communicates and exhibits, for purposes of study, education and enjoyment, material evidence of people and their environment.".

[2] They include: restoration à l'identique, in which interiors are restored so that they resemble their original state, with a limited number of communication tools; the addition of separate spaces, either linked to or adjacent to the residence, in which a sort of visitor's centre is set up or where the contents of the house are displayed; turning the home into a "living museum" where its residential function is retained, even only partially; the transformation of the living space into an exhibition space.

[3] Basso Peressut 2005, 18.

[4] Jeremy 2006, 8-30.

[5] De Fusco 1964, 143.

[6] Rossi 1979, 100-1006. Rossi underlines the comunicative value of the models used by Le Corbusier, as manufatured representations of a "semantic communication [...] which, as a representation of the laws of shaping space and as a typological and technical demonstration of the mechanism tends to appear as a cross-section or dissection of the executive process of the project.".

[7] Sardo 2004, 161-162.

[8] Szambien 1988.

[9] Dulau, Mory 2007.

[10] Zevi, 1964, 651.

[11] Fernando Marzà, 22.02.2007 interview.

[12] Pierre-Antoine Gatier (architect of Monuments Historiques, oversaw the construction of the model), 10.01.2007 interview.

[13] Dulau, Mori op. cit., 129-157.

[14] Szambien 1988, 186.

[15] De Fusco 1968, 187.

[16] Nantes. Musée de beaux-arts. 26.10.2006 – 8.1.2007. Apart from Cabanon's lifesize model, to-scale models reproduced by the students under Tadao Ando were also shown.

[17] Mori Art Center, Tokyo 26.5.2007- 24.9.2007
Dulau, Mory 2007, 124 "The recreation of the interior of the Unité for the Tokyo

exhibition was prepared with the help of reliefs and plans which were drawn up or the recreation at Palais Chaillot". The way it was configured was the result of curatorial and museographical display choices which differed widely.

[18] The juxtaposition of authentic parts and reconstructions also characterizes the reproductions in the Unité d'Habitation curated by Ruggero Tropeano in 1986 at Karlsruhe in *Synthèse des Arts* and in 1987 at the Centre Georges Pompidou in collaboration with Jean-Louis Cohen for the exhibition entitled, *L'Aventure, Le Corbusier*.

[19] *L'Esprit Nouveau. Le Corbusier et l'industrie 1920-1925*. Strasbourg 11.7.1987–31.10.1987.

[20] Alison 2006.

[21] Alison. 15.12. 2004, interview.

Bibliography

Aynsley Jeremy. 2006. The modern period room – a contradiction in terms?. In *The Modern Period Room. The construction of the exhibited interior 1870 to 1950*. Oxon: Routledge.

Alison Filippo. 2006. *Le Corbusier. Interior of the Cabanon. Le Corbusier 1952-Cassina 2006*. Milano 2006: TriennaleElecta.

Basso Peressut, Luca. 2005. *Il museo moderno*. Milano: Lybra Immagine.

De Fusco, Renato. 1964. *L'idea di architettura: storia della critica da Viollet-le-Duc a Persico*. Milano: Edizioni di Comunità.

Dulau, Robert and Mory, Pascal. 2007. *Echelle 1 Le Corbusier. Experience & pedagogical realisation*. Paris: Éditions PC.

Gribenski J., Meyer V., Vernois S. 2007. *La maison de l'artiste. Construction d'un espace de représentations entre réalité et imaginaire (XXVII-XX siècles)*. Rennes: Presse Universitaire de Rennes.

Leoncini L., Simonetti F., 1998. *Abitare la storia. Le dimore storiche/museo. Restauro sicurezza didattica comunicazione*, Torino : Umberto Allemandio & C. – 2005. Study seminar Regione Lombardia. Milano.

Rossi, Aldo Loris. 1979. I modelli originali e le riproduzioni de-costruibili. In *C.E. Jeanneret-Le-Corbusier*. Roma: Officina Edizioni.

Sardo, Nicolò. 2004. *La figurazione plastica dell'architettura*. Roma: Kappa Edizioni.

Szambien, Werner. 1988. *Le musée d'architecture*. Paris: Picard Éditeur.

Zevi, Bruno. 1964. Michelangelo in prosa. *L'architettura cronaca e storia*, no. 99, Juanary.

Cristina Fiordimela, PhD in Interior architecture and Exhibition design from the Department of Architectural Projet at the Politecnico di Milano, where she lectures at the faculty of Architecture and Society. A member of ICOM, since 2005 she writes for *Il giornale dell'architettura* (Allemandi) in the section dedicated to museums.
cristina.fiordimela@fastwebnet.it/cristina.fiordimela@polimi.it
T +39 3381401598/ +39 0223995035.
Via Balzaretti 34, 20133 Milano, Italy.

Tactics for alteration

Edward HOLLIS
Edinburgh College of Art

INTRODUCTION – TACTICS FOR ALTERATION

"Anyone can be creative, it's re-writing someone else that's difficult"

(Bertolt Brecht, quoted in Milling and Ley[*])

The relationship between architecture and the interior has long been a fraught one. Interior designers regularly criticise architects for being insensitive, while architects are prone to dismiss interior designers as superficial decorators.

Recently, many interior designers have rebranded themselves as interior architects, in a bid to leave their decorative reputation behind. On the other hand, architects have found themselves working more often on the re-design of the interiors of existing buildings rather than the invention of new ones.

This new practice, somewhere between architecture (invention) and decor has lacked a proper discourse of its own, finding itself beholden instead to the ideologies of conservation or restoration, both wedded to the preservation of historic artefacts and the defiance of the wounds of time.

But the distinction between the decorated interior and the building is less a matter of material or ideology than one of duration. Decor is designed to be ephemeral, architecture to be permanent. Their senses of history, materiality, and professional practice are rooted in distinct notions of time.

And time is a process of change. Not even the pyramids have escaped the depredations

---

[*] Milling, Jane and Ley, Graham. 2001. *Modern theories of performance.* New York: Palgrave.

of the centuries, let alone the cushions in Marie Antoinette's boudoir. This section presents the tools and tactics with which current practitioners and theorists address the alteration of buildings and interiors.

Richard Murphy was an early British apostle of the Italian architect Carlo Scarpa, who worked on a series of historic buildings in the Veneto in the 1950'-70's. Scarpa's practice, and subsequently Murphy's, attempts to systematise the relationship between modern architecture and historical buildings. In both, new additions are expressed as distinct fragments collaged onto ancient structures, both retaining their own autonomy and creating a new and dynamic whole.

This process has been dissected by Fred Scott, in *On Altering Architecture*. First, there is the stripping back of a building to its irreducible shell – a ruination accompanied by forensic excavation. Next, there is the reconstruction of the original building, or the suturing of the wounds previously inflicted upon it; and finally there is the addition of the new architecture into the old: the addition of a building-within-a-building, or the imposition of a new layer onto the repaired ruin.

Graeme Brooker and Sally Stone's essay on the use of *Spolia* subverts Scott's neat model. The construction of new buildings from the fragments of old ones, be it Lo-Tek's shipping containers or Ben Kelly's use of "found" devices from the construction site, disrupts our sense of time, hierarchy and authorship in architecture, asking us to reconsider the relationship of past to present, and original to altered states.

Their paper ends in Venice. It is here that Carlo Scarpa created his most exquisitely altered corpse in the interiors of the Palazzo Querini Stampalia; and it is also here, in a city built from the fragments of other cities, that we find, par excellence, altered architectures, and architectures of alteration.

Edward HOLLIS
Edinburgh College of Art

INTERVIEW WITH FRED SCOTT

"It's a bit like a TV studio, isn't it?" he grins. It is. The pub in which we meet has all the makeshift quality of a set: the raw sound stage provided by the architecture of the museum of London softened by a minimum of patterned wallpaper, furnishing and hangings. Lights hang from gantries on the ceiling.

Fred Scott is a softly spoken man – so softly spoken that I have to strain to hear him over the hubbub of a city office on their Christmas lunch. He seems to ramble, and never answers a direct question directly. He speaks like a man with infinite time on his hands.

Which is what makes it all the more surprising when, from time to time, Fred speaks directly, for his ramblings are labyrinths so cunningly contrived that they lead you unwittingly to exactly where he wants you to be. Nothing he says is, in the end, extraneous, and nothing cynical or meaningless about it at all.

I am here to interview Scott about the genesis of his book *On Altering Architecture* published in 2007 by Routledge. It's a wonderful book – not least because it is beautifully written, in a prose as crystalline and economical as its author's conversation is prolix; and it is the first and certainly the clearest statement about this increasingly important practice.

It is ironic that, in an age in which the bread and butter of architects work (certainly in Britain anyway) is provided by altering existing buildings, rather than inventing new ones, the architecture schools, and architectural critics and writers have so little to say about the practice. There is Kenneth Powell's *Architecture Reborn* (Lawrence King 1999), and Graeme Brooker and Sally Stone's *Re-Readings: Interior Architecture and the Principles of Remodelling Buildings* (RIBA 2004) and that's about it. Aldo Rossi writes about it a little in *Architecture and the City* (Oppositions 1944) and so did Christopher Alexander in *The Timeless Way of Building* (OUP USA 1980); but the alteration of old buildings has traditionally played second fiddle to the invention of new ones. It's definitely the province of the practitioner rather than the theorist. Carlo Scarpa, for example, was well known to be an intuitive practitioner rather than a neurotic theorist.

On Altering Architecture sets this practice into a clear theoretical framework – a sequence of activities: the excavation of an existing building, its "reconstruction" in a ruined form, and then the creation of an armature – the supposedly invisible additions and insertions that enable the old building to perform new functions, to address new technologies, and to help it to conform to new aesthetic preoccupations. It's an important work, but Fred Scott is at pains to point out – or is at least completely relaxed with the fact – that he is neither an architect, nor an interior designer. Indeed, he makes it seem as if *On Altering Architecture* and indeed his own role in the theorising of interior architecture all happened by accident.

Scott certainly didn't start out intending to work in design or education at all. He was going to be an engineer until, just before starting an apprenticeship, a schoolteacher alerted him to the existence of a place called the Royal College of Art.

Ask Fred what he studied at the RCA, and he behaves as he can't really remember. It was product design, he thinks, "but no-one really taught us anything" and it wasn't the reason he was there, really. The seminal RCA moment for Scott was meeting Norman Stevens in the student bar, who introduced the young product designer to a different world. "I fell among painters," Scott recalls.

The RCA was followed by an academic position in Manchester, working on "a non aesthetic basis for design" (Scott doesn't elaborate) under John Chris Jones, the advocate of "A Systematic Design Method", one of the founding documents of user-centred product design. Scott is more forthcoming by far about his boarding house in Daisybank, which was presided over by a spiritualist who fed her dog amphetamines and which he shared with a team of Australian bikers.

After a year, Scott returned to London, and took up a post doing what he had studied to do: designing radio sets for Philips. It's not a task he talks about with particular affection or nostalgia. Rather, it was the social contacts he was making in London at that time that he recalls both with affection and intellectual stimulation. He remembers attending, in particular, a series of dinner parties in the Oakley Square home of Robin Middleton, one of the architects working on the rebuilding of Euston Station under Theo Crosby. They were held on Wednesday nights in a grandiose nineteenth-century dining room, from the centre of whose ceiling a vast Philips lamp cast a pool of light over the assembled company. Here Scott met Cedric Price, the Smithsons and in particular John Miller.

Scott must have held his own at that dinner table, because it was there that he found himself offered his first teaching post, taking a unit in the 5th year at the Architectural

Association. Coming from his background in product design "I was definitely thought of as odd" he recalls. His students included Alan Stanton, and Mike Davies, one of the key figures in the design of the Pompidou centre shortly afterwards. In the late 60s Scott moved to teaching at the RCA, where, he worked alongside Sir Hugh Casson (in his last year at the college), Ed Jones and David Wild.

Later he moved to teaching teaching Architecture at the University of Kingston, where he met Julian Powell Tuck and Dinah Casson, who had been taken on to set up a new programme in a new subject: Interior Architecture. Scott was soon on board, and found in Powell Tuck a real meeting of minds. It was in Milan, awaiting the arrival of their first students on a school trip that the two men engaged in conversations whose repercussions may be read in the arguments of *On Altering Architecture*.It was, in particular, a stroll in the Romanesque basilica of San Ambrogio that, Scott recounts, they made the realisation of what interior architecture was all about. "There were these repetitive old brick arches down each side" he says, "and each one of them housed a chapel of different design and date that had been put in later. The building had been altered, and altered again, from the inside out."

It was certainly a very different conception of what interiors was all about to that which had traditionally been taught in design schools. Scott is clear that it had to happen, and is somewhat dismissive of the more immersive, scenographic aspects of interior design. "Modernism killed the room" he argues, pointing towards the sliding planes and infinite grids of Mies, or the free flowing plan libre, and the modernist insistence that the form of the outside of a building must reflect its interior workings as evidence of this assertion. Indeed, Colin Rowe's famous essay "Raumplan vs Plan Libre" makes much the same point.

I'm not sure I agree on this one, and I point out the office building we can see through the window over the road – an empty spec shell, doubtless in waiting for a fitout that may or may not reflect the architecture of its host building, and will certainly be entirely detached from it. Scott objects: "the room is ideologically impossible in the modern world," he says, "you can't be surrounded all the time by a single argument or point of view. It's an illusion. It's totalitarian."

Interior Architecture, then, is a way of giving spaces the broken, fragmented integrity of a truly modernist, transparent work of art, and, deep down, Fred is still a proper modernist, for all the apparent postmodernity of an argument for altered architectures. There are certain things he just won't do, or allow – changing the style of a building in the process of alteration, for example. Again, I'm not sure I agree – and nor would most of the churches in Italy.

It's time to go, and we leave the TV set of the bar we're in, and go out into the empty studio lot outside. On the way back to his small but beautiful flat in the Smithsons' Golden Lane development we walk down the over-passes, the frozen communal gardens, and the empty carpeted foyers of the Barbican. Scott is writing about communal living now – big houses – and the Barbican, curiously indefinable – a single, vast building or many, a public piece of city, or an exclusive enclave – couldn't be a better illustration of what it's all about.

Fred stops me as we're halfway down one of the overpasses. Leaning over the concrete parapet, we peer down at the ruins of a medieval wall which threads its way through the concrete. Isolated in a pool of water, it touches nothing. Directly below us the wall turns a right angled corner, articulated by a round tower. "That's the original Barbican" he says, "the defensive wall around the medieval city of London."

"Before they altered it," I think.

Graeme BROOKER and Sally STONE

Manchester Metropolitan University

SPOLIA

Introduction

An early scene within the film *Indiana Jones and the Last Crusade* finds Indy on a quest to discover the whereabouts of his kidnapped father. He visits the place where he was last seen, an academic library in Venice. It is a quiet point within the film, intended both to progress the narrative of the story and fill the lull between the episodes of action. It is a period of the film that contains conjecture, speculation and mistaken assumptions, and as always within Indiana Jones' films, it plays upon the ambiguity between illusion and reality.

The sequence of scenes contains a collection of appropriated images, statements and facts. Indy arrives by boat into a clichéd vision of Venice, the surprisingly female Dr. Schneider is the image of Veronica Lake, she says that he "has his father's eyes" and he claims to have "his mother's ears". The flower that Indy swipes from a canal-side stall is a gardenia and is a direct reference to "Summertime", another much earlier film set in Venice, and the library is a re-used church. But it is the interior of this building that encapsulates this attitude of appropriation; Dr. Schneider, when showing Indy and his companion Marcus Brody around, describes how "...these columns were brought as spoils of war, after the sacking of Byzantium after the Crusades".

These "Spoils of War" give the scene an authenticity, they appear to be old, relevant to the study of antiquities, and they are described as Byzantine, and yet they are the only things in this series of incongruous episodes and elements that are openly admitted as out of place.

The very act of appropriating images, elements and facts, and then re-using them with little regard for authenticity or continuity is indicative of today's information age.

Everything is valid, everything is available and everything can be re-used.

The Indiana Jones films are typical of this contemporary "both/and" approach; all styles, traditions and cultures are valid. These "Spoils of War" or *Spolia* could be described as the epitome of the post-modern culture that we inhabit.

Spolia, an archaic term rarely used outside of the study of Roman and Medieval antiquities, describes the recycling of existing architectural elements by incorporating them into new buildings. *Spolia* is derived from the Latin word *spoils,* a phrase used to describe the act of taking trophies, usually armour and weaponry, from the enemy after a battle. The *spolia opima*, the weaponry and parts of ships stripped from the enemy, would either be worn as trophies or used to decorate the victors' houses and temples after battle.

The study of *spolia* is a little known discipline or practice, and one that is largely confined to the fields of archaeology and antiquity. It is usually only referred to by archaeologists when analysing historic monuments, such as temples, churches and fortifications. Within architecture, *spolia* particularly refers to the re-use of the elements of the classical colonnade; the shaft, base, capital and entablature. Roman builders often built a colonnade in fragments, a practice that not only facilitated construction but one that also valued contingency and the potential for re-use [1]. Roman and Greek architecture is characterised by the use of *spolia*. Evidence of *spolia* can also be found in other periods of history such as the Byzantine or Moorish eras.

However, *spolia* can be seen as a thoroughly contemporary tactic. It is an integral element of the process of creating interior design, and is a method that is used by many contemporary interior architects and designers. The appropriation of elements from different sources, the reuse of details or fragments from other contexts, sampling, specifying, and the selection of key elements to be incorporated into a new design, is one of the fundamental skills in the armoury of an interior designer. The act of creating interior compositions assembled from a selection of elements is a fundamental skill. The use of *spolia* is a method of design that has been neglected, and we shall examine various techniques of using it as a tactic for building reuse and the creation of interior space.

Spolia is a tactic that relies on contingency, availability and ease of supply. It relies on the materials that are to hand and the ease of their reuse, and therefore it is a tactic that uses a collage-like approach to reconfiguring buildings. The use of *spolia* accepts traditions, patterns and a particular spatial design language, which suggests the application of a meaningful approach to design which reads and then revises existing meaning in a place.

The many methods and variations of the use of *spolia* can be distributed into three different categories. These are deliberately vague and of course, not exhaustive. They are: Ready-mades; Persistent or Residual Meaning; and Continuity and Permanence.

Ready-mades

> "The ready mades are anonymous objects which the gratuitous gesture of the artist, by the simple act of choosing them, converts into 'works of art'. At the same time this gesture dissolves the notion of work".[2]

Both the designer and the artist will utilise "Found Objects" when creating works of art or interior space. This connection is central to close relationship between interior design and other creative practices, such as painting, sculpture and installation art. The "Ready-made" is an approach to the creative act of making which allows the artist and designer to recreate, reinterpret and reproduce any existing elements to make something new. In his book "Postproduction" Nicholas Bourriaud suggests that this method of creating, taken from the film and TV production terminology, and based on the set of processes applied to recorded material such as montage, voice-over and subtitles after production is completed, is the dominant method of artistic production since the 1990s. He argues:

> "These artists who insert their own work into that of others contribute to the eradication of the traditional distinction between production and consumption, creation and copy, readymade and original work. The material they manipulate is no longer primary." [3]

Of course, Marcel Duchamp first argued the use of the "Ready-made" as Art. He instigated the use of the ready-made, creating artworks from appropriated mundane utilitarian objects such as a bottle rack and a urinal. This deliberately provoked the art world by removing the human hand from the creative or production process. Duchamp coined this method as "Retinal" art as opposed to "crafted" or hand-made, a process that allowed him to elevate mundane or everyday objects by lifting them:

> "...Out of the earth and place them onto the planet of aesthetics" [4]

The use of *spolia* within interior design is a ready-made approach to the re-use of existing buildings and is a tactic that is based on the creation of appropriating and using what is already to hand. Contemporary interior design is characterised by this approach. When using an off-the-peg approach to designing interiors Ben Kelly uses "Ready-mades" such as traffic bollards, factory-standard plastic screens, telegraph poles, industrial glazed bricks and hazard signs appropriated from motorway hard shoulders. Kelly uses "Ready-mades" in order to create distinct interior space, examples of which include the Hacienda nightclub, Dry Bar, and the Science Museum Basement Galleries. The use of contemporary *spolia* creates a distinct collage-like identity for a space. It also poses difficult questions about the selection of objects and taste and value:

> "The ready-made doesn't postulate a new set of values: it is a spanner in the works of what we call 'valuable'. It is an active criticism." [5]

The re-use of a found object can greatly enhance the atmosphere and quality of a space. It can add a sense of nostalgia and remembrance to what would otherwise be a fairly anodyne place or add to an eclectic collection of elements and spaces. The found object may be totally suitable for the interior, but from a different era or culture when it would then become subtly prominent. But it could also be totally alien to the space, when it then becomes a dramatic statement or critique of the space.

The ready-made is a process of *spolia* that can take place at a variety of scales. Bunny Lane House by the Architect and self-titled "American Anarchist" Adam Kalkin is exactly that. Designed in 2001 the existing house on the rural site was a traditional New Jersey two-storey clapperboard house with shingle cladding. Rather than demolish this undistinguished building, Kalkin completely enclosed it within a corrugated steel shed - a massive structure of the type usually found on an industrial estate. Kalkin viewed the house as a found object, a historical fragment that was left entirely intact within the portal frame of the shed.

The building has now become a strange collection of different types of enclosure; interior spaces within other interior spaces. This ambiguity has produced a new building that is both familiar while being equally surreal. What was once the front garden is now the living room and the front porch is the dining room. Walls and roofs that previously battled with the elements have, in a single stroke, now been relieved of that. The scale and brutality of the shed contrasts strongly with the traditional quality of the original house, and also with that of the furniture, which is carefully positioned within the expanse of the ground floor. The shed was positioned to accommodate the house at the northern end and, at the other, a tall very modern three-storey frame structure was inserted, which contains offices and bedrooms. This leaves the "courtyard" of a lounge in-between the two internal structures. Huge sliding glazed doors allow natural light into this central space and reinforce the connection with the scale of the shed and the surrounding landscape. It is an extraordinary approach to a found object that revives and enlarges a conventional structure in a most dramatic manner.

> "We come from a culture of sampling. I'm just out there in the world picking out things and reusing things—sampling—from my experience and from what other people have already invested a lot of time and energy in. I think there's a tremendous amount of richness out there." [6]

Ready-mades can be used as *spolia* purely because they happen to conform to exact sizes or measurements that ensure that they are fit for use. LOT/EK use found objects such as shipping containers to create new elements within or around existing buildings. The Bohen Foundation in New York is a gallery that is inhabited by three moveable shipping crates that become an office, a meeting room and a bookshop; they are flexible and can be moved to create more gallery space. In other projects the designers have used tankers from petroleum lorries to make bedrooms, and stainless steel kitchen sinks to create partitions in a New York publishing house. The "off-the-peg" process of creating spaces and elements by utilising existing objects is very much a process of the assimilation of the designers' context. Contingency and the elements to hand are important for the designers:

"I get inspiration from the view of the West Side highway from the studio windows, the machines for moving meat, the water tanks on the roof, the fire escapes and air conditioners that seem to grow out of the sides of buildings." [7]

Ready-mades suggest a *fit for usefulness* approach or a potential for adaptation to new uses. This type of *spolia* may manifest itself in re-use of a variety of different found objects and elements. The idea of contingency or potential for re-use is important; the reading and then subsequent manipulation of a ready-made can then create distinct identities for the building or interior.

Persistent Meaning

Spolia could be used as a method for creating form by appropriating objects where meaning is lost, inadvertently forgotten or has become obscured over time. This approach often provokes reflections, whether intentional or inadvertent, on the new use or meaning of the appropriated fragment.

The church of Santa Catalina in Valencia is one of the city's oldest churches. The church was built over a mosque in the 13th century and then remodelled in the 18th century in a Baroque style. In the west wall of the church, facing Placa De Santa Catalina, are three pointed windows that were closed during the 18th century remodelling. Two of the windows were sealed with stone and rendered whilst the middle window has been filled in with the rubble of the Baroque era renovation. The *spolia* that is used consists of fragments such as plinths, the head from a statue, the shaft of a column and an eroded entablature. The fragments were deemed as superfluous and therefore they were appropriated into the window to become *in-fill*.

On the small Venetian island of Torcello is the Santa Maria Assunta Cathedral. Rebuilt in the 9th century it was abandoned in the 13th century as the growth of Venice, the silting up of its canals and the onset of malaria decimated its population. The Cathedral pulpit is fabricated from *spolia*. Its steps are made from a series of reliefs that have been sawn and cut to provide an edge and balustrade to the stair. The carvings are datable to the 11th and the 12th centuries and subsequent research uncovered the fact that they were dedicated to Kairos, in antiquity the symbol of time as an opportunity. The reinstatement of these fragments was not an entirely arbitrary gesture and Patricia Fortini Brown suggests:

> "The restitution of the fragments to a certain degree of wholeness within the larger program calls attention to another occurring, and consummately Venetian, concern: to create a density of time within their major monuments through the employment of rediscovered relics." [8]

Both the *in-fill* in Valencia and the steps of the Torcello pulpit have been formulated using a series of leftover fragments. Both sets of remains are valued but for different reasons. In Valencia the fragments are used as *in-fill*; they are no longer of any use, their meaning is lost and they fix a space that needed covering. In Torcello the carvings were also brutally treated. They were cut to fit the steps and then edged with a reclaimed frieze detail, yet they were retained for their residual meaning; their connection to time. In both examples *spolia* is used as a meaningful link to the past but both are treated quite differently.

The historical understanding of using *spolia* is also found in contemporary interior design. One of the fundamental principles of interior design is that the discipline is concerned with the understanding and the subsequent reuse of existing spaces. Objects and spaces are "valued" for their previous meaning and retained or re-used in a space. This principle lends an air of the fetishisation of existing space, as Fred Scott suggests in "On Altering Architecture":

> "The atmosphere of all preserved buildings is unavoidably instilled with the qualities of fetish. The idea of alteration is to offer an alternative to preservation or demolition, a more general strategy to keep buildings beyond their time". [9]

In 1990 the American designer Ben Nicholson made Appliance House, an installation created to reflect the modern home. The house was conceived and designed with the use of collage; the working drawings for the construction of the house are made using appropriated images from a Sears Catalogue. *Spolia* is used in order to generate not only the appearance of the house but also to suggest an exaggerated distortion of a normal house. As Nicholson suggests:

> "By assembling frail and barely recognisable traits of urban existence into firm gestures, the Appliance House is formed into a Sub-Urban Home". [10]

Nicholson conceived the most important room of the house as the "Kleptoman Cell" (the trophy room.) He invented a mythical inhabitant, the Kleptoman, who would decorate this room with his trophies. The room was designed to be an armature that would contract and swell with the contents of the booty which the Kleptoman had collected from his travels. His *spolia* would become the interior content, decoration and eventually the structure of the room as the frame of the space accepted the contents and displayed them as *in-fill*. In the centre of the room was the Telemon cupboard; a device that allowed forty of the Kleptoman's favoured spoils to be displayed. The cupboard acts as a barometer for the space, monitoring the collection and displaying his finds, selecting the most meaningful objects that have an "afterlife" of memories, meanings, associations and connections – an assembly of fetishised objects.

The use of *spolia* can create a particular aesthetic in a space. In a non-descript 1970s school building in Omaha, Nebraska, Randy Brown has installed an autonomous object that has a number of different uses; an office for three designers and a home for his wife and himself. Brown and his wife lived in the building when it was being built and the hands-on approach to project management led to a particular off-the-peg D.I.Y. aesthetic. The elegant timber and steel element is assembled using off-the-peg sections of material from the local hardware store. Its off-the-peg aesthetic lends itself to a temporary piece of furniture, a detail that helped Brown to persuade the local council that it was furniture rather than new-build and hence ease its transition though planning.

In this case the formal or surface properties of the existing building are basic and the anonymity of the school merely provides the container for the new interior. Rather than disguising these attributes, the studio and residence accepts these qualities and therefore places importance on them as a design feature. Brown retained the existing wall surfaces. In fact the bland qualities of the host have informed the off-the-peg solution to its reuse. Whilst assembling the interior Brown would work with plans but then, while the structure was being built, he would move the elements around until they achieved a satisfactory relationship within the space.

Interiors built using elements and objects with an off-the-peg aesthetic are spaces that are designed as an independent element, using the envelope and its qualities as a container that contrasts or juxtaposes with the new space. Persistent meaning is evident in pervasive elements that are often designed as enigmatic one-offs or sequential elements that enclose new functions yet do not make contact with the walls of the existing space. Their character is to appear at odds with the host and heighten the contrast between them.

Continuity and Permanence

> "Artists today program more forms than they compose them; rather than transfigure a raw element [blank canvas, clay etc.), they remix available forms and make use of data. In a universe of products for sale, pre-existing forms, signals already emitted, buildings already constructed, paths marked out by their predecessors, artists no longer consider the artistic field…a museum containing works that must be cited or surpassed as the Modernist ideology of originality would have it, but so many storehouses filled with tools that should be used, stockpiles of data to manipulate and present." [11]

The third category of *spolia* is the enhancement of the narrative of the host building by the appropriation of fragments or objects of distinct meaning. These fragments might have important associations with the past, links to other ideologies or traditions, or distinct meaning or value. Continuity in the making of buildings advocates the reading of a place in order to understand meaning and then act appropriately. This implies an acceptance of patterns, traditions, forms and the language of a site, yet it does not necessarily advocate a straightforward copy of those conditions. Making buildings with *spolia* allowed Roman architects to express their strengths through their connections with the past. As Kinney states:

> "Making had not yet been problematised as creativity, and the crafting of a new object from traditional – perused – elements could give satisfaction. Building with spolia was just the instantiation of tradition, and the knowledge that the language of architecture had already been spoken and could only be repeated, never invented, was contentedly embraced, to the extent that repetition was enacted as verbatim quotation. Spolia are not symptoms of influence, but symbols of the acceptance of the authority of the Latin/Roman past." [12]

In "Postproduction" Bourriaud states that the current artistic practice of making connections to historicist forms and inhabiting past styles is a process of making sense of the vast flows of information in our daily lives. Whereas the Roman builder was happy with carrying on with traditional forms, today the artists and designer is willing to adapt and remix the existing in order to shape it to fit their lives;

> "All of these artistic practices...have in common the recourse to already produced forms. They testify to a willingness to inscribe the work of art within a new network of signs and significations, instead of considering it an autonomous form. It is no longer a matter of starting with a blank slate... but finding a means of insertion into the innumerable flows of production". [13]

When designing the University Library in Ljubljana in 1936, Jose Plecnik's interest in Roman antiquity and Semper's theory of cladding led him to produce a solution that incorporated *spolia* from the site. The library façade is studded with remnants of the old Palais Auersperg and the medieval city walls that once occupied the site. Granite, marble, Podec stone and *spolia* where combined with brick and concrete blocks to complete the facades. Plecnik wanted to ensure that the profile of the building retained its associations not only to its immediate history but also to its allusions to connections with Italy and Rome. He placed Etruscan concrete vessels above the side entrances in order to suggest an association between Slovenian culture and its Mediterranean roots.

The recycling of the existing building and elements can involve the reuse of unusual spaces, sometimes with extremely odd results. Interiors are usually created to service a specific function and the design of the space will reflect the particular activities happening within it. Sometimes the functional requirements are so specific, that it is difficult to convert without completely losing the essence and honesty of the interior. However, the designer can choose to retain the character and indeed the obvious function of a space and use it as the starting point for the redesign. One of the most outrageous examples of the new and old fitting together very well, but each still retaining a distinct and individual identity, is Klein Dytham's project for an advertising agency situated within an operational bowling alley.

In the dense, ever changing metropolis of Tokyo, KDa were engaged to design the new HQ for global, recently-merged, advertising company TWBA/Hakuhodo. This included finding space for the 300 strong workforce. The site was in an eight-storey amusement complex and the company had to share their venture with a reception for the gaudy gaming halls and endure a still-working bowling alley situated around them. The designers adapted the single span, 30-lane bowling hall into a studio for the company. They worked within the existing grain of the building using the extended, timber lanes of the alley for the distribution of work and meeting spaces. Each lane provided a long narrow length of space for work activities and the space between the lanes, previously used for returning the bowling balls, became circulation. A folded office room was positioned in each lane to provide an element of private meeting space for each team.

In both of these projects *spolia* is used to further connections and links with either the past or already established meanings. In all of the projects *spolia* is used as a method of constructing buildings in a way which makes associations with existing meanings. The use of *spolia* accepts traditions, patterns and the language of either a site or an existing object. It suggests the application of a meaningful approach to design that reads and then revises existing meaning in a place; the appropriate use of appropriation as a strategy for re-use.

Conclusion

The use of *spolia* as a tactic for interiors is another element in the attempt to reclaim and distinguish the theory of interiors. Interior Architecture and Design has often been regarded as a superficial practice that lacks any particular histories, design theories or principles. Interior architecture, interior design and building reuse are very closely linked subjects. All of them deal, in varying degrees, with the transformation of a given space, whether that is the crumbling ruins of an ancient building or the drawn parameters of a building proposal. This alteration or conversion is a complex process of understanding the qualities of the given space whilst simultaneously combining these factors with the functional requirements of new users. This distinctive attribute creates a unique set of issues, theories and processes that are different to many other disciplines. *Spolia* is just one of the tactics that can be employed.

The use of *spolia* is an enduring strategy and one that can underpin the creation of interior space, especially within the practice of remodelling existing buildings. *Spolia* is an overlooked and meaningful tactic for reuse, and is a method of designing that is particular and unique to the creation of interior space. Interiors is a subject that encompasses the analysis and understanding of existing buildings, the nature and qualities of an interior space, and an intimate examination of the characteristics of the decoration. The creation of new interior environments from fragments, existing objects, new materials as well as found elements, is a thoroughly post-modern, contemporary process of design.

References

[1] Kinney, D. Roman Architectural Spolia. *Proceedings of the American Philosophical Society.* Vol 145, No 2, June 2001. pp.138-150.
[2] Paz, Octavio. The Ready-Made. *Marcel Duchamp in Perspective.* p.84 (Prentice Hall International, London 1975.)
[3] Bourriaud, Nicolas. Postproduction. (Lukas & Sternberg, New York 2002).
[4] Naumann, Francis. Marcel Duchamp – The Art of Making Art in the Age of Mechanical Reproduction. (Ludion Press, Amsterdam 1999).
[5] Paz, Octavio. The Ready-Made. Marcel Duchamp In Perspective. p.87 (Prentice Hall International, London 1975.)
[6] Kalkin, Adam. Architecture and Hygiene. (Batsford, London 2002).

[7] Toller, Ada. LOT-EK. Blueprint Magazine. May 2002. p.96
[8] Fortini-Brown, P. Venice and Antiquity. (Yale University Press. New Haven 1996)
[9] Scott, Fred. On Altering Architecture (Routledge, Oxford, 2008.)
[10] Nicholson, Ben. Appliance House. (M.I.T Press, Massachusetts, 1990).
[11] Bourriaud, Nicolas. Postproduction. (Lukas & Sternberg, New York 2002).
[12] Kinney, D. Roman Architectural Spolia. Proceedings of the American Philosophical Society. Vol 145, No 2, June 2001. pp.138-150.
[13] Bourriaud, Nicolas. *Postproduction*. (Lukas & Sternberg, New York 2002).

Graeme BROOKER
Senior Lecturer
Interior Architecture
Faculty of the Arts
University of Brighton
Mithras House
Lewes Road
Brighton
BN2 4AT
01273 642362

Sally STONE
s.stone@mmu.ac.uk

Lorraine FARRELLY and Belinda MITCHELL
University of Portsmouth

INTERIOR ROOM URBAN ROOM

Introduction

There are differences between our consideration of space and our understanding of that space – interior space as defined by the individual experience of the interior and urban space as defined by the individual experience in the city. Architecture becomes a mediator between these two scales of experience. The interior is understood at full size, tangible physical space. The urban is understood by maps, models, but also memory and description.

This paper brings together two different realms, the interior and the urban, and uses the "room" as a common language or framework. We often consider the interior experience relative to the building or architecture in which it sits. Architecture is also considered relative to the urban context. This investigation is about the relationship between the interior and the urban, how can they inform and react to one another, what are the common areas of discourse and consideration.

The paper is informed by an interior design teaching programme and an urban design teaching programme at the same school of architecture, and uses different projects to describe methods of understanding and description of interior and urban space.

Scale of Space : Mapping the room, mapping the urban environment

Mapping Interior space

The interior is understood at the human scale of existence, it is the part of the building we touch and inhabit. Its palette is one of materials, colour, light, space, the fabric of

Figure 1: Mitchell Bould. Setting out of Osborne School onto a Victorian Cellar. Setting out drawing by Fred Rees, Site Engineer, Photograph by Dan Keeler, Architect, represented at the Winchester Gallery 2004

a building. We play with surface, form, and structure. Our tools are pencil, pen, paint, card, cutting mat and steel rule, a drawing board and computer. We shift through scales of practice, from objects to rooms, to buildings and into the city.

The interior is interpreted through our bodily responses and our sensory perception of space. It can be mapped through both analytical and experiential processes.

At Portsmouth students have been involved in a project, "The Sensory Experience of Space" [1], which considers the dialogue between the built form, its textural and material qualities, and our haptic response to it. The aim was to develop a new language of drawing to map personal experience of space rather than a more delineated and ordered way of understanding space that comes from conventional ways of recording space.

"The Sensory Experience of Space" is a student project with dancers, artists and designers to investigate space using drawing as a site for collaboration and investigation, drawing through the body, drawing physically, drawing with string, elastic, cling film.

When thinking about mapping of space we begin to think about the texture of space, the sound, the touch and feel, to consider how to record an experience rather than the space itself. Important considerations are the personal narratives we bring to space, the tools we have to work with. During this process we consider how people inhabit buildings and what marks they make in their inhabitation.

Students were encouraged to look at different types of notation, diagrams, language, plans, and maps, and to use Lawrence and Anna Halprin's RSVP cycle to respond to their experience of the space. The intention was to understand how buildings are experienced, by trying to connect the felt and the abstract; students were encouraged to use themselves as a resource in a building. The buildings provide the frame to work within, the container and the contained.

Mitchell Bould, a research collaboration in interior and textile – worked to represent the experience. They produced a stage set, a set contained within a set developed through the representation of student work. They mapped the space through drawing and sound. This experience suggested new ways to record and engage with the interior.

Mapping Urban Space

The analysis of urban space involves mapping, recording and describing. The initial maps of cities were as people perceived and experienced them. Maps were drawn which had no scale, just important features of the city. In the 18th century an exercise was undertaken to create a military survey in the UK, and an early 19th century survey created maps of England at 1 inch to one mile, which used a set scale. This developed into the national grid reference and the digitised mapping system that we use today. This physical mapping is about measurements and scales, creating a defined framework to measure and place buildings and spaces within it. Figure ground mapping uses scale drawings and maps to describe building forms but also spaces between buildings.

There are approaches to mapping cities that involve an understanding of space and movement through it. Gordon Cullen, in his book *Townscape*, introduced the idea of serial views [2] as a way to describe a route or journey through a city. This involves an abstract map or diagram and then a series of images.

Invisible cities by Italio Calvino uses a series of essays to describe the city. It describes imaginary cities, both the characters within them and the places themselves. It deals with life events associated with relationships and the places these events take place.

Bernard Tcshumi describes the city in his book *Event City* [3] as an arena for events to take place and occur.

Other techniques which describe cities have been developed by Dutch architects MVRDV: *Metacity/ Data town*. [4] This book uses strong graphics coupled with a range of statistics to describe urban conditions.

Figure 2: A figure ground map of Chichester allowing an understanding of the spaces left over in the city

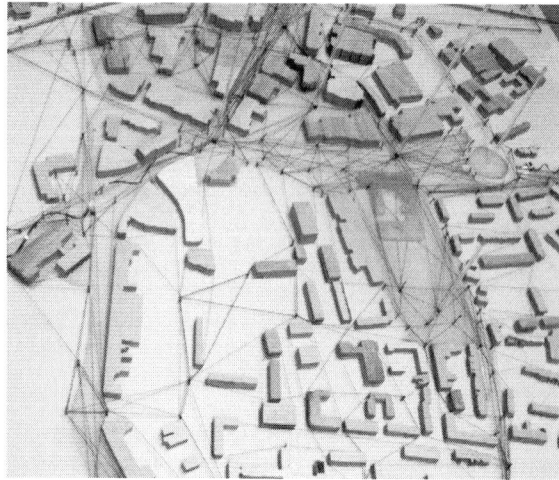

Figure 3: An analytical model of Portsmouth, indicating areas of activity and desire lines or movement patterns across the city

A city can be described with a map, or it can be quantified in terms of a list of buildings, population, density and land area. These analytical approaches to the city record what is there, in both quantitative and qualitative ways. When starting an urban design project one of the important initial exercises is to encourage a personal interpretation of the area, through drawing, modelling and creating journeys of experience and abstract models of the place. The mapping of cities uses information about what exists to inform future design ideas.

Site Context

Interior Context

> "Stripping back in its extended manifestation is the process by which the interventional designer acquires an understanding of the host building with which she or he is engaged. It is to the end of developing a structured affinity, as a preparation for the correspondence between their work and the existing. The host building needs to be understood intrinsically and in terms of its setting, and to be looked at in terms of actualities and provenance. This is an enquiry that will have both architectural and socio-economic aspects." [5]

The interior is analysed through understanding the host building and its many layers, its stories, histories and the lives of people who have inhabited the space, its social and political context. It is also understood through the structures and methods that produced the spaces as well as the physicality, the material that is the building. The designer needs to understand the building's fabric and how it has been occupied to clearly understand the original.

A building is in a continuous process of change. As soon as it is "complete" it is occupied and change begins to take place, the purpose for which the building was built becomes redundant. The interior, as the city, is transient.

Interior designers normally respond to a given context, a site, a building, a room. It is important to consider what the relationship is of our intervention to the building, and also what meaning this gives.

The visual artist is always aware of "site" – the meaning the work has in relationship to the site, the gallery, the installation in the street. The meaning it gives the work, the relationships it suggests. The work needs to be placed within a context.

This idea of understanding the site and revealing its nature is a process that we need to record and use; the recording in itself is a creative experience.

Urban Site Context

The urban condition can be described in emotional and figurative ways; these descriptions provide information that creates the context for an urban idea or master plan.

To create a master plan for a city requires an understanding of the place. This is an understanding of what the city is and what it was. The understanding of the past is important. It can suggest and stimulate design ideas for the future. This understanding needs to be related to function and activity, what happened on site or in a place. It needs to discover stories, narratives about who lived, worked and experienced that place.

The layers of history in most European cities can have physical evidence from Roman periods and beyond. This information can be relevant and inform current design issues and considerations; it is part of the story of the site. The idea of the city as a palimpsest refers to the Roman practice of writing on wax covered tablets, which could be scraped off and written over again and again.

In architecture this metaphor can be understood when we see traces of the past in a city. This may be on a wall or in the road surface. These traces suggest something

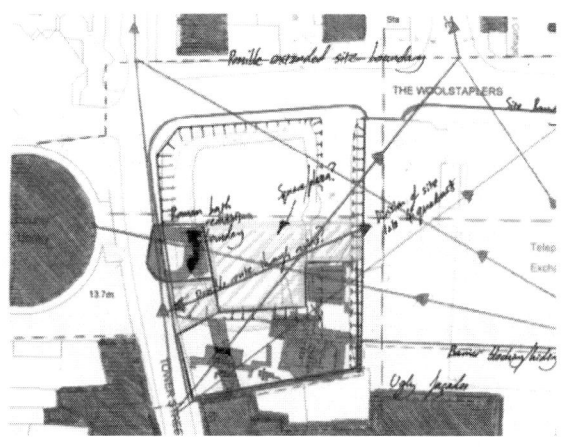

Figure 4: This is a drawing of a site which reveals the roman remains beneath the street: the plan suggests that the site had a past as well as a present

Figure 5: This is a photo of a building that has been partially demolished: this suggests a type of palimpsest, suggesting that there has been a memory to this site, a previous experience that has now been removed

about the past, how a building was used or experienced; tram tracks across a cobbled street; an edge where a building once may have stood. These scars reveal something of the past in the city.

When creating a response to a city, there needs to be a careful understanding of the context and a recording of the information that is there in terms of buildings, activity, and function. This understanding is critical to respond to the site and produce either a master planning proposal or an architectural proposition.

The Room

The Interior Room

The room is the device which we use to contain our human experience; it is defined by function, activity and experience. When we think of buildings, the unit of space we can connect with is the room.

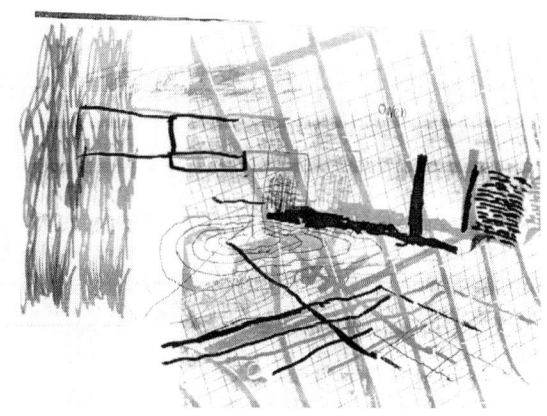

Figure 6: Family Drawing, Mitchell Bould, Site Works

Drawing made layering different scales of the same space together, Library at Osborne School, to form a new space

The interior room is where human activity happens and events take place.

> "we act out to make depictions of space, built form and incident, to invoke true relationship between architecture and human affairs." Fred Scott, *Space and Time in Architecture and Painting.* [6]

The room suggests what we should do within it, sleep, dine, live. Interior designers can create opportunities for this human interaction to take place. To understand the room, an understanding of the potential of a body and how it could engage with its space is important. The room is the container of our activities and interactions.

The Urban Room

This reference is used more and more to suggest that the city and its scale is human, something that can be engaged with. The room metaphor is used to all scale of urban space, from a piazza, to a small courtyard type space. Just as interior spaces can exist at various scales, so too can urban rooms.

The writer Charles Bauldelaire wrote about the "Flaneur", the typical gentleman of who lived around Paris at the time of the French revolution. He considered the city as his home. It existed as a series of rooms, the library was his study, the restaurant his dining room. This reference has been used to suggest that the city has spaces that can be used and considered as different sorts of accessible spaces, but also that the city can be considered like a large house, or a range of interconnected spaces. The urban room can be a piazza or square or a restaurant or library. Interior references such as the "room" become useful metaphors for design of urban spaces, activities can be assigned to urban rooms as with interior rooms to suggest the possibility for interaction. Further metaphors such as "carpet" can be used to suggest surface, these start to connect urban spaces with the idea of habitation and comfort that we associate with interior experiences.

Conclusion: Container/Contained

We have described a range of approaches to the description of the interior and the urban condition.

The language of both environments suggests possibilities for exploration of the urban and the interior. When considering the idea of context there are important connections that can inform the placing of buildings in a city, or the response of an interior to an existing building.

At the start of a project to design an interior space there are methodologies of analysis, both recording and description, which can be applied to the understanding of urban space. Accordingly, methods used in recording urban space can equally be used in the analysis of interior space.

Perhaps one of the most important observations is that design disciplines co-exist; the interior may be connected to the body in space, and how it is "contained" but

Figure 7: Mitchell Bould. Relationship between the drawn and the real. Site setting out drawing

the city, at a completely different scale, also is concerned with the experience of the "containers", or architecture.

The interior suggests borders of experience, the city creates opportunities for events at a range of scales of experience. Some of these are at the scale of the interior, intimate, private, shared and others are collective, work, play. All these experiences need an understanding of the possibilities of our engagement with our environments whether interior or urban.

"To live is to pass from one space to another" [7]

Wherever our experiences start, the room is connected to the architecture that is part of the city. Through mapping the city, buildings and interiors and exploring new ways of connecting and drawing experience we hope to produce new interpretations. There is a synthesis of experience and analysis to create new dialogues in the urban environment; shifting from 1:500 scale of an urban space to describing the touch of a room, the 1:1 detail. The dialogue between the two needs to be explored and developed.

References

[1] Baker, K and Mitchell, B. (2000) Paper "The Sensory Experience of Space" RIBA Conference
[2] Cullen, G. (1971) *The Concise Townscape*, London: Architectural Press.
[3] Tschumi, B. (2004) *Event Cities 3. Concept vs. Context vs. Content*, The MIT Press, Cambridge Massachusetts
[4] MVRDV *Metacity/Datatown* Publisher: 010 Publishers
[5] Scott, F. (2007) *On Altering Architecture*. Routledge
[6] Scott, F. (1988) *Space and Time in Architecture and Painting*. Brief Kingston University
[7] Perec, G. (1978) *Life a User's Manual*. London: Vintage

Acknowledgements

Thanks to the students of the interior design course and the 'European Studio' architecture diploma group for their ideas and inspiration.

Lorraine FARRELLY
School of Architecture University of Portsmouth
School of Architecture
Portland Building
Portland Street
Portsmouth
PO1 3AH
Lorraine.Farrelly@port.ac.uk
02392842083

Belinda MITCHELL
School of Architecture University of Portsmouth
School of Architecture
Portland Building
Portland Street
Portsmouth
PO1 3AH
Belinda.Mitchell@port.ac.uk
02392842087

Material tools and tactics

Andy MILLIGAN

DJCAD Duncan of Jordanstone College of Art and Design
University of Dundee

MATERIAL TOOLS AND TACTICS

Summary

Two opposing but connected research papers help to open up debate on the tools and tactics of materiality between those using design-led thinking and those with an engineering and materials science perspective. In George Verghese's "Material Change Agents and their Dangerous Ideas", the author describes the emergence of think-tanks such as the Edge Foundation and their provocations to seek out dangerous ideas.

As a basis for the development of new and innovative material change agents, Verghese questions why design education might benefit from engaging in similar dangerous thinking which shifts a tendency for design conformity into innovative enquiry and asks "What dangerous ideas can new materials ask about our understanding of interior design?" Although focussed on materiality and change, Verghese describes the interior as a site of constant material, surface and aesthetic change. While products and technologies are effectively "housed" by the interior, material and interactive innovations are set to transform how we dwell, and may well prompt behaviour change. Acknowledging that design is also a change agent, (e.g. it initiates and responds to change), he describes how the disciplinary boundaries of design are undergoing change.

Materials awareness offers designers and their clients important emotional triggers which validate design intentions but which seem against the conventional approaches toward material understanding – particularly so in education where this may remain abstract and limited. Verghese cites Gann's call for more intelligent and flexible environments in a building sector that is not always open to "newness" in materials. He argues for the need to explore materiality and technological paradigms through, "...

waves of innovation in information technology, new materials, genetic and biochemical engineering [to] create possibilities for further economic growth and the need to develop new living places and work spaces".

Verghese argues that we need a massive re-think about how innovation in materiality affects the design process, "...It is material that gives architecture matter....and it is through materiality that a house [interior] gains its soul". Citing Brookes, "...it is only by searching for new discriminations that we shall extend the dimensions of the real", he proposes that engagement with material organisations, or indeed the establishment of a new materials specialism within interior design, may be required to shift thinking from a 20th-century concept of tangible bulk to a 21st century mindset of "...surfaces, monolayers, even single molecules".

Verghese suggests that that the process of spatial investigations driven by material change agents [designers and material organisations] lies in the domain of pedagogy and that dangerous ideas revolving around materiality and spatial interactions – both digital and theoretical future scanning – are important tactics to employ if interior design is to evolve.

In contrast, Sumeet Ballara, representing MADE, the Materials and Design Exchange and IOM3 materials network, describes the materials and engineering science approach toward a functional and quantitative understanding of materiality. MADE brings together the communities of design and materials technology to stimulate innovation, promote the transfer of materials knowledge, and improve the competitiveness of UK business.

Part of the Materials Knowledge Transfer Network (KTN), MADE links designers and researchers with funders and with other sectors concerned with metals, plastics, textiles and the full range of modern materials. Offering the type of physical and virtual materials and process resource identified by Verghese, MADE led the first smart materials and design exhibit including printed electroluminescent lighting, a thermochromic iron and a ski jacket that uses a quantum tunneling composite to control an iPod without wires. MADE's link to material resources and samples offers designers access to samples and to show the connection between materials and design (www.made.uk.net.)

Sumeet Ballara offers an important counterpoint to the more speculative and dangerous ideas discussed by George Verghese, suggesting that function, performance, cost-benefits and sustainability - rather than emotion, feeling or fascination - drives material innovation. Indeed, he claims, efficiency is valued in materials science and engineering and aesthetics is rarely considered.

A deliberate tactic of the Interiors Forum Scotland "Tools and Tactics" conference was to bring together opposing views of shared territory and thus to expose gaps and opportunities between researcher communities. This is illustrated by Verghese and Ballara's distinctive approaches to materiality. Whereas many of the materials innovations developed by materials scientists and engineers can result in hiding, embedding or coating materials to enhance efficiency, durability and performance, within architectural and interior contexts, materials are celebrated and overt.

The way that "research" has evolved across these communities is also significant, shifting from knowledge for its own sake to applied research, a demarcation that is clearly reinforced in current UK research funding where knowledge may be classified as "basic" research whilst "applied" research is often more highly valued to GDP and manufacture. Verghese's call is to establish material specialists within larger interdisciplinary practice, and it is clear that interior designers could evolve into this role, and would transform material understanding.

Andy MILLIGAN
DJCAD Duncan of Jordanstone College of Art and Design
University of Dundee
Interior Environmental Design
Perth Road
Dundee
DD14HT
SCOTLAND
a.milligan@dundee.ac.uk
44 7929 136 580

George VERGHESE

University of Technology Sydney

MATERIAL CHANGE AGENTS AND THEIR DANGEROUS IDEAS

Introduction

In his seminal book on theatre design, Peter Brook states

> "… it is only by searching for new discriminations that we shall extend the horizons of the real."[1]

These words have followed me for many years, framing my thinking on design and design education. Although Brook's comments are about design for theatre, the idea of spatial design, place-making, and human-centred design are central in his mind as they are in the minds of interior designers. His expression highlights one very strong tendency in design: the principle of change. This principle is constantly tugged upon by the notions of continuity and tradition. Regardless of your own approach, all design, traditional or not, involves change. Designers are change agents and they accomplish change through the use of tactics and tools.

Change in its most basic form means to move from one state of affairs to another. Krick talks of design problem statements that are a resolution of state A to state B.

> "A problem arises from the desire to achieve a transformation from one state of affairs to another" [2]

The movement from A to B is a diagram of the design process in its simplest form. Design process, design strategies, and design tactics all describe methodologies taken by designers to accomplish the desired changes needed for a design outcome. Change implies movement, dynamism, and to some degree, the unknown. Risk and the control of risk are fundamental to design.

> "All design deals with unknowns, risk is always apparent and the degree of exploration can vary. Design is about amending the future and moving forward." [3]

We now live in a world in which we do not have any luxury of being complacent. As a civilisation we have squandered the environmental inheritance left by previous generations who also need to accept some of the responsibility for their actions in the environment. Our generation now needs to act, a sentiment shared by James Martin in his opening sentence of his insightful book of our world which states:

> "At the start of the 21st century, human kind finds itself on a non-sustainable course — a course that, unless it is changed, could lead to grand-scale catastrophes" [4]

A change is definitely needed, however this paper will not discuss the disastrous global environment condition but will focus on the link that the profession and industry has with the principle of change. As Cilla Robach comments:

> "...the field of design is changing dramatically and that design is in the midst of a paradigm shift." [5]

She follows this comment by further support of the relationship of design and the applied arts to the rest of society, and how design initiates change and also responds to change. Today the emphasis is on a dynamic society in which economies, environments, society, and relationships are called on to look away from stability as being a desirable pathway. The scope of this paper does not allow for a thorough trace of these histories and relationships. However as a starting point we need to talk about key issues on this continuous road of material-driven design innovation. These will allow us to outline some dangerous ideas that will alter our perspective and interior tactics when designing.

Materials Innovation in a Changing World

An architectural spatial enclosure captures a volume of material matter within a condition that is called an interior. This enclosure, cloaked in material assemblages, establishes roofs and ceilings; walls and openings; and, floors and fittings; all together describing interior spaces. The gaps in material allows for a dialogue with the external world via the passage of air, moisture, sound and light.

> "Materiality is the stuff of architecture. While structure and form give space and dimension to architecture it is material that gives architecture matter....In the domestic realm materiality takes on a new role. It is through materiality that a house gains its soul" [6]

This material world that we inhabit is full of substances and forms that we have fabricated, each constructed with the aid of some level of technology and all providing a response to our senses. It is our response to technology that provides it with a context and purpose.

New materials have influenced design for many centuries, both affecting society, and equally being driven by social pressures. The term "new materials" should not be restricted to just sophisticated materials, but should also include new material thinking that responds to the advances in technological processes and the social demands on technology - in short, the entire gamut of transformation in which material matter resides. It is the application of new materials that constitute a change in the era, and not solely the existence of an advanced material technology. Change gives rise to change, as extending the discriminations of our reality has led us to search for new technologies. These technologies are always incorporated with material advances.

When we consider the histories of technological paradigm shifts we immediately go back to the Industrial Revolution that occurred in Britain in the mid 18th Century. During this period, new technologies, new markets, new methods, and new materials all rapidly started to appear which would all become driving factors for the industrial growth in Britain in this period. However there were numerous smaller revolutions that occurred beforehand. Glass manufacturing, coal production, and shipbuilding were but a few industries that grew from capital investment and an increased labour force. New markets were generated through the growing middle class merchants. New materials and technologies began to develop such as Ormolu, Queensware pottery, and transfer printing – all catering for this growing market that demanded a sense of style based on their neo-classical aspirations.

> "Taste in the eighteenth century was disseminated by 'upward emulation' " [7]

The world has grown up since the days of those early pioneers of the Industrial Revolution in the early 1750s.

> "They were practical men – neither aristocrats nor scholars but manufacturers who came together because they were excited about ideas." [8]

James Martin progresses this argument by talking about the continual growth and impact of these ideas and that

> "...each wave of technology brought with it new ideas for improving things, and the waves picked up speed and followed one another increasingly quickly." [9]

Their ideas challenged complacency and tradition, broke the social bonds, and

> "...transformed attitudes: for the first time, the idea that something was 'new' made it attractive, preferable to something that was traditional, familiar, tried and tested." [10]

These were all brave men chasing dangerous ideas because they believed them to be true.

Succeeding ages beyond the Industrial Revolution have seen fluctuations between the inherent qualities of a material substance used in design, and those of the associated qualities of materials. The former supported functional and rational thought, and the latter lent towards poetic application and decoration. The divide between decoration and design began. The turn of the century saw this dichotomy expanding between traditional approaches to interior decoration and design and an opposing design ethos that engaged with technology which set out to embrace change by looking to the future. It was with this latter direction that the term early modernism applies. Materiality, in both fabrication and structure, was innovatively explored through the work of Wright, Corbusier, Gropius, Chareau, and others who investigated new spatial organisations, shapes and forms, and the integrated use of new materials and manufacturing processes. Their dangerous ideas were an expression of the turn-of-the-century and of the spirit of the age, but quite often they were not fully appreciated for their visionary ideas. In the 1930s a cleaner, more functional interior was desired which led to a greater sense of efficiency for a healthier future. This desire was supported by a host of new materials. In the 1960s economical and practical aims were met with the development of gypsum-board panels. These panels revolutionised the construction industry and presented a new way of thinking about interior spatial fabrication and design. Advances in painting technologies, fabrics, and polymers have also shifted designers' thinking about approaches to spatial design.

The digital age began with the invention of the computer and has greatly advanced in recent decades. Moore's Law which notes the capacity of microchips to double every 18 months, whilst the production cost halves, is a powerful indicator of the speed of progress. This understanding is being addressed by the construction and design industry, but only in a very rudimentary manner. Currently the advancement of information systems and interactive technologies are laying the foundation for a massive re-think of design processes. David Gann talks about the historic proportion of change now needed in the building industry to support changes in society:

> "If the pressures for change in buildings, structures and infrastructures seem great now, they are unlikely to relent as the forces that shape society continue to ebb and flow. Waves of innovation in information technology, new materials, genetic and biochemical engineering create possibilities for further economic growth and the need to develop new living places and work spaces." [11]

David Gann's thorough study of innovation in the building industry discusses the histories of innovation from the machine age through to the digital age. He also argues

> "... pressures for innovation are strongest when there is demand for radically new types of building structures. This usually occurs during periods of general and widespread technical and economic change." [12]

Gann continues his general introduction by discussing the importance of material research, and the fact that customers with larger projects who fund research and development activities are thereby supporting the innovation process. Gann discusses the concepts of innovation within the entire building industry, from designers to manufacturers, and prefers to combine them all into the *construction process;* which gives it a dynamic nature. He does note that some organisations are not passive in their engagement activities and they provide vital feedback to others in the building industry. His prediction of the advance of intelligent buildings concluded that

> "[s]killful integration of new technologies by designers and engineers creates possibilities for the production of more flexible buildings. But the pace of technological and spatial change has not been spread evenly across markets for different types of buildings..." [13]

It is clear from Gann's work that change is occurring and the whole construction industry needs to keep abreast with the changes. He indicates that innovation progresses through organisational change, as he cites the significant reduction in the number of British brickworks from 1950 to 1980 that illustrates the economic advantage of centralisation and modular fabrication. He also openly discusses the role of leaders of the building industry being usurped by the leaders in the electronics and telecommunications industry, who are the champions of innovation. Profitability is aligned with research towards innovation, and larger organisations have the ability clearly to invest in research and development without hindering the bottom line. Some parts of the industry still seem to be slow on the uptake as

> "[t]he introduction of any 'new' material to construction projects requires careful long term planning. The industry is not generally receptive to 'newness' in materials. However, material development is an essential part of innovative design concepts..." [14]

The UK-based Materials Innovation & Growth Team produced a report in March 2006 providing a sense of scale to the concerns stating that

> "...[t]he UK must build on its strengths in material science and technology and accelerate the pace of innovation if it wants to stay competitive." [15]

The report also notes that

> "material businesses in the UK, companies that produce and process materials, have an annual turnover of £200 billion...15% of the country's GDP". [16]

Governments, small business, and the media are all starting to engage with research and development activities and "innovation" is quickly becoming a key driver in all the discussions.

The driving assertion of this paper is that the developments in advanced material science are continually forming platforms for change. However, the change that we now need to prescribe must be of a fundamental paradigmatic magnitude.

Edge Foundation

In 1988 a group of individuals came together from their previously informal gatherings to establish the Edge Foundation. This group included intellectuals from a variety of fields and disciplines such as science, philosophy, technology, business and the arts, who met to discuss issues that aimed to raise deeper meanings to our lives, and in the process question and define who we are as human beings. Part of this foundation is the annual feature of The World Question Center. This Center was established to ask the members to address specific questions. In 2006, Steven Pinker asked the question:

> "What is your dangerous idea? An idea you think about (not necessarily one you originated) that is dangerous not because it is assumed to be false, but because it might be true?" [17]

These were intended to be ideas that challenged the collective decency of the age but not ideas that were harmful or were the basis of evil ideologies.

This question is the basis around which this paper is written. The essence of design education, albeit all education, must surely be to stretch the mind and to ask the difficult questions. Challenging the student in a design studio is part of developing the designerly ability of enquiry. Asking the dangerous questions must be a core tactic of all design education. The educational challenge is not only to ask these questions that initiate change, but also to be cognisant of the beauty of tradition and of continuity. This will allow students to be able to take calculated risks and to explore ideas intelligently. In doing so they can move forward objectively to amend the future. Risk and uncertainty are domains in which design meanders around. As design is an activity that deals with change and the unravelling of the unknown, designers are often knowingly in dangerous terrains. Designers need to be aware of the domains of risk in which the domain material myth must be constantly challenged by the domain of proven facts and material knowledge. These domains are always featured in the domain of material context. [18]

Designers as change agents are not necessarily a new idea. However, if we take this as a basis, the question must be asked: why is there such a propensity towards equilibrium and tradition? Comfortable thinking is surely not part of a designer's ethos. Yet, as we ponder the notion of tactics and tools for interior designers we do not see the provocative visionary paradigm shifts, but rather measured thoughtful approaches to design. I am not proclaiming that we should throw defiance to the stars as the Marinetti stated, but as interior designers, what should we saying about our future? It is time for the conformist to be dislodged through the challenge of innovation. We need to appropriate Pinker's question and ask: what dangerous ideas can new materials ask about our understanding of interior design?

New Material Discriminations within Interior Design

Interior design is a discipline that has a focus on the human being. It aims to understand and provide for the psychological and physiological needs of the users through meaning, symbolism, safety, enjoyment, and ease of operational use. Safety and welfare are all very important, and codes are established to maintain the standards. But inherent in this whole notion of "standard" lies the challenge of searching for the new. "Shifts in the gestalt" is the description that Thomas Kuhn uses to discuss the elementary transformations in the scientific world as

> "...during revolutions scientists see new and different things when looking with familiar instruments in places they have looked before." [19]

As designers we are constantly looking at familiar places and seeing the new; we have looked at material science for hundreds of years, and now designers need to look at materials with new eyes.

> "We predict that the development of innovative materials must take place in parallel with new approaches to engaging human senses." [20]

In saying this Toshiko Mori clearly equates new material innovation with change through a human-centred approach as she connects sensory engagement with material interaction.

> "New materials by themselves do not constitute change, or design innovation. It is the application of these materials within a context that issues forth a new era in design, and this new era must coincide with the implementation of new materiality into the process of design and not solely as an aspect of the outcome." [21]

When materiality does become a central theme in interior design, the discipline will lift itself out of its currently outdated paradigm that it now finds itself. If the 20th century was focused on tangible bulk materials and the manipulation of them into various forms, then

> "...the 21st century will be that of surfaces, mono-layers, even single molecules, and the new functionality that these will allow." [22]

New steel, ceramic, and wood technologies can also fit within this new definition as do biotechnology, nanotechnology, and smart materials.

The process of spatial investigations driven by material change agents lies in the domain of design pedagogy. It is here that shifts have to occur. A degree of discomfort and unfamiliarity needs always to be present in a design brief. This leads to a tactic to be alert to the present with an eye to future design resolutions. The discomfort is in the form of ideas that will re-align the thinking of spatial relationships, and adjust the inherent education needed to produce spatial outcomes. Discomfort is not an easy topic to embrace with delight, as quite often we want our teaching to inspire joy in the student's experience as they become awoken to the world of design. However, built within the fabric of our discipline lie the seeds for change.

The scope of this paper restricts further elaboration on techniques used in a design studio to encourage innovation, but it must be built into the graduate profiles and not just lost in individual learning objectives for subjects. However, it is worth noting that the online assessment tool called Re:View ® includes as one of five attributes: Creativity and Innovation.

> "This criteria category includes assessment criteria that encourage inventiveness, versatility, thoughtful risk-taking, imagination, creative problem solving, natural curiosity, creative experimentation, innovative use of materials and technologies." [23]

If the world of design is changing so rapidly, educators must prepare the students for these challenges.

Conclusions and Dangerous Ideas

"We will build intelligence into materials and liberate form from matter. Material has traditionally been something to which design is applied. New methods in the field of nanotechnology have rendered material as the object of design development. Instead of designing a thing, we design a designing thing. In the process, we have created superhero materials and collapsed the age-old boundary between the image and the object, rendering mutable the object itself." [24]

The collapsing of boundaries and establishment of new paradigms are all bold statements and, perhaps, even dangerous, but the brief overview of recent history of material advances has attempted to show how new materials have affected the methodology of design and in doing so have provided new tactics and tools for the generation of new spaces.

All of the information on new materials is quite clearly stating the obvious. Most designers, if they subscribe to innovation in materials or not, are well aware of their impact as they see advanced materials on the horizon. All the sources of new materials: Material Connextion®; Materia®; and, Transmaterial®, to name three of the most popular, exist in the marketplace and are growing daily. With over 100, 000 materials to choose from, and that number increasing annually by at least 1000, the question that is often asked is: "How do designers select?" But this research has led to a conclusion that it is not the right question to ask. More appropriately the question is: "Who will make the selection of new materials?" It is David Gann's research on building innovation that really sets the stage for the future and sheds light on the answer, an answer best described as a *dangerous idea*.

Dangerous Idea: Material Agencies

New materiality and innovation hold the seeds to future designs and must now be elevated to be the driving force in design. This idea needs to be implemented at all stages of the design process, profession, and discipline. Design education needs to address innovation at all levels. Design project briefs must instil the excitement about materiality and innovation so that graduates are capable of dealing creatively in the world of tomorrow.

Most importantly there needs to be a paradigm shift in the thinking about how designers practice. Gann has assembled an impressive document that illustrates growth in various sectors. He clearly argues that the growth of larger organisations that can afford the risk of research and innovation points to models in the telecommunication industries. It is time that the individual and small-scale design companies start to reorganise into a network, or even collapse into large units. This is needed to create a greater critical mass to afford research and development time.

Also, the larger organisations, if structured appropriately, can attract larger clients and larger funds for research into materiality. Herzog & De Meron and OMA are two larger organisations that can afford to release some staff to research into material innovation. These investigations push the manufacturer who in turn responds with innovative materials. Continuing to exist in the current, almost craft-like approach will see interior designers left behind in the wave of material driven innovation that is upon us. Fashion designers, visual communicators, and industrial designers all work equally well in larger organisations, without stifling their creativity and innovation. Of course there is the argument that interior design requires site-specific outcomes, but even that viewpoint is fading with the growth in more flexible spaces and interactive environments. Larger organisations will mean larger teams available to support all projects; and, the viewpoint stressed here is that there be a mandatory inclusion to the in-house specialists of a team of material scientists, together with all other specialists common to design practices who offer their support. Individuality will not be lost as there is still a designer looking after a client, but this designer will be able to concentrate on what they do best, design.

References

[1] Brook, P. *Empty Space*, p.108 (Penguin Books, New York, 1980).
[2] Krick, E. *An introduction to engineering and engineering design* (2nd ed.), p. 3, (John Wiley & Sons, Toronto, 1969).
[3] Verghese, G. Strangers in a Material World. In McCarthy, C. and Matthewson, G. eds., *Inhabiting Risk*, p.157. (Interior Design/Interior Architecture Educators Association, Wellington, 2007).
[4] Martin J. *Meaning of the 21st Century — A vital blueprint for ensuring our future*, p. 3. (Random House, Sydney, 2006)
[5] Robach, C. Critical Design —forgotten history or paradigm shift. In Emanuelsson, H. and Sarstad, M. eds., *Shift—Design as Usual or a new Rising*, p.31. (Arvinius Förlag, Stockholm, 2005).
[6] Watson, F., ed. Material Matters. Monument, 2007, 81, 19.
[7] Sparke, P. *Design in Context*, p. 17. (Quatro Books, London, 1987)
[8] Martin op cit, p. 18.
[9] Martin op cit.
[10] Watson, P. *Ideas — a history from fire to Freud*, p. 553. (Weidenfeld & Nicholson, London, 2005)
[11] Gann, D. Building Innovation — complex constructs in a changing world, p. 1. (Thomas Telford, London, 2000)
[12] Ibid. p. 10
[13] Ibid. p. 109
[14] Manning, J. Risks associated with the use of new materials in construction. *Technology, Law and Insurance*, 1999, 4, 57.

[15] Department of Trade and Industry, UK, Materials Innovation and Growth Team, *A strategy for materials London, Engalnd*, [PDF] Available: http://www.dti.gov.uk.URN06/651 [Accessed on 2007, 21 March],(2006). p. 35
[16] Ibid. p.5
[17] Pinker, S. Introduction. In Brockman, J. ed., *What is your Dangerous Idea?*, p.xxix. (Pocket Books, London, 2007).
[18] Verghese, Strangers, op cit. p.161
[19] Kuhn, T. S. *The Structure of Scientific Revolutions, 3rd edition*, p.111 (University of Chicago, Chicago, 1996).
[20] Mori, T., ed. *Immaterial/Ultramaterial—Architecture, design, & materials*, p.63 (George Braziller, New York, 2002).
[21] Verghese, G. Sensual Spaces Through Material Abstraction. In Gigli, J., Hay, F., Hollis, E. Milligan, A., Milton, A., Plunkett, D. eds., *Thinking inside the box — a reader in interiors for the 21st century*, p.199. (Middlesex University Press now Libri Publishing, London, 2007).
[22] Ashby, M & Johnson K. *Materials and design: the art and science of material selection in product design*, p.10 (Butterworth-Heinemann, Boston, 2003).
[23] Thompson, D.G., 'Integrating Graduate Attributes with Student Self Assessment'. In *Proceedings of ConnectED 2007, International Conference on Design Education*, pp. 1-6.(University of New South Wales, Sydney, 2007).
[24] Mau, B. *Massive Change*, pp.140-141 (Phaidon Press, London, 2004).

George VERGHESE
University of Technology Sydney,
Faculty of Design Architecture and Building,
P.O. Box 123
Broadway,
NSW, 2007
Australia
George.verghese@uts.edu.au
+61 2 9514 8964

Andy MILLIGAN

DJCAD Duncan of Jordanstone College of Art and Design

University of Dundee

Written on behalf of

Sumeet BELLARA

formerly of IOM3/MADE

MATERIALS AND DESIGN EXCHANGE (MADE)

Dr Sumeet Bellara's considerable contribution to the *Interior Tools Interior Tactics* debate offered new perspectives on material innovations through his unique experience as a curator of the MADE Materials Resource Centre at 1 Carlton House Terrace, London. MADE, the Materials and Design Exchange network, brings together the communities of design and materials technology in order to stimulate research and manufacturing innovation, promote the transfer of materials knowledge and improve the competitiveness of UK business through material knowledge. MADE is an important component of the Materials Knowledge Transfer Network (KTN) funded by UK Government through the TSB, the Technology Strategy Board. In the UK, the TSB continues to play a very significant role in driving opportunities for interdisciplinary research and development between industry, wider organisations and academics. MADE exists to connect designers and other sectors of the KTN Knowledge Transfer Network who share a concern with metals, plastics, textiles and the full range of modern materials. The core partners of MADE are the Institute of Materials, Minerals and Mining (IOM3), the Royal College of Art (RCA), the Design Council, the Institution of Engineering Designers (IED) and the Engineering Employers Federation (EEF South).

IOM3 is a major UK engineering institution whose activities encompass the whole materials cycle, from exploration and extraction, characterisation, processing, forming, finishing and application, to product recycling and land reuse. It exists to promote and develop all aspects of materials science and engineering, geology, mining and associated technologies, mineral and petroleum engineering and extraction metallurgy, and is a leading authority in the worldwide materials and mining community. IOM3 has an individual membership of over 18,000, and represents a combination of scientific, technical and human resources which links industry, government, research and the academic world. Members of the Institute come from a variety of backgrounds, from students to company chief executives. As a core contributor to the MADE magazine, a materials consultant, a materials science engineer, and materials advisor for IOM3, Sumeet provided a critical counterpoint to more visionary insights of George Verghese's discussion on dangerous material possibilities. Addressing an alternative knowledge base and materials perspective, Sumeet's role also as curator and contributor to academic materials research events, embodied the collaborative strategies, (as opposed to the more disciplinary specific explorations of materials for interior contexts), and drew upon his own industrial experiences in working with non-technical fabrics, plastics, metals and ceramics. His expertise in fibre reinforced plastics, tile and sanitary ware glazes, pavement and construction materials including recycled and secondary materials, chemical analysis, assessment of non-metallic materials in harsh environments, bioremediation, waste minimisation, and alternative technologies for road surveying also highlights a particularly deep professional body of knowledge around material applications.

A central provocation of *Interior Tools Interior Tactics* was to bring these material connections and philosophical differences into focus. In responding to George Verghese's thought provoking paper, "Material Change Agents and Their Dangerous Ideas", Sumeet's perspective locates these materials change agents and dangerous ideas themes as more of a design phenomenon. For materials professionals, materials choices are governed by quantitative performance, economics and social issues, such as their sustainability, and function is far more important driver than emotional response. However, as emotional beings, we may also learn to "love" that functional reliance that good materials science provides. Efficiency is highly valued, while aesthetics is, not surprisingly rarely considered though one wonders whether in Sumeet's role as curator of the MADE's Material Resource Centre, those encountering, touching, smelling and encountering those innovative materials both "hear" the quantifiable engineering characteristics of those materials whilst also gaining an emotional buy-in to those materials simultaneously and tacitly.

Sumeet also touches on some other key distinctions between the materials science and the interior design communities, suggesting that, for the materials science and engineering perspective, the fact is that, generally speaking, most of the materials remain hidden and their quantative performances are engineered and "embedded" rather than highlighted, whereas for designers the materials immediacy and impact are valued through their visibility. In general, engineers and material scientists spend time covering and protecting materials; for example, with coatings whilst designers indeed celebrate those surface, skin and transient material characteristics through thematic and sometime theatrical affect. How both communities examine the temporal nature of materials also differs. Material scientists tend to look at change and transience through different disciplinary lenses, of durability, wear and tear, hardness, brittleness whereas the engineer perceives, (rightly or wrongly), interior design and architecture's application of materials as being prone to continual cyclical change; what George Verghese describes the interior as a site of constant material, surface and aesthetic change. Research on materials has, however, moved from knowledge for its own sake, toward projects which have the potential for industrial applications, economic gain and collaborative development for new markets – and indeed, this suggests that the interior research community, (like that being pursued by the smart home / smart technology research), are outside those research and collaboration cultures and need to engage. Sumeet also identifies other disparities between the differing material perspectives; engineers tend, he feels, to be much more conservative as their work is controlled more by regulations, standards, specifications, performance criteria and legislation. However, it is important to note that engineers and material scientists are the people that help to create standards and specifications. So, proof is needed to confirm that the chosen material is equivalent or better but what this ignores is those intangible human responses to the materials that surround, envelope and enclose us. We can, and do, value even apparently dysfunctional materials through investing those materials with meaning beyond their functional role.

Dr Mark Miodownik, Head of the Materials Research Group at King's College, London also recognises this perceptual materials gap exposed across various communities concerned with materials and their quantative and qualitative values. Whilst engineers may favour material performance tables, these however fail to capture the wider human material experience. Here there is an undeniable multi modal spectrum of how we experience the world. As Miodownik identifies, "Such properties have a huge effect on our use and enjoyment of products, [interiors and environments]. Characteristics of smell and feel are almost impossible to capture in numerical data, and, he noted, many modern products show evidence of the fact that these properties were ignored during their design. The only way that people can gain an understanding of these other material properties, suggests Miodownik, is by experiencing the materials directly – touching them, manipulating and interacting with them in different ways. "Touching a material changes your way of thinking about it."

Sumeet also suggests that part of this proof finding mission of a material's likely performance in-situ is the ability of materials science engineers to apply testing regimes set out in the standards and specifications that are unnecessarily harsh or restrictive can also bring about material change, and with global competition for jobs, contracts, and research funding, materials professionals in the UK are working together to speak with a single voice, greater visibility and impact. Speaking with a single voice means that the community as a whole is taken more seriously by government policy makers and funders and can achieve more positive benefits. There are however practical limitations that locate superb MADE Materials Resource Centre's and events that are perhaps too "London-centric" but far from expressing a geographical frustration, this helps explore how the immediacy of encountering "real" materials can be transferred, experienced across different geographies whilst being sensibly based in London. This raises some useful points for future debate: first, the innovations, opportunities and future interior applications of intelligent and responsive materials and finishes, (from thermal, charged to digitised), and second, how a better balance can be developed between materials science and design material change agents in collaborating on material developments. Having prepared responses to media queries can be an advantage, so that the materials side of the story is told. By talking to the media, material scientists and engineers can help promote and raise awareness of material technologies and innovations, turning a possibly negative story into a piece of positive publicity. Materials libraries, such as the MADE Materials Resource Centre together with their links to organisations and their associated activities each play a vital role in breaking down the language barrier between the materials community and the creative industries. These libraries will have an impact on the change agents and their dangerous ideas. Unfortunately materials professionals have been slow to embrace these libraries though geography presents a real problem when dynamic initiatives like this remain rooted to one place.

So, what will be the future for material change agents and innovative networks like IOM3 and MADE to migrate, celebrate and sell material awareness more fully? In response to George Verghese's proposal that larger organisations could have in-house interior materials specialists linked perhaps to a team of material scientists is seen by Sumeet as a very encouraging proposal. Considering the number of design consultancies this would, Sumeet feels, create jobs for many and give the more creative materials professionals an outlet for their ideas and promote materials as a subject worthy of deeper investigation. Working as technology translators for designers could also lead some of those new materials professionals, (interior material change agents) to make a substantial contribution to the MADE network and could allow wider resource arguments to be made by educators to reintroduced lost material sample resources and for interior researchers to develop funding proposals. The reverse, with designers working in materials organisations, is happening in companies that produce products rather than just sell component parts or precursors; such as, sheet materials. Sumeet feels that those materials companies that have not embraced this practice may be slow to take up in-house designers. However, there is also a perceived lack of understanding of how changes to their business plan can benefit them. Survival in the global market for UK materials companies, for example, will ultimately depend on quality, service, design and intellectual property and the UK will not be able to compete by just selling at the cheapest price so new innovations are needed. Ultimately it is the emergence of new models for business that will promote opportunities for materials change agents to emerge and encourage dangerous material ideas to surface. Central to this may be developing new educational strategies that combine a necessary understanding of materials functional and performance factors, alongside experimenting, (rather than "abstracting") through actual material making, prototyping, (e.g. experience and / or traditional prototyping), and emotive making and by celebrating a creative play ethic where discovery and playful practices enable students, researchers and public to interact with material possibilities. This also suggests opportunities for future design research in which interior design plays a key role, and that enables interior design to develop a new breed of material change agents, capable of working across boundaries and able to meet the needs of business.

Dr Sumeet Ballara
formerly of IOM3 / MADE
sumeet.bellara@iom3.org

Julieanna PRESTON

Massey University, Wellington, New Zealand

TOOLING A FEMINIST INTERIOR PRACTICE

By and Large

Gender issues are no stranger to the discipline of interior design. While searching existing literature for theory specific to interiors to be included in *INTIMUS*, I was struck by the number of texts written about women, often by women, with regard to interiors.[*] This should not, in itself, be surprising as there has been a proliferation of gender and women studies research in the past several decades, nor for the surge of architectural research on gender, and interdisciplinarity in the 1990s. Several observations can be drawn from these texts. First, women's historical and cultural association with domestic environments dominates the literature, often conflating the home with the interior. The evidence suggests that the interior is exclusively situated within the domestic sphere, in many cases within a house, occupied by a family, and the house is run and decorated by a woman. It is her domain, but she does not control, own, design or build it. Examples extend across history from Praz's recount of upholstery's transformation to the home-hobby of interior decoration, to Colomina's reconstruction of Eileen Gray's battle with Le Corbusier over her Cap Martin house and Karen Burn's essay on Loos' Josephine Baker House. Even Virginia Woolf's seminal text, *A Room of One's Own* and Beverly Gordon's essay, "Women's Domestic Body" demonstrate the extent to which women are housed. There is a sense that interior and women have been successfully branded as synonymous entities.

---

[*] Of the 1137 items reviewed for *INTIMUS*, 189 address gender issues, more than 75% were written by women, and 95 were about women. Of the seventy-nine chapters in *INTIMUS*, 26 are specific to interiors and gender, of which 16 were written or co-authored by women and 14 are about women.

Second, these texts also revealed numerous significant female designers who use textual discourse to explicate their own interior or an architectural practice, often embedding a response to gender bias into their house designs. Alternatively, the research highlights women who use design as a means to theorise on feminine space, female modes of knowing and processes of writing and making that serve to advance women's role in professional and academic spheres. These contributions are numerous, significant and insightful to the various points of view on the link between architecture, interior and gender issues.

As early as 1869, when women's suffrage campaigns were escalating, Catharine Beecher and Harriet Beecher Stowe published *The American Woman's Home*. Incredibly modern in their approach to house design, this pair challenged social norms of living with an ergonomic and pragmatic sensibility capable of popular acceptance without significant uproar. On the other hand, Elsie de Wolfe's infamous identity as an actress, talent agent and interior decorator drew as much attention to her public image as to the light-hued suitable, simple and well-proportioned interiors she designed for wealthy clients. I suggest the works by these women marked an inroad for women in professional terms but perhaps only in so much as it claimed the right to manipulate the inside of the house. However, Dorothy Draper's bold, brash and shocking designs, and behaviour, shifted ideals of good taste from the home to the public sphere. Her 1939 book, *Decorating is Fun! How to be your own Decorator* predates an extensive career in refurbishing hotel interiors in major American cities. Her lavish designs occurred at a time marked by an aesthetic (and many would say cultural and ideological) battle between opulence and modernism.

In another time and place, Jennifer Bloomer questions ornament's relegation to women as a denigrating quality. She contests the limits of containment through the generative employment of rhetorical tropes, autobiographical anecdotes and a subversion of canonical methods of constructing history. Both her essays and her architectural works wage a clever and multi-faceted skirmish against the stereotypes and cultural identity markers that have historically cast women to the margins. Casting doubt on what was assumed to be a safe and comfortable interior, Bloomer works to un-do normative (and culturally reinforced) notions of a woman's relation to public life, professional endeavour and thought processes. Her theoretical and creative practice exemplified in *Abodes of Theory and Flesh: Tabbles of Bower* and *Natura Morte* has been inspiring to many young and female students, myself included, and the subject of strong retort by as many male critics.

Although I have omitted significant references for the sake of brevity, these examples and others collectively attest to a growing consciousness amongst designers towards gender as an informing factor in an interior spatial and political built environment. Further evidence of this activism is found in the work of scholars including Hilde Heynen and Gulsum Baydar, Shirley Ardener, Alice Friedman, Jane Rendell, Barbara Penner and Penny Sparke. With acuity, these researchers construct critical speculation on what happened, what was there and how it came to be, all serving to script compelling commentary on Western European culture's propensity to cast women to the inside, not as central, but as peripheral figures. Knowing the significance these works play towards forming histories and theories of interior design, I note the rare occasion that the word 'feminist' or 'feminism' is used to either describe the author, the work or its method. I ask, with limited innocence (and no immediate response): Is my apprehension of feminist values and ideals in these works merely the mirage of my own biased agenda or are these values and ideals latently fuelling the work as motivating agents?

To the Point

A shift of office recently prompted me to organise papers and portfolios which have accumulated over twenty-five years as an academic, architectural designer and spatial artist. A nostalgic sift through that body of work revealed a reoccurring theme: to employ feminist values to construct spatial design and textual discourse related to those designs. I am now curious as to how an interior might serve a political agenda and how feminism might behave as a spatial force. If design has the tendency to look to the future, towards innovation or what could be, how might interior design be propelled by an intention to reorder social and spatial hierarchies, upset power relations and imagine environments based on difference? Such a cause leads to other questions: Is there such a thing as a feminist aesthetic? Is the interior environment too laden with femininity and privacy to offer an alternative without resorting to dualistic reactions? Is the active advocacy and dissent associated with feminism compatible with the tangible and material vocabulary of interior design? While these questions raise doubts as to the appropriateness of testing interior design as a site for feminist agency or feminism as an expressive theme or style for interior design, they also identify positive friction between two forms of speculative action. More central to this conference's theme, what modes of tooling are useful to draw out these questions?

The text that follows considers these questions in light of three projects completed between 1994 and 2008, each offering further insight to the issue of what I am dubbing "alterior femme-space". Advanced by virtue of a strategic tool aligned with specific forms of feminist activism and interior construction methods, these projects outline an emerging feminist interior practice situated at the confluence of gender, politics and technology. Brandishing the wedge/shim as a multi-purpose low-tech building device, this essay shies away from the military rhetoric associated with tactics to focus on the instrumental nature of tools to 'make work'. Such purpose is literally and conceptually founded in the unassuming artefact of a sliver of material typically called a wedge. Inverted from its role to 'pull asunder', the wedge is also a shim, a notably delicate, often make-shift wad inserted in order 'to make up the difference.' Because of its tapered double-face, this single tool serves to bolster, shore up, level and stabilise as readily as it bifurcates, fractures and dislodges. Its effect is directed by intent managed by the force of the hand that wields the mallet behind it.

Rhetorical Tooling

"Blaze" structures metaphoric and experiential associations between body, building and landscape. Deep within Canada's interior lies a large territory riddled with lakes and waterways named Algonquin. As a provincial park occupying a large part of Ontario's landscape, such territory serves as a contemporary recreational wonderland as well as a historically significant site of trade between the French Voyageurs and the Algonquin Indians. I came to know this place first-hand between 1990 and 1994 during annual canoe trips. Each visit was an experience that extended the archetypical narrative of "journey" and tested the limits of my own body and practices of space-making and place-finding. I entered this territory as an architectural designer with a special affinity for construction and material inquiry. Each time I returned from this wilderness, I gained, not just greater skills as a canoeist, but insight of how such travel was specific to being female. I gathered embodied intelligence about how my body - its posture, its movement, its spatial extension - was associated through semiotics and metaphor to the act of portaging between lakes with a canoe on my head following a path blazed by hatchet marks on tree trunks. I was struck by the poignancy with which such violent marks knitted various aspects of my world-body view together.

These eight drawings are the actual site of processing observations, reflections and findings, ordering them and making them public. Structured by the blaze marks of one particular portage, each sheet drew associations between areas such as patching walls, stitching wounds, reading maps, building structure, and spatial enclosure. As fields of lateral musing, the drawings are the result of pasting bits of found images and data, a practice of prompting meaning through adjacency and relation, a technique well documented by feminist artists and authors.

What began as the wielding of a heavy metal instrument to cleave and scar so as to blaze a trail amongst the forest concluded with a sliver of tapered timber used to level or find balance. A shift of scale, material, purpose and power structure signifies a variable convergence between wedge and shim, a space and action of gendered difference. This transformation of instrumental meaning has had a profound impact on my creative and professional practice whereby the smallest of design gestures have the capacity to lever significant change.

"Blaze" capitalises on a generation of feminist works where the artist's female body explicitly exploits sites of biological and cultural forms of wilderness and wildness, ultimately a retort against the male (artist) gaze of the female nude. While "Blaze" is constructed with a belief that we carry our sex, our sexed body and sexuality with us everywhere, a belief that infuses cultural geographer Robyn Longhurst's research on pregnant bodies, it also draws from Rebecca Solnit's effort to rethink landscape as

> "...ubiquitous—as the environment, a landscape that includes the microscopic as well as the macroscopic, economies as well as ecologies, the cultural as an extension of

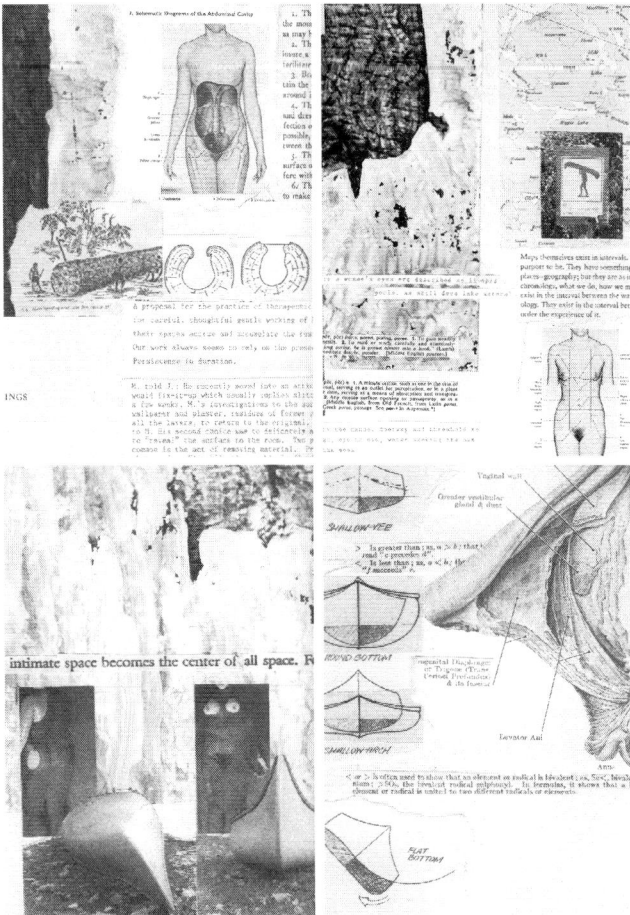

Figure 1: Detail images of "Blaze" drawings

the natural, our bodies as themselves natural systems that pattern our thoughts, and our thoughts as structured around metaphors drawn from nature".*

Both writers are drawing on the theories of Luce Irigaray and Hélène Cixous, French feminist philosophers, who posit a woman's body not exclusively in terms of biological anatomy but with reference to morphology,

"meaning the way in which the shape or form of the female body is represented in culture".†

---

*   Solnit, R. As Eve Said to the Serpent: On Landscape, Gender and Art (University of Georgia Press, Athens, GA, 2001), p. 47.
†   Gatens, M. Feminism and Philosophy: Perspectives on Difference and Equality (Polity, Cambridge, 1991), p. 115.

For these philosophers, the notion of being everywhere and ever-present are attributes that are reinforced by their use of language that is

"deliberately ambiguous, paradoxical, poetic and metaphoric"

and meant to undermine "the dominance of the phallic, the well-formed, clarity, singularity of meaning..."[*]

Instead of transcending a trapped and "mere body" condemned to a life of reproduction, as Simone de Beauvoir promotes, the specificity of one's body and gender is a vehicle with which to produce meaning and value.[†]

"Blaze" is also inspired by Judith Fryer's literary comparative analysis of Willa Cather's sense of the desert as a space of emancipation and Edith Wharton's fixation on the "room of the undressing me", an interior figured as a flight of fantasy amongst architectural details. While Cather credits her allure to vast, open, and unobstructed space as the means to find a centre and hence, a spatial circumference, Wharton's particularised fetish with the intimate and envelopment of place signals her willing surrender to disorder, which for her is an interior of passion.[‡] "Blaze" constructs a virtual interior that oscillates between these polarised extremes. The shift between scales and its paste-up nature form an image that resists commodity and re-representation – it is difficult to view all the drawings at once and impossible to photograph without losing the detail. In this case, the wedge/shim is shown to be a rhetorical tool capable of simultaneously cleaving and joining imaginary structures made accessible by a visceral and corporeal female body, my body, in the process of trans-disciplinary migration.

Tooling Dissent

In 1996 Emily and Mike Donovan purchased a house on the fringes of an historic neighbourhood close to the centre of Des Moines, Iowa. The house and its immediate surroundings wore vestiges of the urban blight that to this day still plagues huge pockets of the city. The house was but a frame without full enclosure, heat, windows, doors, plumbing or internal linings, effectively a carcass of a past inhabitation. After braving the elements and the local drug scene, the Donovans were informed by council that, as a historic landmark building, any plans to improve the house must comply with standards of preservation, the cost of which was more than ten times the purchase price and beyond their means. As architects themselves, the Donovans invited fourteen artists to make installations within the house. The ensuing exhibition raised public awareness of the issue and subsequently waged a productive protest - the policy minders decided it was better to have the house renovated and occupied than empty and derelict.

---

[*]   Gatens, p. 117.
[†]   Gatens, p. 54.
[‡]   Fryer, J. Feliticious Space: The Imaginary Structures of Willa Cather and Edith Wharton, p. 292-293 and p. 60 (University of North Carolina Press, Chapel Hill, 1986).

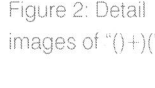

Figure 2: Detail images of "()+)("

(the) (sek re ter i) (ov) (the) (in ter i erz) (stan derdz) (for) (r...

(wun) (a) (prop er ti) (wil) (be) (juzd) (az) (ti) (woz) (his tor i kal i) (ov) (be) (gi) (too) (itz) (dis tingkt tiv) (ma ter i alz) (fe turz) (spas ez) (and) (spa :

(too) (the) (his tor ik) (kar ak ter) (ov) (a) (prop er ti) (wil) (be) (tand) (and) (ma ter i alz) (or) (ol ter a shun) (ov) (fe turz) (spas ez) (and) (spa sh ti) (wil) (be) (a void ed)

(thre) (ech) (prop er ti) (wil) (be) (rek og nizd) (az) (a) (fiz i kal) (re kord) (ov) (tols) (sens) (ov) (his tor i kal) (fle vel up ment) (such) (az) (ad ding) (his tor i kal) (prop er tiz) (wil) (not) (be) (un der tak en)

(for) (chanj ez) (too) (a) (prop er ti) (that) (hav) (a kwird) (his tor ik) (sig ni zurvd)

(fiv) (dis tingkt tiv) (ma ter i alz) (fe turz) (fin ish ez) (and) (kon strul ship) (that) (kar ak ter iz) (a) (prop er ti) (wil) (be) (pre zurvd)

(siks) (de ter i o ra ted) (his tor ik) (fe turz) (shal) (be) (re pard) (rath er) (tha shun) (re kwirz) (re plas mant) (ov) (a) (dis tingkt tiv) (fe tur) (the) (G (teks tur) (and) (hwat) (pos i b'l) (ma ter i alz) (re pad) (or) (re p at ed) (bi) (dok u ment ta ri) (and) (fiz i kal) (ev i dens)

(sev en) (kem i kal) (or) (fiz i kal) (tret mentz) (if) (a pro pri it) (wil) (b'l) (tret mentz) (that) (koz) (dam i) (too) (his tor ik) (ma ter i alz) (tv

(at) (ar ke o loj i kal) (re sors ez) (wil) (be) (pro tekt ed) (and) (pre zurvd) (mit i ga shun) (mezh erz) (wil) (be) (un der tak en)

(nin) (nu) (a dish unz) (eks ter i er) (or) (re lat ed) (nu) (&c alz) (fe turz) (and) (spa shall) (re la shun shipz) (that) (kar ak ter iz shi at ed) (from) (the) (old) (and) (wil) (be) (kom pat i b'l) (with) (the) (pro por shun) (and) (mas sing) (too) (pro tekt) (the) (in teg ri ti) (ov

My collaboration with Deb Scott adopted a grass-roots approach, where many small acts (and voices) serve to overwhelm a dominate power structure. The parable of a mouse who overcomes a fear of being devoured to remove a thorn from a lion's paw was reconceptualised as the insertion of many small conciliatory details figured as political irritants. Two hundred pewter-capped timber wedges and shims were inserted into the dilapidated house literally to pry open gaps and shore up walls, stairs and flooring. While the house could easily have benefitted from thousands of these tools, the reflection of silver caps on the exhibition opening night spoke to the distressful situation.* Each individual cap signified a point of contention and weakness. Collectively, they signalled the extent of repairs needed to simply stabilise the frame by virtue of their cutting (critical) edge.

Our installation, entitled "()+)(", included a poster plastered to a piece of plywood temporarily serving as a front door, traditionally the site of public notices such as quarantine, eviction, condemned or more familiarly, "go around to the back," "door bell not working, please knock" and "please leave the package on the porch". The poster was a copy of the historic landmark mission statement rewritten phonetically in order to emphasise spoken (immediately present) over written words (officially sanctioned), as well as to locate the wedge/shim as a tool shaping a protest language and a political and economic argument. Each hyphen, accent, long and short vowel sign and parentheses marked a detail of similar weakness to the house.

Re-Tooling

One of the strongest points of difference within feminist theory and activism is whether or not one can work within an existing context; whether the existing context is susceptible enough to be undermined, sabotaged or even simply used as the foundation for its own critique. This point appears to mark the difference between radical feminists, poised to wage public protest and overturn political establishment for a cause, and liberal feminists, who deal with matters within an existing process of dispute. "SHEET GOODS" is a series of architectural constructions playing out operations that link actions of civil disobedience to standardised unit materials specific to interiors such as plywood, Medium Density Fibreboard (MDF), T&G flooring and gypsum board. It is designed to test the boundary between radical and liberal feminist strategies, effectively seeking to work within the context of a given material as a means of subverting it and, possibly, even replacing it. In this case, the wedge/shim tool serves as a conceptual mediator between complete destruction of material structural integrity and subservience to dominant cultural norms in order to measure the limits and influences of industrial building products proliferating domestic interiors.

Like most post-industrialised countries, New Zealand's building industry is still geared to standardised unit materials that by virtue of their modularity, uniformity and pre-designed integration, theoretically ease production costs. It is no wonder that the economy of the country is driven by the construction industry, in particular the housing sector, for as a small nation we rely almost exclusively on importation of these goods. And in turn, as a result of New Zealand's value on a second degree of thriftiness and expediency, our built environments, particularly interiors, tend to become a consequence of material sheets goods joined by generic details. I observe an overpowering trace of the 1200 x 2400mm sheet, a smooth, rigid and homogenous surface applied in uniform thickness to a structural frame. Interior space is regulated visually and experientially by this unit. The difference between inside and outside is reduced to a functionally driven membrane.

---

*   The exhibition, Re: BIRTH, occurred at 905 Eighteenth Street Des Moines, Iowa, USA, November 16, 1996.

As a reiteration of industrial tenets, interior space becomes unresponsive to inhabitation of the particular, site-specific and anomalous: the body. In this scenario, design of the interior is at risk of becoming the mere specification of surface appearance, much akin to rendering a wall texture in a digital model – just pick an image texture.

Handbooks on civil disobedience highlight several forms of non-compliance and protest, in particular, modes of resisting police arrest in a non-violent, passive yet uncooperative, posture. The most instructive piece of advice stated in the Civil Disobedience Manuals put out by ACTup[*] is to "go limp", a posture which makes carrying a protester away more difficult and in many political states, not interpreted as a crime. "Go limp" assisted my material exploits to take on parallel processes such as draping, distressing, cutting out and relaxing. Primarily used by fashion and textile designers, these material processes induce a greater degree of pliability, tactility and variable density to a given textile whereby structure, pattern and surface texture are indistinguishable. To presume these are simply applied tempering acts dismisses the instrumental form of (creative) violence. The process of increasing weight and vulnerability while exponentially increasing surface area, selectively slicing structural threads to tinker with the integrity of the weave, and bringing "a perfectly good material" to the brink of failure with the intentional application of heat and chemicals offer modes of fertile protest..

To date two of five works have been completed. "HUNG" plunges towards the floor as a bundle of fragile wafer-thin strips compressed by a horizontal beam recalling the decorative figure of curtain, drapery, pelmet and valance. This furnishing reconstitutes a sheet of cabinet grade birch veneer plywood, 25mm thick x 2500mm long x 1200mm wide, successively ripped into 1.5mm strips, the finest slice before the alternating layers of ply start to disintegrate. Typically reserved for a highly visible interior architectural feature, the veneer finished plywood sheet's structural value, married with its natural wood grain surface, lends to its prudent and judicial application as an interior finish. And yet it also serves as a mask for the storage cabinet behind the thickness of its face. Such economy is not specific to NZ. The fact that more than 65% of the sheet was lost to the dust extract system and it took two people more than eight hours to slice the sheet upset the New Zealand building ethics associated with its extravagant $400 price tag.

"Tread" is a cantilevered section of tongue and groove pine flooring, a common product designed to provide diaphragmatic strength when the two edges are coupled. Each individual stick has been tapered at one end by the use of an electric hand plane, orbital sander and hand spoke-shave. At the far end of the cantilever their tips succumb to gravity where the removal of material has breached the limit of the section modulus. Lightweight is ironically figured as heavy. As an elevated level, perhaps a terrace or plateau, it suggests a step up yet its frail edge gives way. Worn thin, the down-turned riser obstructs physical transcendence. As "Tread" refuses to be tread upon, it highlights the artificially of interior floor surfaces and the inappropriateness of considering floors as stable and level or even, synonymous with ground.

---

*   http://www.actupny.org/documents/CDdocuments/ACTUP_CivilDisobedience.pdf. Website sourced 22 April 2008, 12:38 p.m.

Figure 3: "Hung"

In the freshness of this recently completed work I reflect upon the manner in which it draws comments about the labour it required in light of the absurdity or foolishness of wasting material for the sake of testing an idea or advancing a theory. For labour here was laborious - many hours expended working between hand and machine, adopting systems of working that should have made it easier, but didn't, and tending to the character and properties of pieces as they became more and more individuated. A few days into the project I already knew that its making was a performance that tracked the consistency at which I could set the fence a fraction between two fine hairlines 1mm apart or how much I could repeatedly hand plane the flooring without it turning to shavings. What could have been a challenge to automate my actions became a ploy to disturb the mandate to be rigid, flat, proportional, and reliably consistent. The fruits of this sacrificial labour contest the underlying principle of contemporary interior construction to do more with less; to seek a material solution that maximises surface coverage, minimises surface differentiation, contributes to structural rigidity and incorporates "honest" decoration with the least possible investment of craft.

While these three projects chart individual agendas about interiors, they collectively assert the speculative and productive nature of "tooling" as the basis for an interior design practice that prioritises gender, politics and technology with an aim to reform

Figure 4: "Tread"

interiors as sites of political upheaval. As products, they are less consumable than objects but perhaps more strategic as material "thinks". That they showcase the diversity of one tool, the wedge/shim, to act or to work upon interior design as a form of feminist activism challenges assumptions about the interior's predominant identity as a docile, domestic, passive and subservient environment.

References

[1] Ardener, S. *Women and Space: Ground Rules and Social Maps* (Berg Publishers, Oxford and New York, 1993).

[2] Beecher, C.E. and Beecher Stowe, H. *The American Woman's Home: or Principles of Domestic Science; Being a Guide to the Formation and Maintenance of Economical, Healthful, Beautiful, and Christian Homes* (JB Ford and Company, New York, 1869).

[3] Bloomer, J. Natura Morte. In Hughes, F. ed. *The Architect: Reconstructing Her Practice*, pp. 236-251 (MIT Press, Cambridge, Mass, 1996).

[4] Bloomer, J. Theories of Flesh: Tabbles of Bower. *Assemblage*, 1992, 17, 6-29.

[5] Burns, K. A House for Josephine Baker. In Baydar, G. and Thai, W. C. eds. *Postcolonial Space(s)*, pp. 53-72 (Princeton Architectural Press, New York, 1997).

[6] Colomina, B. Battle lines. In Hughes, F. ed. *The Architect: Reconstructing Her Practice*, pp. 2-25 (MIT Press, Cambridge, Mass, 1996).
[7] de Wolfe, E. *The House in Good Taste* (Ayer Company Publishers, Stratford, 1913).
[8] Draper, D. *Decorating is Fun! How to be your own Decorator* (Rizzoli International, Italy, 2004).
[9] Friedman, A. *Women and the Making of the Modern House: A Social and Architectural History* (Abrams, New York, 1998).
[9] Fryer, J. *Feliticious Space: The Imaginary Structures of Willa Cather and Edith Wharton* (University of North Carolina Press, Chapel Hill, 1986).
[10] Gatens, M. *Feminism and Philosophy: Perspectives on Difference and Equality* (Polity, Cambridge, 1991).
[11] Gordon, B. Women's Domestic Bodies: The Conceptual Conflation of Women and Interiors in the Industrial Age. *Winterthur Portfolio*, 1996, 31(4), 281-301.
[12] Heynen, H. and Baydar, G. *Negotiating Domesticity: Spatial Productions of Gender in Modern Architecture* (Routledge, New York, 2005).
[13] http://www.elc.uvic.ca/projects/199901/civil_disobedience.html (21/04/08)
[14] Longhurst, R. (Re)presenting Shopping Centres and Bodies: Questions of Pregnancy. In Ainley, R. Ed., *New Frontiers of Space, Bodies and Gender* (Routledge, London and New York, 1998).
[15] Penner, B. *A World of Unmentionable Suffering: Women's Public Conveniences in Victorian London*. Journal of Design History, 2001, 14(1), 35-51.
[16] Praz, M. *An Illustrated History of Interior Decoration from Pompeii to Art Nouveau* (Thames and Hudson, London, 1964).
[17] Rendell, J. *Gender Introduction*. In Gender Space Architecture: An Interdisciplinary Introduction (Routledge, London and New York, 2000), pp. 15-21.
[18] Solnit, R. *As Eve Said to the Serpent: On Landscape, gender and art* (University of Georgia Press, Athens, GA, 2001).
[19] Sparke, P. *As Long As It is Pink: The Sexual Politics of Taste* (Pandora Press, London, 1995).
[20] Taylor, M. and Preston, J. *INTIMUS: Interior Design Theory Reader.* (John Wiley & Sons, London, 2006).
[21] Woolf, V. *A Room of One's Own*. Barrett, M. ed. (Penguin Books, London, 1929).
[22] Wood, D. and Beck, R. *Home Rules* (John Hopkins University Press, Baltimore and London, 1994).

Acknowledgements

I gratefully acknowledge research assistant Jane Apthorp, photographer Paul Hillier and workshop technician John Hawkins for their contributions in the making and documentation of the SHEET GOODS project.

Julieanna PRESTON
College of Creative Arts,
Massey University,
Wellington, NZ
j.preston@massey.ac.nz

ABOUT THE EDITORS

Frazer Macdonald Hay is an internationally established designer & educator, currently teaching in the Netherlands, Belgium and Britain. Frazer's research and publications range from areas such as, 'interiors', 'working with a building's memories', 'architectural surgery' to 'intervention methods and systems of practice'. Frazer is the Director of, Big Stone Collective ltd, an international design and architectural consultancy, specialising in building regeneration

Frazer is Chairman of the SBID's (Society of British Interior Design) Educational panel

Frazer is the British Educational Representative for ECIA (European Council of Interior Architecture) and is currently leading the ECIA'S Educational Initiative in Britain

Frazer has worked for architectural and design practices internationally, from high profile projects like the New Scottish Parliament building to local design consultancy, Frazer is currently a member of the Scottish Parliament: Cross Party Group on Architecture and the Built Environment

Email: contactcrrb@aol.com

Goethe described architecture as frozen music, but in fact buildings, interiors, landscapes evolve over time, only so slowly that we hardly see it happen. **Ed Hollis**, Head of Interior Design at Edinburgh College of Art is a journalist, the author of *The Secret Lives of Buildings*, (London and New York 2009), and an academic. His writing, teaching, and research attempt to find ways of talking and writing about the ways in which the environments around us change and grow over time.

Email: e.hollis@eca.ac.uk

Andy Milligan is an interior researcher and Course Director of Interior Environmental Design at Duncan of Jordanstone College of Art and Design at the University of Dundee. He initiated, and is co-founder of the Interiors Forum Scotland and is also a Fellow of the Higher Education Academy. He is the European coordinator of GIDE, Group for International Design Education, and has led interdisciplinary and international collaborations and published widely at international conferences. He is a researcher on UK-funded research council projects focusing on community urban green spaces, and in energy efficiency interventions in existing buildings. He is a designer mentor to schools on Go4SET Engineering Development Trust, and has been an academic external examiner at Domus Academy, Liverpool LJMU and Lincoln amongst others.

Email: a.milligan@dundee.ac.uk

Joyce Fleming is an active Interior Design practitioner and Interior Designer educator on the BSc (Hons) Degree course which is run jointly by Glasgow Metropolitan College and Glasgow Caledonian University. Joyce trained at Duncan of Jordanstone College of Art and Design, Dundee. She worked as Interior Designer within Edinburgh City Architects Department where she contributed to a variety of prestigious capital projects including Edinburgh City Arts Centre, and the refurbishment of the Assembly Rooms and the Lyceum Theatre. She managed the redisplay of several of the cities' museum collections and was heavily involved with the restoration of a number of the historic interiors under the care of the Local Authority.

Email: joycefleming.design@virgin.net

Drew Plunkett is former Head of Interior design at the Glasgow School of Art. He has previously taught at the University of Ulster and SGIHE in Cardiff and has been a visiting lecturer at the London Institute, University of Westminster and the New York School of Interior Design. He was elected a Fellow of the Royal Society of Arts in 1996.

Since 1981 he has practised as an interior designer based in London and Glasgow. He primarily designs restaurants, exhibitions and domestic interiors and a recent major job was a restaurant at Dubai Marina. Previous commissions include the British Airports Authority (with colleague Patrick Macklin) to establish a Scottish identity in the international arrival area. Drew is also active as an exhibitor, curator and critical writer.

Email: Drewplunkett@live.com